THE

GOOD GERMAN
OF NANKING

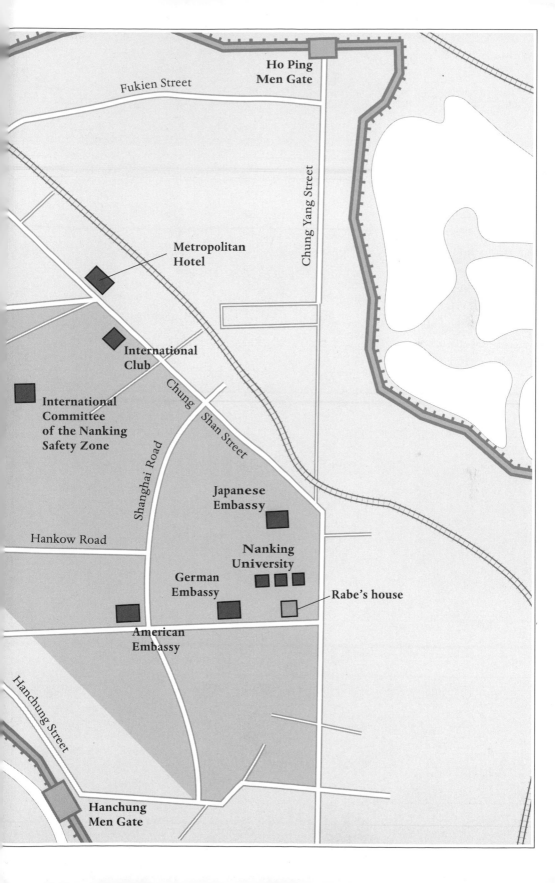

THE
GOOD GERMAN
OF NANKING

The Diaries of
JOHN RABE

EDITED BY ERWIN WICKERT

TRANSLATED FROM THE GERMAN
BY JOHN E. WOODS

LITTLE, BROWN AND COMPANY

A *Little, Brown* Book

First published in the United States in 1998 by Alfred A. Knopf, Inc.
This edition published in 1999 by Little, Brown and Company
by arrangement with Alfred A. Knopf, Inc.

Originally published in Germany by Deutsche Verlags-Anstalt
GmbH, Stuttgart, in 1997 as *Der gute Deutsche von Nanking*,
edited and with a Preface and Afterword by Erwin Wickert.

Grateful acknowledgment is made to the Jiangsu People's
Publishing House, Nanking, for permission to reproduce the
illustrations in the text.

A CIP catalogue record for this book
is available from the British Library.

ISBN: 0 316 64807 8

Typeset by Palimpsest Book Production Limited
Polmont, Stirlingshire
Printed and bound in Great Britain by
Clays Ltd, St Ives plc

Little, Brown and Company (UK)
Brettenham House
Lancaster Place
London WC2E 7EN

CONTENTS

PART 2 JOHN RABE IN HIS GERMAN HOMELAND

FOREWORD

JOHN RABE WAS BORN in Hamburg, Germany, on 23 November 1882. His father was a ship's captain; he died while his son was still young, so that John had to leave school after passing general exams. He then worked for a Hamburg export firm, first as an apprentice for two and a half years, and then as an office clerk. At his boss's recommendation he was sent to Lourenço Marques in Mozambique, a Portuguese colony in southeast Africa, where he worked for a well-established English firm. There he learned to speak fluent English.

A bout of malaria forced him to return home in 1906, but he was on his way again by 1908, this time to Peking. In 1909 he went to Shanghai, where he married his childhood sweetheart from Hamburg. With only a few brief interruptions, he lived in China for the next thirty years. At first he worked for a Hamburg firm, and then in 1911 joined the Siemens branch in Peking, where he remained throughout the First World War, even though, under pressure from the Allies, China declared war on Germany in 1917. He was able to convince the Chinese authorities, however, that it would be in both China's and their own best interest if he continued to run the Siemens office in Peking during the war. That sort of thing was possible in China.

But in 1919, under pressure from the British, he was repatriated to Germany along with all his fellow countrymen. German competition was not wanted. A year later, however, he returned to China via the backdoor of Japan and reestablished the Siemens branch in Peking under the cover of a Chinese firm, until Siemens China Company was permitted to reopen, with its main office in Shanghai. At first he worked in Peking and Tientsin, but from 1931 on, he was the director of the Siemens branch in Nanking, which at the time was the capital of China. The firm called him home in March 1938 and transferred him to its main offices in Berlin, where, however, he was not given any position of real responsibility. In 1947, he retired at age 65; two years later, on 5 January 1950, he died.

The life of an international businessman, then, nothing unusual, nothing particularly exciting—had not John Rabe outgrown that mundane role for a period of six months when he placed, and often risked, his life in the service of 250,000 Chinese. In the Memorial Hall of the city of Nanking, there is a tablet erected in honor of his exemplary humanity. Those who may think humanity is unknown in China are wrong.

> The student Fan Chi asked the Master what "jen" (humanness) means. "To love men," Confucius replied.

In the philosophy of Confucius, *jen* is the central ethical concept. Confucius returns to it again and again. What he taught and what the Chinese people learned for two and a half millennia has never ceased to be a challenge to humankind.

John Rabe was a simple man who wanted to be no more than an honest Hamburg businessman. He was always ready to help, was well-liked, showed good common sense, and maintained a sense of humor even in difficult situations, especially then. He always found ways to come to an amicable agreement, never thrust himself to the fore, and was more likely to do the opposite. If he records some complaint in his diary, he usually adds: "But it's the same for others" or "Others are a lot worse off." He often writes about people who are in need, and how he helped or tried to help them. He saw that as his task, and it distinguished him from his fellows.

He had a great many friends in China, both among the Germans and the other Westerners there. We know that he spoke excellent English; but his written French is impeccable as well. He wrote a whole series of books, mostly about life in China, embellishing them with photographs and little humorous drawings. The books are mostly of a private nature and have never been published, but the bound manuscripts are still extant. He knew a good deal about Chinese art, without ever becoming an expert. Literature, music, and the sciences were not his strong points, but sentimental poems could move him to tears. He had a soft heart, but didn't like to show it.

He was a practical man, both adept and lucky in practical matters. He was only moderately interested in politics, essentially only to the extent that it concerned China, German commerce in China, and German foreign policy in Asia. But he was a patriot, and for a long time he thought Hitler wanted peace.

In 1934, he founded a German school on his property in Nanking—and not for his own two children. His daughter was already past school age, and his son was at a boarding school in southern Germany. As chairman of the school board, which had to work through official channels of the Reich and get approval of the Nazi Party for teachers and funds, he joined the NSDAP in 1934.

A simple man whom people prized for his common sense, his humor, and his congeniality, but certainly not in any way a conspicuous man—and yet he earned people's highest admiration for the way that his love of his neighbor, of his Chinese fellow men in their plight, grew and outgrew itself, for the way he not only rescued them as a Good Samaritan, but also displayed political savvy, a talent for organization and diplomacy, and unflagging stamina in their cause. Working closely with American friends and often at the risk of his life, he built a Safety Zone in Nanking that prevented a massacre and offered relative security to 250,000 Chinese during the Japanese occupation. That he also found time to keep a diary is almost incomprehensible. What he did and saw during the six months between October 1937 and March 1938 is the topic of this book.

He was highly praised by his friends, revered as a saint by the Chinese, respected by the Japanese, whose acts of misconduct he constantly resisted. And yet he remained the same modest man he had been before, who nevertheless could lose all his gentle humility when he saw a wrong being committed; who erupted into hot fury when he saw a soldier about to rape a woman, roared at him in German, held his swastika armband under the man's nose, grabbed him by the collar, and threw him out of the house. And by all accounts he was also a figure of strict paternal authority in his own home.

He was modest, yes, but now and then a little vanity shines through, as, for instance, when he sits down dressed in tails and adorned with medals to pose for a prominent Berlin photographer. Or in the hurt he felt when the editor of the Shanghai *Ostasiatischer Lloyd* simply blue-penciled a joke with which he had spiced up an article.

He left Germany in 1909 when Kaiser Wilhelm was still on the throne. He returned in 1919 for a brief period—when the German empire had been replaced by a republic that still rested on very uneasy foundations. When the Communists took over the town hall in Hamburg, John Rabe was beaten up because—in characteristic fashion—he tried to help a man who had been trod underfoot by the mob.

In Berlin he saw machine guns appear on the street during a strike by Siemens workers. He began to keep a diary. It became his great passion, and not always to his wife's delight, for even after office hours he was often not available to the family. A constant theme of the entries is Rabe's worry that in such unsettled times the volumes of his diary might get lost. They were his most precious possession. He had preserved his times and his life in them.

He wrote about that year in Berlin:

> Then came the Kapp putsch. I knew and understood nothing about domestic politics. Only later did it become clear to me that those days in Germany were far worse than they had appeared to me at the time. To my left, in the Music Hall on Stein Platz, was the army, to my right, the Communists were quartered in the Riding Academy on Uhland Strasse, and they shot at each another during the night, so that I had to move my family from the bedroom out into the corridor.
>
> It was not very pleasant in Berlin. Those were the days of the General Strike and the Organization for Maintenance of Supplies, the days when starving students became gigolos and opera singers sang for pennies in the back courtyards. Those were the days of hoarding and want. At the Siemens offices there were days for using bacon ration cards and days for using boot-resoling ration cards. I never missed a one. Herr Brendel, a friend and coworker at Siemens, had told me about a place inside Siemens where you could get cheap beans and peas. I tried to haul two large bags of peas home, but it began to rain and there were no streetcars. My bags turned soggy and I got home with about half. I really didn't fit in Berlin!
>
> I shared my food on the streetcar with a young girl who fainted because she had nothing in her stomach. I remember another gross example of the misery that I ran across almost every day. Herr Braun, our bookkeeper in Shanghai, had returned from vacation and invited Herr Brendel, me, and a few other friends, to share a pint of beer and some Bavarian snacks he had brought from home—white bread, butter, and

sausage—at the Pschorr Beer Hall on Potsdamer Platz. We had all eaten our fill, and Herr Braun gave everything that was left to a little girl of perhaps eight, who carried matches in her apron and sold them for one mark a box. With a great sob the little thing let her entire stock of wares fall to the floor and ran with her treasure to her mother waiting at the door. The beer didn't taste good to us after that.

Who can blame me for heaving a sigh of relief when I received news that I would be able to return to my old workplace in China.

Over the next two decades Rabe was in Germany only twice, both times briefly—first in the twenties, the second time in 1930, when he came home to get over a "head flu," as he called it. After that he became the director of the Siemens branch in Nanking, China's new capital city. He did not see Germany again until his firm recalled him in 1938.

Nanking had been China's capital since 1927. By 1937, it had a population of about 1.3 million. Siemens had built the city's telephone system and the turbines of its electrical power plant; it had also supplied the hospitals with German equipment. Chinese technicians trained by Siemens serviced these facilities round the clock. Rabe spent his days at various governmental ministries trying to win contracts for Siemens.

There was a German hotel in Nanking. The famous German bakery Kiessling & Bader in Tientsin had a branch here. The German embassy under Ambassador Trautmann had made the move from Peking to Nanking, and the other foreign embassies had set up shop in Nanking as well. Based in Nanking, the Transocean News Agency kept the world abreast of political events in China, while Shanghai remained the nation's financial center—a relationship something like that between Washington and New York.

Marshal Chiang Kai-shek, the generalissimo, governed from Nanking, and wanted to modernize a backward country that had disintegrated into spheres of influence, most of them controlled by various warlords, each in charge of his own private army, and one, the province of Yen-an, by Mao Zedong, who had set up his headquarters there at the end of his famous Long March. There were thirty to forty German military advisors stationed in Nanking, most of them retired German officers, some with their families. Chiang Kai-shek had begun to bring them in under private contract as early as 1927. They were supposed to turn his army into an elite fighting force that could resist both Mao's revolutionary forces and the Japanese.

The chief advisor from 1934 to 1935 had been retired Colonel-General

Hans von Seeckt, the former commander in chief of the Weimar Republic's army. His successor was General Alexander von Falkenhausen. They began the training of several elite divisions, which in fact were able to hold their own against the stronger Japanese for much of the autumn of 1937.

Housed in a separate colony, built for them by the generalissimo, the German officers in Nanking kept to themselves for the most part. They lived much the same casino-based life that they knew from home. They normally signed up for only a few years and had little interest in China, its land and people, its culture and history. Their main topics of conversation were their work, servants, transfers, war stories. Since these men came from very different political backgrounds, there were frequent enough serious arguments for Colonel-General von Seeckt to have to set up a court of honor.

For the businessmen of Nanking, who often did not leave China for years, home was far away. Eurasia, a subsidiary of Lufthansa, was the only airline in China, but as yet there was no direct link by air to Europe or America. The voyage from Shanghai to Genoa, where most Germans disembarked to complete the trip home by rail, lasted four to six weeks; the trip via the Trans-Siberian Railway took ten to twelve days. Most people preferred the comforts of a sea voyage.

John Rabe had no clear picture of what had happened in Germany since his last brief stay in 1930. He learned of Hitler's seizure of power, the Röhm putsch, the fundamental changes in the political landscape, only from newspapers. He read the British *North China Daily News,* China's most serious English-language daily, published in Shanghai. He also subscribed to the *Ostasiatischer Lloyd,* based in Shanghai as well, which essentially restricted itself to passing on the dispatches from Transocean and from the official German news agency. Its editorial policy therefore reflected the standard jargon of the Reich Propaganda Ministry.

This little German paper knew only good things to say about Germany, its Führer, and its party. But even the *North China Daily News* was generally rather sympathetic, if somewhat condescending, in its reports about Germany and its policies. German newspapers from home were usually two to three weeks old when they arrived in Nanking and thus of little interest. But these newspapers, too, had nothing negative to say; they reported about a new German nation that had risen up and broken the humiliating chains of the Versailles Treaty, that no longer paid reparations, and, with the defeat of 1918 behind it, that now demanded and got the same respect as other nations. The Jews were often attacked. Why?—that wasn't very clear in China's world of international business, where you dealt daily with people of the most diverse religions, races, and nationalities. And at first there was very little in the German press about the actual measures taken against the Jews in Germany—nor in the *North China Daily News* for that matter. For years most of the foreign press treated Hitler's policy of anti-Semitism as a disagreeable topic of German domestic politics in which outside nations would do better not to meddle.

Far more important to the press were Germany's foreign and economic policy, its rearmament, and, after 1938, increasing worries about whether Hitler's policies might lead to war. In China people learned details about the treatment of German Jews only toward the end of the thirties, when increasing numbers of them began to emigrate to Shanghai. After that, however, it was impossible not to have some idea of what was going on.

John Rabe, who had lived in China for almost thirty years, was more at home there than in Germany. He was one of the fabled "old China hands," who could speak fluent English but no Chinese, conversing instead with the Chinese in Pidgin English, and yet who could think like locals and who understood, admired, and loved the Chinese. These old China hands were an inexhaustible source of anecdotes and experiences, living pieces of history who could offer vivid accounts of the Chinese and China's otherness. When they returned home to Europe, however, they found it difficult to settle back into a homeland that now felt strange. The same thing happened to John Rabe.

His home in Nanking was open to every guest. I was there in the autumn of 1936, returning from studying at an American college, traveling on a shoestring through Japan and China, and wanting to see and know everything.

In Shandong province I had visited Herr Klicker, a remarkable German who lived far in the interior, where life was made insecure by army deserters and bands of thieves, including those who had pulled off the legendary robbery of the Shanghai Express—later to be turned into a successful movie. He was the director of a mining company owned by a Chinese corporation and had provided the workers of this large enterprise with many social services and benefits, so that it would have been considered a model operation even in Germany. He had given me a letter of introduction to John Rabe. I could stay with him, and he could tell me a great deal about China.

By the early light of dawn on a November morning, I arrived in Pukou by train, took the ferry across the Yangtze, rode a ricksha through an imposing gate of the Nanking city wall, and pulled up before Rabe's house, a modest villa with an office attached. Everyone was still asleep. I walked up and down the street and didn't ring until breakfast time.

John Rabe and his wife immediately had a third place set at their table and a bed made up for me in the guest room. They kept me with them for over a week, longer than I had originally planned. We went to the movies once and saw an American film. Otherwise our evenings were spent sitting in the living room, while Rabe talked about his years in China, about the Chinese, their ways of thinking and living, about China's curious domestic politics, the regime of Chiang Kai-shek, the corruption, the German military advisors. He had even experienced the final years of the Ch'ing dynasty and the infamous Empress Dowager Tz'u-hsi, the Imperial German "Kiaochow protection zone," and the building of the city of Tsingtao.

John Rabe spoke in concrete terms, emphasizing and explaining for me what is often incomprehensible about the Chinese. He read from his diaries: humorous verses or observations on the life of his servants and their families or on business practices in China. In those days before television, people had much more time for conversation.

I had to tell him about the United States and my trip through Manchuria. He was outraged to hear that Japanese army trucks were racing with impunity about Peking, even in the legation district to which the Chinese government had granted extraterritorial status.

Like all Germans in China, he was worried that Hitler was making approaches to Japan. The Anti-Comintern Pact that Joachim von Ribbentrop, the German ambassador in London, had initiated and signed without any participation of the Foreign Ministry, proved it. Nonetheless John Rabe did not believe the rumor that Hitler would withdraw German military advisors from China, for they had all signed private contracts with the Chinese government. (Hitler did it all the same in 1938, and von Ribbentrop threatened the advisors and their families with "serious consequences" if they did not return posthaste.) We did not talk much about conditions in Germany itself—back then it was a faraway place for him. Nor did he mention that he was a member of the NSDAP or that he had temporarily stood in for Legation Councilor Lautenschlager as the party's local group leader. He probably saw it as a formality not worth mentioning. I heard of it myself only long after the war.

The Rabes took touchingly good care of me. I had exchanged some of my money in Shandong. But the currency was not accepted anywhere in

Nanking, because it had been issued by a northern Chinese warlord. John Rabe found a bank, or so he said, that would exchange it for valid currency. Nowadays I ask myself if he didn't simply replace my currency with money out of his own pocket.

The Rabes drove me out to the tomb of Hung-wu, the founder of the Ming dynasty in the fourteenth century, to the huge mausoleum of Sun Yat-sen, the founder of the republic, and to Nanking's other historical monuments; or they simply let me roam the city alone, which in some places did not even look like a city. There was a center, where new large ministries had arisen along with broad avenues and squares, like the ones that the Nanking Germans called "Potsdamer" or "Leipziger Platz." But wide expanses of fields, lakes, ponds, and thickets, where not a house was to be seen, were also part of Nanking.

All of it—Purple Mountain, Lotus Lake, the rock formations of the Stone Citadel—was enclosed within the magnificent city wall that the first Ming emperor had ordered built around his capital, the largest and longest city wall in the world, the work of two hundred thousand people over twenty years. It is twenty-one (some say more than twenty-five) miles long, and from North Gate to South Gate measures six miles. The wall was already too big for the city when the first Ming emperor had it built. It would have taken an entire army to defend its circumference. Despite its wall,

Yangtzekiang and the Nanking city wall.

Nanking has been conquered and razed several times in its history. The last time had been in 1864. Even in 1936, it still had not completely recovered from that most recent devastation.

Around the middle of the nineteenth century, Hung Hsiu-ch'üan, a village school teacher in southern China, had a vision in which he was told that he was the younger brother of Jesus. He collected about him a group of fanatically religious revolutionaries, and their number quickly grew. They soon constituted a small army, and moving northward, they defeated the Imperial forces sent out against them and took Nanking. This "brother of Jesus" now called himself "Heavenly King" and named Nanking the "Heavenly Capital" and his empire *Taiping Tienkuo,* the "Heavenly Kingdom of Great Peace." It was, as we would call it today, both a fundamentalist theocracy and a cruel dictatorship.

The leaders of the Taiping Rebellion (1852–1864) came close to conquering the whole empire and toppling the Imperial dynasty. But the Imperial government raised new armies and, after a long series of battles, finally defeated the "Taipings," whose leadership was now falling apart. It was the most deadly civil war in world history; some thirty million Chinese died in the struggle for the Heavenly Kingdom.

When Imperial troops retook Nanking in 1864, they engaged in a bloodbath that lasted for days, not only slaying the Taiping rebels, but also murdering almost all the inhabitants of the city, looting their homes, and finally burning everything to the ground. Nanking perished. Only what was made of stone remained.

The Taiping rebels had themselves already blown up the Great Pagoda of blue, green, and red porcelain, with its one hundred fifty bells that rang in the wind, one of the wonders of the world in the early fifteenth century. A small portion of the palace in which the Heavenly King had perished, plus a little park and lake, still remained, but at the time were considered Generalissimo Chiang Kai-shek's official residence and could not be visited.

Taking Rabe's advice, I took a stroll along the city wall, which in some places is over fifty feet high and up to forty feet wide across the top. The city gates were themselves great fortifications, each containing a sequence of gates and courtyards, so that troops who broke through one gate would find themselves facing yet another and surrounded on all sides. The top of the wall was wide enough for two wagons to drive abreast easily.

About two-thirds of the wall was still standing. It led almost down to the Yangtze, which is three-quarters of a mile wide here, yet far upriver from Nanking still remains navigable—for a total distance of well over six hundred miles from its mouth at Shanghai. There is a bend in the river here, and in that bend, as if in a protecting hand, lies Nanking. From the wall you could look out over the city, which was almost lost in the green of trees, meadows, fields, and ponds.

I saw a child's bright red cap lying in the tall grass growing on top of the wall, picked it up, but then dropped it again at once in horror. Beneath it lay the half-decomposed head of a child. The worst part were the fat white maggots.

That evening when his wife had gone out, I told John Rabe about it. He was very upset.

"In Shanghai," he said, "that sort of thing happens every day—dead bodies of poor people who die on a cold night are lying in the streets come morning. But not in Nanking. There are no dead bodies lying around here!"

The next morning he called the chief of police. That was at the end of 1936. About one year later, he was to write in his diary: "We literally climbed over dead bodies. It was worst at Christmas."

But during that December of 1937, *he* was, as he wrote this, to all effects the chief of police, indeed the mayor of the city of Nanking.

And how that came to be is what he describes in his diary, from which the following chapters have been taken. He typed a clean copy of it during the war and added certain materials: documents, public notices he had himself written, notes to embassies, proclamations, newspaper clips, letters, and photographs. As a way of protecting himself from the Gestapo, who had forbidden him to write or speak in public, he added a foreword to his final copy:

This is not intended to be read for entertainment, though it may perhaps look like that at first; it is a record of facts, a diary, which was not written for the public but for my wife and the closest circle of my family. Should its publication, which for obvious reasons has at present been prohibited, ever seem appropriate, that should be done only by permission of the German government. All reports and correspondence of the International Committee of the Nanking Safety Zone to the Japanese embassy have been translated by me from English into German, which is also the case of correspondence exchanged with American authorities.

Berlin, 1 October 1942

A NOTE ON THE TEXT

THE FOLLOWING PORTION of this book contains excerpts from the two volumes of John Rabe's diaries, which he assembled during the war by combining selected documents and what he considered the most important entries from the private diary originally written for his wife and family. His experiences in Germany after returning from China have been taken from accounts he wrote for his family and a small manuscript diary from the postwar period.

I have attempted to select passages that show John Rabe in all his many facets and have also included material that he himself might have left out today because the period in which he lived is in so many ways no longer understandable. To those who make an effort to grasp what the conditions of that period were, John Rabe will not appear any weaker for it. Since he wrote his diary for his family, I have occasionally recast careless sentences into more standard language and have omitted entries that concern only his immediate family.

In his diary, Rabe included accounts written by his German helpers, Krischan Kröger and Eduard Sperling, as well as some reports from the German embassy. These have been supplemented with a few accounts by

other eyewitnesses. I have added still other documents taken from the political archives of the German Foreign Ministry, the Federal Archives, and
the Military Archives in Freiburg, which, although they express different
views of these same events, also complement and confirm what Rabe himself observed and described. In an afterword based on documents of the
period, I have attempted to sketch the general political background, various perspectives in Berlin concerning German policy in the Far East, and a
summary of what information was available to Rabe himself, in order to
make his own position more understandable, particularly his relationship
to Hitler and National Socialism as he understood it.

The transcription of Chinese characters has always presented problems. I have generally followed Rabe's spelling of Chinese names, though
not without a few minor changes here and there.

Summarizations and remarks by the editor within the text of the diary
are set in italics.

PART I

FROM JOHN RABE'S
NANKING DIARY

CHAPTER I

HOW IT BEGAN

In 1931, after meeting no opposition worth the name, the Japanese army occupied Manchuria, China's northernmost region, and declared it to be the sovereign state of Manchukuo, though in reality it was totally under Japanese control; nor did it become any more independent once the former Chinese emperor P'u-Yi was placed on the throne. A few years later, the Japanese army advanced into other northern Chinese provinces. Early in June 1937, there was a skirmish in Peking with Chinese troops on an old marble bridge that foreigners called the Marco Polo Bridge—and at first no one attached any real importance to the encounter.

It marked, however, the beginning of Japanese aggression against China, the goal of which was to subjugate the entire land and its people. In terms of international law, both sides spoke only of an "incident," although the Japanese would go on to conquer Nanking, Hankow, and large parts of China. As a result, diplomatic relations were not broken. Even after Japanese troops had occupied Nanking and the Chinese government had long since retreated to Hankow, or later to Chungking, Japan's embassy continued to function in the old capital, if only at lower levels. The ambassador himself resided in Shanghai.

Summers in Nanking are unbearably hot. The city, along with Hankow and

Chungking, is called one of China's "three ovens." With the onset of the summer heat, John Rabe's wife, Dora, had departed for the coastal resort of Peitaiho, north of Tientsin. John Rabe joined her there at the end of August. He writes:

Chinwangtao had already been conquered by the Japanese by then, and with them came an unrelenting stream of troop trains heading for Tientsin, some equipped with antiaircraft artillery, which gave me pause for thought. Things looked much more serious than I had expected.

In Peitaiho, about an hour north of Chinwangtao, there was no evidence that Japanese occupation was now an accomplished fact, but there was a certain tension in the air that convinced me to book my return trip to Shanghai from Chinwangtao right away. I was told: "Booked full for two months." While I was still considering the quickest way to arrange to get back, we heard news that the Japanese had attacked Shanghai, so that for the moment a return trip via its harbor was out of the question.

Good advice was scarce. When word leaked through that Nanking was under attack by Japanese aircraft and had been heavily bombed, I realized that the situation was truly serious. My only option was to travel by boat from Tientsin via Cheefoo or Tsingtao and from there by train to Nanking via Tsinanfu. On 28 August 1937, I said good-bye to my wife in the dark of night.

On 7 September 1937, after an eleven-day journey that in peacetime would have taken forty hours, Rabe reached Nanking. Because he did not want his wife to share the risk of air raids, he had left her behind in the resort town of Peitaiho. She remained in the north for a few months and then later moved to Shanghai.

21 SEPTEMBER 1937

All the rich or better-off Chinese began some time ago to flee up the Yangtze to Hankow. In courtyards and gardens, in public squares and on the streets, people have feverishly been building dugouts, but otherwise everything remained calm until two days ago, when I received my baptism by fire during four air raids on Nanking.

Many Americans and Germans have departed as well. I've been seriously considering the matter from all sides these last few nights. It wasn't because I love adventure that I returned here from the safety of Peitaiho, but primarily to protect my property and to represent Siemens's interests. Of course the company can't—nor does it—expect me to get myself killed here on its behalf. Besides, I haven't the least desire to put my life at risk for the sake of either the company's or my own property; but there is a question of morality here, and as a reputable Hamburg businessman, so far I haven't been able to side-step it.

Our Chinese servants and employees, about 30 people in all including immediate families, have eyes only for their "master." If I stay, they will loyally remain at their posts to the end. I saw the same thing happen before in the wars up north. If I run, then the company and my own house will not just be left deserted, but they will probably be plundered as well. Apart from that, and as unpleasant as that would be, I cannot bring myself for now to betray the trust these people have put in me. And it is touching to see how they believe in me, even the most useless people whom I would gladly have sent packing during peacetime. I gave Mr. Han, my assistant, an advance on his salary so that he could send his wife and two children to safety in Taianfu. He quite frankly admits: "Where you stay, I stay too. If you go, I go along!"

The rest of the poor servants, most of whom are actually from northern China, simply don't know where to go. I wanted to send off the women and children at least, offered their husbands money for the trip, but they don't know what to do. They want to go back home to the north, but there's war there, too; and so they would rather just huddle here around me.

Under such circumstances, can I, may I, cut and run? I don't think so. Anyone who has ever sat in a dugout and held a trembling Chinese child in each hand through the long hours of an air raid can understand what I feel.

Finally—subconsciously—there's a last, and the not least important, reason that makes my sticking it out here seem simply a matter of course. I am a member of the NSDAP, and temporarily even held the office of local deputy leader. When I pay business calls on the Chinese agencies and ministries who are our customers, I am constantly asked questions about Germany, about our party and government, and my answer always is:

> Yes indeed—
> We are soldiers of labor;
> We are a government of workers,
> We are friends of the working man,
> We do not leave workers—the poor—
> in the lurch when times are hard!

To be sure, as a National Socialist I was speaking only about German workers, not about the Chinese; but what would the Chinese think? Times are bitterly hard here in the country of my hosts, who have treated me well for three decades now. The rich are fleeing, the poor must remain behind. They don't know where to go. They don't have the means to flee. Aren't they in danger of being slaughtered in great numbers? Shouldn't one make an attempt to help them? Save a few at least? And even if it's only our own people, our employees?

And so we have put our filthy dugout, which the Chinese had excavated during my absence but that was already close to collapse, back in top-notch order.

I've equipped the dugout with my personal first-aid supplies, plus some from the apothecary in the school, which closed down some time ago. We plan to use vinegar compresses as face masks in the case of gas attack. I've also stored food and drink in baskets and thermos bottles.

22 SEPTEMBER

Once the long wail of the siren announced the end of the second attack, I went for a drive through the city. The Japanese had made a particular target of Kuomintang party headquarters, where the offices and studios of the central broadcasting station are also located.

My war diary begins as of this date.

DURING THE WORST of the bombing on 19 and 20 September, I sat with my Chinese in our homemade dugout, which is certainly not bombproof, but at least provides protection against shrapnel and bomb fragments. Out in the garden we've also spread a 20-by-10-foot piece of canvas with a swastika painted on it.

The government has set up a very good alarm system. About 20 to 30 minutes before an air raid, sirens start howling loudly, and by the time a certain shorter signal sounds the streets must be cleared. All traffic stops. Pedestrians crawl into dugouts that have been built alongside all the streets.

The final bomb intended for the Kuomintang party landed behind the buildings, making a direct hit on a dugout built into the clay of the city wall. Eight people were killed. One woman had been peering out of the dugout—her head was nowhere to be found. Only a ten-year-old girl miraculously survived, and she herself has no idea how. She could be seen running from group to group, telling her story. The area was cordoned off by the military. Sacrificial paper was burning beside the last coffin.

23 SEPTEMBER

Herr Scheel, the baker at Café Kiessling, had moved into the home of one of Hapro's[1] former employees in the new residential section, which was considered a particularly safe area until yesterday's attack badly stained its reputation, so that he has had to move again—I've been unable to find out where to. The worst part is that Scheel has closed his bakery. There is no more bread.

I just returned home with an order in the amount of 1,500 pounds sterling from the National Resource Commission. Not bad in the middle of a war, if only as a moral success. There's a very nice letter from the board of directors in Shanghai, expressing concern about my well-being and giving me permission to take any measure I consider appropriate for my personal safety, even to leave Nanking if necessary. Many thanks! The letter did me good.

Rabe in his garden with the swastika flag, which he hoped would deter Japanese bombers. It later became a makeshift tent for some of his Chinese refugees.

24 SEPTEMBER

In the long hours of crouching in the dugout during the recent bombardment, I turned on Radio Shanghai to take my mind off things with a little music, and they were playing Beethoven's Funeral March, then to make matters worse they announced to their listeners: "This music is kindly dedicated to you by the Shanghai Funeral Directors."

25 SEPTEMBER

According to an article in the *Ostasiatischer Lloyd*, Germany's ambassador, Dr. Trautmann, has made arrangements to provide for the safety of those Germans still remaining in Nanking. We're all very curious how he is going to manage this.

At a conference in the embassy yesterday he disclosed his plan, and it's not all that bad. He has chartered the *Kutwo*, an English steamship owned by the Jardines line, which is to transport those of us Germans not needed here farther up the Yangtze and so out of danger.

26 SEPTEMBER

Yesterday evening Mr. Chow, an engineer from Shanghai, arrived after spending 26 hours on the train. He has been ordered here by Mr. Tao of the Communications Ministry to repair the telephone system. Chow is one of our best people.

When I asked if his family was worried that something might happen to him on the trip, he answered—and a remarkable answer it is: "I told my wife, if I am killed you can expect nothing from Siemens and should go to my relatives in the north where you and the children can live from the yield of our little parcel of land there. I undertook this trip not only in the company's interest, but also, and above all, in the interests of my fatherland."

It reveals an attitude one generally doesn't credit the Chinese with having, but it is there, and it is gaining ground, especially in the lower and middle classes.

3 OCTOBER

It's said that people at the highest levels, especially Madame Chiang, have no great sympathy for Germany, because we have concluded a pact with

Japan against the Soviets and have refused to take part in the [Nine Power] Conference in Brussels, since we don't want to sit at the same table with the Soviets.

He who is not for us is against us, Madame Chiang is reported to have said. And what about the German advisors? Who introduced the flak battalions and antiaircraft artillery that the Chinese are so proud of today? German advisors! Who trained the troops fighting so bravely near Shanghai, while untrained soldiers in the north are simply fleeing? German advisors! Who are staying at their posts in Nanking? German advisors and businessmen! From our perspective here, my countrymen are staying on in the capital at a considerable sacrifice, something the Chinese here in their own country simply do not appreciate.

I was just at the bazaar and for 80 dollars bought four suitcases in which I want to pack the 16 books I've written. Chow, our Chinese engineer, who will be coming back from Hankow in about two weeks, wants to take them back with him to Shanghai. Perhaps they can be stored more safely there than here.

Medicine is in short supply. The Tien Sun Apothecary was badly damaged by the blast from the most recent bombs and is closed. Every bottle on its shelves was broken. And it was the only shop that still had six bottles of insulin. Why didn't I snap them up before the bombing began? Because I wanted to save money. What nonsense! We're always wiser in hindsight! I am going to try to get 20 to 30 vials shipped from Shanghai. Let's hope it works. Soon there won't be a single shop open in Nanking. I just managed to scare up two bottles each of ether and alcohol, plus a package of cotton wadding, at a wine shop.

Trucks are arriving daily now full of those not too severely wounded, but what a sorry sight they are. They're covered with filthy bandages and crusted with mud as if they have just come from the trenches. I'm glad we have Dr. Hirschberg with us here at least. His family is still here, too—they have returned, or perhaps they never left.

6 OCTOBER

Ambassador Trautmann was here for tea from 5 to 6 o'clock. We sat together for an hour and discussed the general situation. We are both in a rather pessimistic mood. The north is lost, and nothing will change that. The Chinese appear to regard Shanghai as the main theater of war because Shanghai protects Nanking. But for how long?

9 AND 10 OCTOBER

Rain, putting everyone in the best of moods. Sunday afternoon, just for a change of scenery, I went on board the *Kutwo* again for coffee. There were only a few visitors. Dr. Rosen from the embassy has now become a permanent guest on board. In his own way, the man impresses me. He frankly admits that he is frightened by the bombardments and is acting accordingly. Not everyone can be as candid as that. I don't love being shelled either; but I simply cannot bring myself to save my skin just yet.

13 OCTOBER

Scattered clouds and sunshine. The forecast for a very unsettling day. But it all took place at some distance. The alarm sounded at eight o'clock, but then was called off fifteen minutes later. At each alarm, a large number of poor neighbors—men, women, and children—all come running past my house, fleeing in the direction of Wutaishan Hill, where dugouts have been built into the slopes. What a wretched sight, I'm tired of just watching their torment, especially the women with little children in their arms. The crowd stormed past here three times today.

I'm experiencing some growth in my dugout, too. Mr. Sen and Mr. Fong, who both speak German, have been sent by their former branches to Nanking and are living close by, so that they take refuge here whenever the alarm sounds. Plus the two postmen who have always brought my mail are now among my permanent guests. I'll soon not know where to put all these people. I've made no appearance in the dugout the last few days. Herr Riebe, a Siemens engineer sent here from Shanghai, came home ill today—*dutzebuhau.*[2]

14 OCTOBER

Radiant sunshine at 7 a.m.—splendid weather for flying! Herr Riebe is doing better, thank God, it was only an upset stomach, and is happily returning to work today, that is, to the electricity works in Hsiakwan.[3]

Herr Riebe has never seen Sun Yat-sen's tomb, so I drive him out to see it. Good luck! The gates are surrounded by bamboo scaffolding draped with cloths. Even the old Ming grave is off limits. The entire memorial park is filled with military trucks, all of them empty but ready to go, because in each one sits a dozing Chinese driver. Word is that the marshal is living somewhere near the Great Pagoda. No one has ever resided in the Chia Hung Chang, the actual presidential palace, which has been painted black from top to bottom. Looks awful!

There's a lot of talk about the Japanese using gas. An article in a local paper announced that the hospital here has determined that some Chinese soldiers who have been admitted are suffering from gas poisoning.

We're all very worried about the possibility of a gas attack, because Nanking's civilian population has not been issued gas masks. There have been some announcements about how you can protect yourself by soaking a cloth in vinegar or some other liquid and using it as a face mask, but that's all just a poor makeshift that would be absolutely useless in a real emergency.

17 OCTOBER (FROM A LETTER)

People want to be taken so "dreadfully seriously," and that's not my way. I just happen to have an unfortunate talent for tripping people up with my so-called humor at the oddest moments.

I don't mean to claim these are not serious times. They are serious; they are very serious and will probably get even worse. But how are you supposed to deal with all this dreadful seriousness? It seems to me by gathering up some last snatches of humor to defy fate's absurdities. Which is why my prayer each morning and evening goes: "Dear God, watch over my family and my good humor; I'll take care of the other incidentals myself."

You want to know, I'm sure, what we are still doing here and what our lives are like. Well, let's admit it: At such a time a man tries to behave decently and doesn't want to leave in the lurch the employees under his charge, or the rest of his servants and their families, but to stand by them in word and deed. It's the obvious thing to do really!

LATER

All the movie houses, most of the hotels, the majority of shops and apothecaries are closed. Impeccable order reigns in the streets. The military, the police, and civil defense do their duty modestly and correctly. Westerners—there aren't that many left, among the Germans maybe 12 women and 60

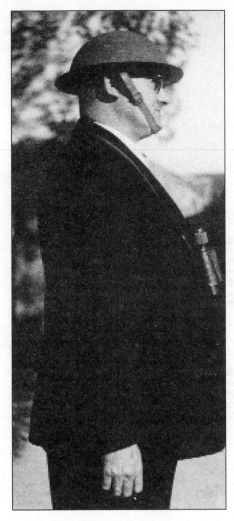

Rabe, with characteristic lack
of pomposity, in plane-spotting gear.

men—are not harassed, on the contrary! People show amazing goodwill toward those of us still staying on here as their guests.

People are scrambling for a spot in my dugout! I really don't know why. It simply has the reputation of being rock solid. When I built it I was figuring on 12 occupants at most. As things turned out once it was finished, I had badly miscalculated: There were 30 of us in all, and there we sat like sardines in a can.

Where do all these people come from? Very simple. Every "boy" has a wife, children, a father, mother, grandfather, and grandmother, and if he doesn't, then he adopts some. A very profitable business, might I add! In addition, my neighbor, a cobbler with whom I had been feuding before the war because he always calculated a 20 percent "squeeze" into the price of his boots, had to be included, along with his family, after it turned out that he was one of my boy's relatives. What could I do? I let them all in. I didn't want to lose face!

Someone had placed an office chair in the little cellar for me; all the others squatted on low benches. It was perfectly clear to me that I had to join the others in the dugout, at least when bombs were falling too close and making too much racket, and as I sat there, and saw how the women and children were reassured simply by my poor presence, I knew that I had done the right thing in deciding to return as quickly as possible from Peitaiho.

If I were to write that I was not afraid, I'd be lying. When the dugout began to do some respectable shaking, a feeling came over me, too, that said, "Damn—we'll be lucky to get out of here!" But fear is there to be conquered. A few cheerful words, a really rotten joke, grins all around—and the bombs had already lost much of their effect.

Women with nursing babies have priority in the dugout. They are allowed to take the seats in the middle; then come the women with bigger children, and then the men: an arrangement on which I always stubbornly insist, much to the amazement of the men.

Whenever there's an increase in the number of bombs landing too close, everyone just sits there in the dugout, silent, mouths open. Women and children get wads of cotton for their ears. As soon as things calm down a bit, one hero after the other emerges from the cellar to have a look around. And how the Chinese applaud happily whenever an enemy bomber takes a hit from antiaircraft fire and plunges to the earth in a beautiful fiery arc. Only the funny, inscrutable "Master" is behaving strangely again. He silently touches the brim of his hat and mutters, "Hush! Three men are dying!"

18 OCTOBER

Herr Riebe spent the whole time standing beside his turbines at the electricity works, the silly ass! But he had only just got the machines running today and didn't want to shut them down again. If the Japanese had really come any closer, he said, he would have taken cover of course. Yes indeed, my friend, if there's still time!

19 OCTOBER

The Japanese really mean business today! Alarm at 2 a.m., and by the time I was pulling on my other boot, bombs were already falling, setting the whole house shaking. Riebe, however, was not to be disturbed, but went right on sleeping as if nothing was happening. Just as I shouted, "Hey there, Riebe! Second alarm!" a couple more bombs exploded, and our friend Riebe calmly replied, "Yes, I hear."

Riebe did a fine piece of work in getting the power going again. Turbine II is running at full power (5,000 kW). He's working on turbine III now. All we have are our old Borsig boilers that have been in constant use since being delivered six years ago. We couldn't even get our renowned American boilers to fire up again.

We saw our Siemens searchlights shining again tonight. I had to establish some order while we were "boarding" the dugout. There's a fat, well-fed telegraph operator from the Transocean News Agency who always takes the best middle seats from the women and children. I was forced to set him straight a bit. And in the fervor of the moment I ended up in groundwater and got the seat of my pants soaked.

As of this morning a huge sign in German, Chinese, and English adorns the entrance to the dugout. It reads:

A Bulletin for My Guests and Members of My Household:

Anyone using my bomb shelter must obey the rule giving the safest seats, meaning those in the middle of the dugout, to women and children—whoever they may be. Men are to make do with other seats or stand. Anyone disobeying this instruction may not use the dugout in the future.

JOHN RABE   Nanking, 19 October 37

The fat telegraph operator took the message very much to heart!

20 OCTOBER

Herr Hoth from the German embassy is lying in Kulou Hospital. On a hunting trip in a sampan on the Yangtze, the man behind him put a load of buckshot in his calves. He was not given first aid until they were on board an English warship. The things that can happen to a person in war! In the calf of all places! I've been wondering whether I ought to award him the Order of the Garter for his ailing legs. I think I'll do it!

21 OCTOBER, 9:15 A.M.

I'm on my way to the electricity works, when the *ying bao*—the alarm—sounds. I barely make it home in the car, and find everything in an uproar. The German-speaking officials at Shanghai Com-Sav Bank have received word that the Japanese have been dropping gas bombs along the highway to Nanking. We have no gas masks, only primitive muslin face masks. I check to see if all my guests are outfitted with the things. The women just have handkerchiefs or little towels. I screw up my courage.

22 OCTOBER

Herr Woltemade arrives at 8 a.m. He got to Nanking at one this morning, but rented a room at the Metropol Hotel rather than disturb me. The drive from Shanghai to Nanking took 18 hours. He had entrusted himself to the Central China Express Company, which promised to get him here in eight hours. The allegedly German chauffeurs of this company, however, are in fact out-of-work Jews, who maybe don't know much about driving but are that much better at making money. The trip costs 75 dollars a person. One chauffeur's behavior has been offensive, and the embassy wants to remove the swastika flag from his car, since a Jew has no right to fly it.[4]

24 OCTOBER

Evening brings news on the radio that the Japanese are said to have broken through the Shanghai front at Tazang. If it's true, which we hope it isn't, we shall soon be cut off entirely from Shanghai.

Hurrah! A letter has just arrived from Otto[5] in Salem, dated 26 September: cheerful, without a care in the world. He's busy harvesting plums and apples and is delighted that Otto Rabe, laboring member of the service corps, is soon to become a soldier.

25 OCTOBER

Our wounded Herr Hoth was a good sport about receiving his "bulletproof Order of the Garter," that is, a white garter with an attached medal displaying two crossed rifles (from my little medal box) and the inscription *honi soit qui mal y pense*. I packaged it in a cigar box covered in blue silk and lined with white. It was a whopping success! Hoth almost laughed himself well again, and—what was not at all my intention—everyone says: Only Rabe could have come up with that!

26 OCTOBER

Herr Riebe has finished the job at the electricity works. He could have left for Changsha, but a telegram arrived from Shanghai: "Letter to follow—don't rush the work!" In all my twenty-seven years with Siemens, I have yet to receive such a lovely telegram.

27 OCTOBER

The Japanese breakthrough at Tazang has now been confirmed by the Chinese. They have now retreated to their so-called "Hindenburg Line."

Rabe's dugout in his garden.
The sign reads:
OFFICE HOURS: FROM
9:00 P.M. TO 11:00 P.M.

28 OCTOBER

Alarm at 9:10 a.m., but a false one. Otherwise an active business day that was quiet until evening when something happened after all: Tsao, my rascal of a cook, was supposed to serve bread and cheese for supper, but had none, got scolded, became angry, and gave notice as of the first. He lost the battle, but saved face. Let him go—I don't care! I won't weaken, I want my cheese!

29 OCTOBER

Dr. Lautenschlager has returned from Peitaiho by way of Shanghai and has brought me the insulin that Mutti bought for me in Tientsin.

In a moment of some reasonableness, I wrote the following verses and have inscribed them on my heart:

To whom it may concern

Now's the time and now's the season:
Damn it man, do use your reason!
Crouching at your dugout door
Is witless foolishness and more!
First because the bombs that drop
Are known to travel from up top,
And that shrapnel from on high
Is said to hurt the stander-by.
Once it booms and it's too late,
You tell yourself: Oh heck, I'll wait,
There's surely time enough to duck,
I only wanted one last look. . . .
Stuff and nonsense, Curly, think
A little faster, hero! Slink
Into your shelter there!
Reason calls you to beware!

6 NOVEMBER

Making my business rounds today, I came across some rather ugly news. A "*nitchevo*-mood" appears to be gradually spreading among the Chinese. Herr Riebe told me recently that the workers at the electricity works asked him directly whether a man wouldn't be a lot better off if he became a Communist. And today a businessman told me in confidence that all educated Chinese believe that they ought to join the Bolsheviks.[6]

LATER

It's amazing to read how bravely the Chinese army—and remember, they're hirelings, because although Nanking declared a general draft, it was never set up of course—is fighting against well-disciplined Japanese troops in Shanghai. It's true that only the best Nanking troops, trained by German advisors, were sent to Shanghai. Two-thirds of them are said to have fallen in battle already; but what can the best troops do without adequate equipment. The modern Japanese army, outfitted with heavy artillery, countless tanks, and bombers, is simply vastly superior to the Chinese.

7 NOVEMBER

Meals of late leave something to be desired. Chang, our number-one houseboy, has taken a three-day vacation. He sent a substitute to fill in while he's gone, and to my inexpressible joy the man speaks classical, unadulterated Shanghai Pidgin English. The following conversation is taken from today's breakfast:

> MASTER: Boy! Ham and eggs taste all same like fish—how fashion can do?
> BOY: Chicken no can help, Master. Present time no got proper chow. Only got fish.
> MASTER: But butter taste all same. You thinkee cow all same chow fish?
> BOY: My no savee, Master. My wanshee ask him.

In English:

> MASTER: Boy! The ham and fried eggs taste like fish. Why is that?
> BOY: The chickens can't help it, Master. There's no regular feed for them, so they get only fish.
> MASTER: But the butter tastes of fish, too. Do you think the cow's eating fish as well?
> BOY: I don't know, Master. I'll have to ask it (i.e., the cow).

Well, I'm curious to know what the cow has to say! If the skillet were ever cleaned, maybe we'd get rid of that oily fishy taste. The entire population of my dugout is probably using just one skillet, meaning: mine.

Otherwise, no news.

8 NOVEMBER

I've been told that the Japanese have about 600 airplanes in Shanghai at present. If an air force that large attacks Nanking, it will achieve what it sets out to do.

Modern warfare is simply pandemonium on earth, and to think that what we're experiencing here in China is child's play compared to what a new world war would mean in Europe, from which heaven preserve us.

10 NOVEMBER

About nine Japanese airplanes are flying over the city. They've been under heavy fire, but without success. Except for Riebe, who's standing at the gate to the school and scanning the sky through my Zeiss binoculars (factor of 18), I ordered everybody into the dugout the moment the roofs of nearby houses started rattling under the rain of flak fragments. I'm always happy when we all come out of these thunderstorms unharmed. It's becoming increasingly difficult to get people to take cover in time. Since nothing has happened thus far, thank God, they've become careless and don't think they're in danger anymore, unless I go into a nice tirade now and then. Our dugout is getting terribly soggy. We're having trouble keeping groundwater out. It requires hours of bailing.

German military advisors returning from the Shanghai front report that a number of lightly wounded (Chinese) soldiers are no longer under military discipline and are marauding behind the front lines; if you travel at night you need a Mauser pistol in your hand.

11 NOVEMBER

The bombs were like a hailstorm. Suddenly a whoop of joy from outside. The flak batteries have made a hit. The dugout empties out in no time. Everybody wants to see. The bomber breaks in two and plummets in a swirl of flames and smoke. We see two men, of what was perhaps a five- or seven-man crew, leap out of the fire and smoke. Without parachutes! Within 20 seconds there's nothing left of the proud bomber but debris and corpses.

12 NOVEMBER

A German woman, whose name I don't even know, called me on the telephone just now: "Ah, send your engineer at once! My sewing machine is broken!"

"My dear lady," I reply, "this is Siemens, not Singer."

"I know that," she says, "I've already tried Singer, but he's too stupid. Now I'm trying you. After all, it is an *electric* sewing machine!"

What am I supposed to do? I'll send Sung, our telephone installer, over tomorrow. Business seems to be improving.

The sewing-machine woman calls again: She would prefer that I send the engineer in the afternoon, please.

14 NOVEMBER

Splendid sunny Sunday, and no bombs! Han says the Japanese don't like to fly on Sunday. He doesn't know why, either, maybe they want to rest. That reminds me of Young, who used to be our comprador in Tientsin; he was

Rabe and an unidentified colleague watching Japanese aircraft overhead.

so lazy that we made him keep a diary listing the customers he'd called on and what shops he'd entered. Every Sunday his entry read: "Today being Holy Sunday. All day no business can be done!"

Herr Riebe had hoped to leave for Hankow this morning, but the only places left on any of the Jardines steamers were in steerage. In his shoes I would have bought a seat in steerage and then I would have sat down in the 1st class salon and waited until the 1st officer provided me with suitable accommodations. The English always treat Europeans courteously.

15 NOVEMBER

A visit to the Communications Ministry convinced me that the government is about to retreat from Nanking. The corridors and offices there are full of trunks and boxes. They intend to move to Changsha on the upper Yangtze. I stop by the Railway Ministry and get one of the boys to tell me in confidence that they, too, will be packing tomorrow.

I have tea with the German ambassador and his wife, Frau Trautmann. There I meet General Speemann, who has just arrived from Tayuanfu. It appears that the *Kutwo* will first take the ladies and other valuables to Hankow, then return for the embassy staff and the rest of the Germans. The embassy has to leave the moment the Chinese government bolts, they say, because otherwise it would be left behind in enemy territory.

16 NOVEMBER

All day I have been firmly resolved to hold out here. But now I hear that Soochow is being badly plundered by defeated and retreating Chinese troops. That makes you stop and think. Besides which, people believe that Nanking will try to defend itself against the advancing Japanese, even if the city is shelled from the river by Japanese naval artillery.

On the other hand: What's to become of all the many Chinese clinging to my coattails? Mr. Han asked for another advance. He wanted to send his wife and children as soon as possible via Tsinanfu to Tsingtao, where he has friends. But now he hears that the route is no longer open. The Chinese have blown up one of the railroad bridges outside Tsinan in order to slow the Japanese advance. Meaning that the Japanese will soon be, or already are, on the Yellow River. And now Han, too, will probably have to send his family to Hankow. He's still waiting for another family of friends who are to join them. I hope he doesn't wait too long.

There is no point in pursuing any kind of project whatever. No one is available to talk business. Everybody's packing. But then so am I! I've already packed up the books I've written. And next come my suits, then the silver. How strange it all sounds! The few remaining items can be quickly thrown into a trunk, then you just paste an address on it. I'm going to withdraw money from the bank, since I've been advised I'll need cash. The banks will be closing, too, in any case.

17 NOVEMBER

There was heavy traffic on the main road all night: car after car, trucks, even tanks. All rumbling ponderously past. The government has begun its evacuation. Word is that Mr. Lin Sen, the president of the Chinese Republic, has already left. I'm worried about Han's family. They have to leave, as soon as possible.

Hundreds upon hundreds of rickshas piled high with baggage are on the road to Hsiakwan, their Chinese owners alongside, all trying to make it to safety on the few steamers still sailing upriver. Several columns of new recruits were a pathetic sight: all in more less ragged civvies, each with a bundle on his back and a rusty rifle in hand.

I have now also learned why the Japanese were able to advance so quickly of late. Outside Soochow about 5,000 soldiers of the Chang Hsueliang (the Northern Troops) refused to obey orders. They say Chiang Kai-shek himself took one of his crack regiments to Soochow and disarmed the whole mutinous bunch. The marshal doesn't have an easy time of it. A tip of the hat, just to the sheer energy! Now that the marshal has personally intervened, the Chinese front is said to be holding again. The Japanese have skirted around the "Hindenburg Line," however, so it's been lost, which also probably means the end of that lovely defense strategy drawn up by General von Falkenhausen.

18 NOVEMBER

There was no Nanking edition of the *China Press* today. The printers have probably all fled. Day and night a steady stream of rickshas, carts, wagons, cars, and trucks, all piled high with baggage, rolls out of the city, mostly in the direction of the river, since the vast throng is trying to flee upriver to Hankow and beyond. At the same time many regiments of new soldiers are arriving in the city from the north. It would appear, then, that the plan is stubbornly to defend the city. Many of the soldiers look awfully wretched. Entire columns arrive without any footwear. They all march by in total silence, an endless mute procession of weary figures.

Yesterday I felt much the way Mutti felt recently when she was in Peking helping Gretel and Willi[7] pack up. I wandered from room to room trying to choose the things I wanted to pack and store on board the *Kutwo*. And as I did it came to me how very much our hearts hang on such things.

Every bag and trunk had to be brought down from the attic, and then we packed for a good part of the night. At 10 o'clock this morning the first six trunks were ready and could be sent down to the harbor in two *mashaws*,[8] at 5 dollars a piece. Our boy Tung took charge of transporting them. The launch is scheduled to leave the Chung Shang Mato wharf for the *Kutwo* at 11 o'clock.

This afternoon Herr Siegel from Kunst & Albers arrived with a truck and was able to fetch 3 more trunks, as well as 5 pieces of baggage that belong to Rilz the teacher and that were stored here with me when Rilz was transferred to Spalato.

When Tung our office boy had not returned by 7 in the evening, I drove out to Hsiakwan, pulling up just in time for the arrival of the launch that was scheduled for 11 this morning. When they started loading the baggage it turned into a general mess. To keep both baggage and boys from falling into the water I had to intervene with a loud shout of "Stop!" Result: a hell of a row with one of the boys, who assaulted me with the following response:

"*Shegoan*—out of my way! You have no say here. I am carrying the carpet of his excellency the ambassador, and it comes first!"

He didn't get any farther than that, because I simply shouted him down.

By 8 o'clock most of the 600 pieces of baggage that had been assembled on the pier were successfully loaded on the launch. After 20 minutes in the dark and by a driving rain, and after finally sorting out and delivering on board the various ladies with their babies and then the baggage, we were all swearing like sailors. Exhausted and drenched to the bone, I arrived home at 9, and then we went on packing and packing until after midnight, as much as the trunks could hold.

From the Diary of Horst Baerensprung[9] (excerpt)

"The fleeing army stealthily bore naught but its honor and the weapons of war"—those verses kept coming to my mind as I watched those endless columns in the rain. From a suburb of Nanking, I watched for almost seven hours as troops passed along the rutted muddy road. One company after the other. Even most of the officers were on foot, only a few rode drenched and matted Mongolian ponies. The rain whipped at them mercilessly, incessantly, and most soldiers carried umbrellas made of simple oilpaper. The clouds hung so low that you could almost grab hold of them. The Purple Mountain and Lion Hill, the hallmarks of Nanking, were lost in thick fog. The weather had a good side however: No air raids were to be expected.

The soldiers bore modern rifles on their shoulders, and hand grenades hung from their belts, but they had only straw sandals for their feet. No backpack, no coat, only thin summer uniforms despite the icy wind. Each man carried a rolled-up blanket or piece of canvas slung over his shoulder, that was all. What princes our soldiers were in contrast, each with his own backpack! A number of heavily laden coolies formed the baggage train. Everything was carried on bamboo poles. In lieu of a field kitchen, two coolies carried one huge kettle. Then came several mules with modern machine guns and quick-firing rifles, well-protected by canvas. As I looked at these carefully wrapped machine guns and then at those soldiers, who were soaked to the bone and—as you could see right off—had spent the night in some rain-drenched field, I was reminded of the motto that on the marshal's order has been engraved on every firearm, from simple rifles to howitzers: "Never forget, my son, that this weapon was bought with the sweat and blood of our people!" Most coolies will never earn as much in their whole life as one of the weapons they carry costs. There is no money for clothes, shoes, and other comforts, only for guns. Christ probably was thinking of times like these when he advised his disciples: "He that hath no sword, let him sell his garment and buy one." (Luke 22:36)

CHAPTER 2

THINGS GET SERIOUS

The International Safety Committee

19 NOVEMBER

IT'S STILL RAINING, and we are still relentlessly packing. I'm trying to close the company books, but work keeps getting in the way of work. Han has drawn out a large sum in cash. I'm transferring most of the company's money and 2,000 dollars of my own to Hankow. All the employees will be given their full November salary now, so that they can buy food before the last shops close. I can store only one ton of coal and four canisters of petroleum, there's simply no more to be had at present. The servants walk about with large, terrified eyes, because they think I'll be leaving on the *Kutwo* as well. They'll be happy again once I explain straight out that I am definitely staying on in Nanking, come what may.

An International Committee has been formed, made up primarily of American doctors from Kulou Hospital and professors from Nanking University, all missionaries. They want to try to create a refugee camp, or better, a neutral zone inside or outside the city, where noncombatants can take refuge in case the city comes under fire. Since word has got around that I intend to stay on, I was approached about whether I would like to join the committee. I agreed and at dinner this evening at Professor Smythe's home, I made the acquaintance of a good number of the American members.

Three people from the German embassy are remaining behind for now: Hürter, Dr. Rosen, and Scharffenberg. It's unclear to me why they're keeping Dr. Rosen here. When I learn that he did not volunteer, I ask Frau Trautmann to intercede with the ambassador, who is still here for the moment, to get the order reversed. Frau Trautmann will do what she can. What good to us is someone whose heart is not in this? Dr. Rosen knows nothing about my intervention yet and he never needs to learn. Melchior of Carlowitz & Co. tried to talk me out of my decision to stay. I thanked him, but declined.

I am not walking into this enterprise with my eyes closed. My decision has been made. Don't be angry with me, Dora dear. I cannot do otherwise! By the way, Dr. Hirschberg and his family, as well as Frau von Schuckmann, are all staying on; so is Mr. Hansen, the head of Texas Oil Co. So I'm not the only one risking his hide. Mr. Han is determined to stay by me through thick and thin. I expected no less of him. A fine fellow!

20 NOVEMBER

At 6 p.m. an extra edition of a Chinese newspaper announces that the Chinese government has been moved to Chungking. Nanking Broadcasting confirms the news and at the same time declares that Nanking will be defended to the last drop of blood.

21 NOVEMBER

I'm worried about my dugout. The water keeps on rising. I'm afraid we won't be able to use it for the next few days, since we don't have time now to bail it out. I'm on the lookout for a better dugout. There really must be several bombproof shelters in the city now. If I could find something for me and my charges, what a fine thing that would be!

Mr. Pai, the manager of the electricity works, asks if he can live at my house. Agreed! And now here comes the first engineer, Mr. Loh Fatsen, who wants to live here, too, along with his wife and servants. Once the Transocean Agency has left on the *Kutwo,* the schoolhouse will be empty and available again.

At 1:30 this afternoon I drove to Chung Shang wharf to check on my baggage, hoping to take the launch scheduled to leave for the *Kutwo* at 2 o'clock. The launch finally arrives at 4. I have only 10 minutes on board the *Kutwo* to race through the baggage room. Much to my satisfaction, I find the last crates that were sent off this morning. After a brief good-bye to the passengers, who are calmly sitting there playing cards and drinking beer, I take the launch, which is honking impatiently now, back to Hsiakwan. My last bridge is burned.

I visit Dr. Baerensprung, the successor to Freiherr von Lamezan, who is currently in charge of the police. I would like a pass to be able to drive my car without being stopped after the second alarm sounds, and after 10 p.m. as well. Baerensprung is likewise leaving for Hankow tomorrow, he has just received his orders from the marshal. He gives me his calling card to present to General Wang Kopang, the chief of police, whom I am supposed to visit tomorrow—that's if he hasn't already left as well.

22 NOVEMBER

My neighbor the cobbler can go to hell! Whenever the *ying bao* sounds, he comes running with his wife and children, grandfather and grandmother, and God knows how many other relatives, but now that there's three feet of water to be bailed in the dugout he's nowhere to be seen. Just wait!

A call from Dr. Rosen: We few Germans who have remained behind are to discuss our future at the now empty embassy at ten o'clock. Meanwhile I've drummed together all available hands and backs to bail out the dugout. As for the cobbler, all is forgotten and forgiven. He, his wife, his three children, and a half dozen of his relatives have been busy bailing away. We finally got the pit emptied out, but then discovered that unfortunately part of the dugout, the west wall, has collapsed.

In between two alarms, a conversation with Dr. Rosen at the German embassy. Rosen is staying on after all. My intercession did no good.

Five p.m. meeting of the International Committee for Establishing a Neutral Zone for Noncombatants in Nanking. They elect me chairman. My protests are to no avail. I give in for the sake of a good cause. I hope I prove worthy of the post, which can very well become important. The German ambassador, to whom I introduce Dr. Smythe shortly before he leaves to board his ship, gives his consent to the text of a telegram to be sent to the Japanese ambassador by way of the American consulate general in Shanghai, which has a wireless. We already have the permission of the

English and American ambassadors. The committee decides that the text of the telegram should not be published before the Japanese ambassador in Shanghai has received it. We truly hope our appeal is not in vain. France is not represented on the committee, since there are no French here. The same is true of Italy. The text of the telegram reads in part as follows:

> An international committee composed of nationals of Denmark, Germany, Great Britain, and the United States, desires to suggest to the Chinese and Japanese authorities the establishment of a Safety Zone for Civilian Refugees in the unfortunate event of hostilities at or near Nanking. The International Committee will undertake to secure from the Chinese authorities specific guarantees that the proposed "Safety Zone" will be made free and kept free from military establishments and offices, including those of communications; from the presence of armed men other than civilian police with pistols; and from the passage of soldiers or military officers in any capacity. The International Committee would inspect and observe the Safety Zone to see that these undertakings are satisfactorily carried out. . . .
>
> The International Committee earnestly hopes that the Japanese authorities may find it possible for humanitarian reasons to respect the civilian character of this Safety Zone. The Committee believes that merciful foresight on behalf of civilians will bring honor to the responsible authorities on both sides. In order that the necessary negotiations with the Chinese authorities may be completed in the shortest possible time, and also in order that adequate preparations may be made for the care of refugees, the Committee would respectfully request a prompt reply from the Japanese authorities to this proposal.

LATER

Returning home from the committee meeting, I am asked by our houseboy Chang to find a doctor for his wife. Dr. Hirschberg comes to examine her and determines that Chang's wife must have had a miscarriage about three or four days ago; she must be taken to Kulou Hospital as soon as possible.

23 NOVEMBER

My fifty-fifth birthday—congratulations, Rabe! At first my mood was somewhat gloomy and overcast. We could use some overcast weather, too, right now! I received a telegram from Mutti and a very lovely scarf. Many thanks! The scarf however has not yet arrived. Frau Trautmann was supposed to bring it with her, but I haven't been able to make much sense of her explanations. Presumably the little package was sent by mail, and it never got through. So that's that!

Around 5 a.m. I was roused from bed by a phone call from Cavalry Captain Lorenz. He is just returning from the front and wants to board the *Kutwo;* but it steamed away yesterday evening. At 7 o'clock Herr Huldermann, editor of the *Ostasiatischer Lloyd,* and Wolf Schenke were at the door. Both have made their way here from Shanghai and want to speak to the ambassador. They take Hürter's car to drive to Wuhu, where they hope to catch up with the *Kutwo.* At 8 o'clock I take Chang's wife to Kulou Hospital. The poor woman is in terrible pain.

A steady stream of wounded men are arriving at Hsiakwan station. Dr. Smythe sends some student volunteers to the station to receive them. I have to lend the students my car.

Mr. Han arrives with some good news. A Chinese friend of his wants to give me two trucks with 100 canisters of gasoline and 200 sacks of flour. Now that's a birthday present! We can do something with that, particularly since the committee will have urgent need of food and vehicles. If only the news turns out to be true!

5 p.m.: Tea party given by Mr. Chang Chun, the former foreign minister and now chief secretary of the Ministry of Foreign Affairs. In addition to about 50 Americans and Europeans from various countries, the party was attended by: General Tang, who is in charge of the defense of the city, General Wang Kopang, the chief of police, and Mr. Ma, the mayor. The "main idea" is that all of us remaining Europeans and Americans are to gather each evening between eight and nine o'clock at the International Club, so that we can remain in contact with leading Chinese figures or their representatives. A good idea. We had a "roundtable" of that sort in Peking, too, during the world war.

My marvelous birthday present of two trucks plus drivers, gasoline, and flour has turned into one empty truck with no driver, etc. All the rest is supposed to be standing somewhere behind Ho Ping Men, the closed city gate.

Wolf Schenke: Nanking's Final Days[10]

On my return I found remaining behind: three members of the embassy staff who had been assigned to stay at their posts and Herr John H. D. Rabe, in whose house I had always been a welcome guest on earlier visits to Nanking. Herr Kröger from Carlowitz & Co. and Herr Sperling had likewise remained behind, though I did not have occasion to meet them. Each painted the most dreadful picture of the imminent capture of the city. Each was aware that his remaining behind might well prove to be a matter of life and death. It was less that they feared the shelling of the city by Japanese artillery and airplanes. That danger was really nothing compared to what was to be expected from the flood of retreating Chinese troops. They considered all eventualities, but the results of their deliberations were anything but hopeful. Had not the troops of the Kuomintang under Chiang Kai-shek murdered foreigners and raped foreign women upon their arrival in Nanking in 1927?

They had seen the Szechuan soldiers march to the front, looking like the semibandits they were. In previous wars it had been standard practice for Chinese soldiers, especially those of defeated and retreating armies, to burn, sack, and pillage the local population. They pictured the retreating army, defeated and demoralized by the Japanese, flooding through Nanking. Would not their rage and hate be directed against the whites? The old xenophobia would surely break out anew.

They recalled events that had occurred in Canton a decade before. These included scenes of bestial cruelty beyond the imaginings of a European brain. It is not easy to brazen out that sort of future. But that is what those who remained behind in Nanking did.

Unless I obtained a press card from the Chinese foreign ministry, it would be impossible for me to send press telegrams home. After a long conversation with the remaining staff at the embassy, it was agreed that I should continue on to Hankow.

Herr Scharffenberg quickly scanned the mail I had brought with me (from Shanghai), culled out what was secondary, and put the important items in a new envelope. We wanted to take them on with us to Wuhu, where the German ambassador Dr. Trautmann was on board the *Kutwo*.

Despite our haste, I wanted to say goodbye to Herr Rabe. Hürter turned off the main road toward "Siemens City," as the Germans in Nanking called the grounds of Siemens China Co., where there was a little German school, which owed its foundation primarily to Herr Rabe. Johny Rabe was sitting at his typewriter in his office, writing his diary. Rabe had not remained in Nanking for business reasons, but in order to erect a zone of refuge for the 200,000 noncombatants of Nanking, similar to that created by Pater Jacquinot in Shanghai.

I was personally very skeptical of the plan, since the committee lacked the authority to maintain law and order and prevent either Chinese or, later on, Japanese soldiers from entering the zone. Rabe said: "Well, after working here for 30 years and spending most of your life here, it's worth taking the risk."

In our brief conversation he still kept his old good humor, but it seemed to me to be more of a gallows humor now. Although I had every good reason to leave Nanking, somehow in the presence of Rabe and Hürter I felt like someone who is saving his own neck while others march toward an almost certain death.

24 NOVEMBER

Reuters has issued a premature report about the International Committee's plans. Dr. Rosen heard on the radio yesterday noon that Tokyo is already protesting on account of the Reuters telegram. They want to know why the American embassy, which has already left Nanking, should have anything to do with such plans. Upon learning this, Dr. Rosen sent the following telegram, via the American Navy, to the German general consulate in Shanghai:

> Local international private committee with English, American, Danish, and German members, under chairmanship of German Siemens agent, Herr Rabe, applied to Chinese and Japanese for creation of civilian safety zone should Nanking become directly involved in hostilities. Via general consulate, American ambassador passed suggestion on to Japanese ambassador in Shanghai and to Tokyo. New safety zone to be safe refuge only for noncombatants if needed.
>
> Given German chairmanship, I would ask unofficial, but no less warm support of humanitarian proposals.
>
> Have only phrase book[11] here. Please pass on to Tokyo and send both your response and answer from Tokyo via American Navy.
>
> ROSEN

Dr. J. Henry Liu, chief of staff at the Central Hospital, has departed, and two of the doctors that he left in charge have likewise bolted. If the American missionary doctors don't hold out, I don't know what will become of all the many casualties. Meanwhile, I have got the one truck I was given up and running. Liu, our chauffeur, is driving under a German flag in order to keep it from being commandeered. The Chinese soldiers are now commandeering every truck they come across. I hear from Christian Kröger (who works for Carlowitz) that a *ming lin* has been issued, that is, an order for all the inhabitants of Nanking to leave the city.

25 NOVEMBER

We're worried about the doctor problem. We've telegraphed the Red Cross in Hong Kong, Shanghai, and Hankow to send us doctors and medicines. We couldn't ask for foreign doctors because the telegram was sent via the American embassy, which, like all other embassies, has ordered its citizens to leave Nanking.

I never dreamed that I would be called upon once again to save the old Imperial Chinese curio collection,[12] and yet it has come to that. The truck, my birthday vehicle from the I-Ho-Tung Brick Works, after having been used for a while to transport students to care for the wounded, has been placed at the disposal of Dr. Han Liwu,[13] who has assembled a whole parking lot full of trucks in order to take to the harbor, would you believe, 15,000 crates of curios that the government wants to ship to Hankow. They're afraid that if they fall into the hands of the Japanese, they'll be taken to Peking. Where they actually belong!

It was reported yesterday on Shanghai radio that the Japanese command is receptive to our attempts to create a neutral zone here for noncombatants. No official reply has arrived as yet.

Han's dugout has now collapsed as well. He has to build a new one. Besides which, he has been getting a room in the school ready for his family to move into. Frau Ella Gao has sent a number of crates and trunks for me to take care of, among them two wall clocks wrapped in paper and inscribed: "Fragile, Clocks!"

My neighbor, the cobbler, that miserable cobbler, has now become my friend. We are bosom buddies. He and his family have been bailing water from the dugout all day, and on the side he has made me a lovely pair of brown boots for ten dollars. I volunteered an additional dollar to further cement our friendship.

According to the radio, the Japanese have thus far given no definitive answer to the question of a neutral zone for noncombatants. I have decided to telegraph Hitler and Kriebel[14] via the German general consulate in Shanghai and Lahrmann, the national group leader there. I managed to get off the following telegram today:

German Consulate General Shanghai

I respectfully ask National Group Leader Lahrmann to send on the following telegram stop

First to the Führer stop

Undersigned Deputy Group Leader Nanking, chairman of local International Committee, asks his Führer kindly to intercede with the Japanese government to grant permission for creation of a neutral zone for noncombatants, since imminent battle for Nanking otherwise endangers the lives of over two hundred thousand people stop

With German greetings Rabe Siemens agent in Nanking stop

Second to General Consul Kriebel stop

Urgently request support of my petition to the Führer for his intercession with the Japanese government concerning creation of a neutral zone for noncombatants, since dreadful bloodbath otherwise inevitable in imminent battle for Nanking stop Heil Hitler!

Rabe Siemens representative and Chairman of International Committee in Nanking stop.

Since I am not sure if Herr Lahrmann may not perhaps be alarmed at the high cost of these telegrams I have asked that the cost be advanced by Siemens China Co. Shanghai against my account.

All bus traffic has been suspended today. All buses, I'm told, have been sent to Hankow. It will probably be somewhat quieter in the streets, although over 200,000 Chinese—noncombatants—are still in the city. By God, I hope Hitler helps us so that we can set up the neutral zone at last.

In answer to my question, Dr. Han Liwu has just told me that we need not worry about the Chinese government's approval for setting up a neutral zone: The generalissimo has personally given his consent.

We have now found a foreign director for our committee, Mr. Fitch of the YMCA, Nanking. All we're waiting for now is Japanese consent.

A telegram for me from the company's main Shanghai office has arrived at the German embassy; it reads:

For Siemens. Local Siemens branch advises: You are free to leave Nanking—Avoid personal danger—Suggest move to Hankow—Telegraph your intentions.

I told the embassy to reply:

For Siemens Shanghai from Rabe stop Thank you for your telegram of 25 November—have decided to remain in Nanking—have accepted chairmanship of International Committee for creation of neutral zone to protect over two hundred thousand noncombatants.

Mr. Han has managed to fetch the 100 canisters of gasoline from the I-Ho-Tung Brick Works, as well as 20 sacks of flour. They are working to build a new dugout in the garden. I'll have to find somewhere else to store the gasoline. One hundred canisters in the garden seems somewhat too risky even to me.

Dr. Smythe telephones that a Tokyo newspaper has suggested that a neutral zone in Nanking would make it more difficult to take the city, and/or delay its being taken. . . . What are we to do if the plan doesn't work. The danger is truly great. My hope is Hitler.

Rosen is very concerned that if the city is bombarded we shall all still be able to get away in time on the *Hulk,* a Jardines lines steamer that, if need be, the Hirschbergs plan to flee with as well. That's all very reasonable of course, but it's so discouraging when all you think or hear about is getting out. The Chinese around me are so calm and composed. To them the main thing is that the master doesn't cut and run, everything else will take care of itself. And I can't rid myself of the feeling that I simply and absolutely must hold out. Except, I admit, I would indeed like to be somewhere a little safer than this house.

Perhaps I can find another place to live. Dr. Rosen has been offered the house of Minister Chang Chun, which has a marvelous shelter. I need to go over and have a look at the fortress, and then the big question will be: Move or not? I can't take along all the people that have gathered here around me. But I can't be in two houses at once, either, and ultimately it's my poor presence that counts.

27 NOVEMBER

Tsao the cook is still sick. He had a prescription for Jacopral, but couldn't find any, since the pharmacists have all scattered. Today, five days later, it suddenly occurs to people to tell me. For now, I've given him some from my own small supply. Moreover, the man's been sleeping in an unheated room for a week (just to save money, I'm sure). So I lend him a kerosene stove. When I ask why he hasn't bought a coal-burning stove, he replies: There are no more stovepipes to be had, the tinsmiths have all closed shop.

A great lover of jokes, John Rabe sits at his desk with helmet and field glasses.

I think that's a white lie, but I'll have to check on it. Our good Tsao has not made himself very popular with the rest of the staff—which is why they let him get into this state and that, of course, can't be permitted.

It's touching how Dr. Rosen worries about me. Of all the Germans who have stayed behind, I am his biggest problem child. He is quite rightly afraid that I'll remain here and not want to flee with him and the other Germans and English, etc. on board the *Hulk*. He personally handed me a pass that was issued by Prideaux-Brune, the English consul, and that permits me to board the *Hulk*, which is to be tugged upstream shortly. He has also arranged to pass the house of ex-minister Chang Chun on to me, just in case—no matter whether I can use it or not. In short—he does everything he possibly can! We had a long conversation yesterday afternoon, that is to say, he told me about his life. His grandfather[15] was a friend of Beethoven's. He showed me a letter Beethoven wrote his grandfather. His family has been in diplomatic service for almost a hundred years. His father was once foreign minister, but he will probably stay a legation secretary all his life—a Jewish grandmother in his family has ruined his career. A tragic fate!

From Georg Rosen's Personal File

Because of his fate, which was hardly unique in those days, Georg Rosen deserves a more detailed account:

Georg Rosen, Dr. jur., was born in Teheran in 1895. His father and his grandfather Rosen had been important Orientalists, both having also worked for the Foreign Service, the grandfather in the service of Prussia, the North German Confederation, and the Empire. His father, Friedrich Rosen, was foreign minister from May to October 1921.

Both of Georg Rosen's grandfathers had married daughters of the pianist and composer Ignaz Moscheles, one of Beethoven's pupils and confidants late in life.

"Beethoven's last letter," Georg Rosen wrote in an account of his life, "was to him, as were the letters of those who were at Beethoven's bedside as he lay dying. Everything posterity knows about Beethoven's final hours comes from a letter he wrote to my great grandfather (Ignaz Moscheles), who was living in London at the time."

Georg Rosen entered the foreign service in 1921. After Hitler assumed power, he was considered "related to Jews." For the moment, however, he was allowed to remain in service, since in 1917 he had voluntarily left Portugal to serve in the war for Germany and had fought on the western front; he was never promoted, however, and was left in entry-level positions until he resigned.

From 1933 to 1938, he was legation secretary at the embassy, first in Peking, then, after it moved, in Nanking in 1936 and finally Hankow in 1937. Rosen was temporarily charged with consular duties. But in 1938 he was placed on the inactive list; because of his wartime service in 1917–18, however, he was not released from the civil service, so that he continued to receive moneys owed him. With the official approval of the Foreign Ministry, he moved to London in 1938. At the start of the war, he was first detained there, but in 1940 was able to move to the United States, where he taught at various universities during the war. His wife and children, whom he had left behind in Germany, lived from his pension; when Frau Rosen was killed in an air raid, the money was then transferred to the children's guardian. Apparently the Foreign Ministry used every legal means available to ease his circumstances.

He returned at the end of the war and entered the Foreign Service for the Federal Republic of Germany; he first became secretary of the embassy in London and was then ambassador to Uruguay until his retirement in 1960. He died one year later.

Georg Rosen was a German nationalist with right-wing views. He often spoke his mind candidly, could be touchy, and also short-tempered on occasion; he did not believe in compromise. He approached the Japanese in Nanking with head held high and, in contrast to the more diplomatic John Rabe, was sometimes very blunt as well. He was greatly hurt by the discrimination he suffered under Hitler's race laws and shared his sorrow with Rabe.

"A tragic fate," John Rabe wrote. On the day when he spoke to Rabe, 27 November 1937, did Rosen know that only three days before a telegram had been signed by the director of personnel at the Foreign Ministry and sent to the embassy in Hankow? It read:

Telegram

(In secret code)
For the ambassador only.

Please tactfully inform Rosen that there can be no question of his returning after vacation and that due to his non-Aryan ancestry he will be placed on the inactive list.

PRÜFER

27 NOVEMBER, EVENING

A meeting at 69 Peking Road at 6 p.m., General Tang, the city commandant, is present and gives a speech. He points out that some disorder may arise among his troops during the impending battle to defend the city. To the extent that it is within his power he will provide protection to all foreigners. The gates of the city are closed, but until the very last moment we foreigners will have the chance to pass through them.

Dr. Rosen, Prideaux-Brune, the British consul, and Atchinson, secretary of the American embassy, are with Generalissimo Chiang Kai-shek this afternoon. They want to hear the unvarnished truth about plans to defend the city. A very good idea!

Since our International Committee has not yet received an answer from any Japanese officials, another telegraph message was sent today to the

Japanese ambassador in Shanghai by way of the American embassy. There is, of course, no telling whether my telegrams to Hitler and Kriebel did any good. But they should be in Berlin by now I think.

We have scheduled a meeting of the International Committee for 2 p.m. tomorrow. Even if we do not receive any answer from the Japanese, we must make some arrangements, at least draw up plans for insuring the general safety.

28 NOVEMBER

Dr. Rosen shared with me the following results of yesterday's conference with the generalissimo:

Question: "Will the defense be limited to areas outside the city or will the battle continue inside the city walls?" Answer: "We are prepared for both."

Another question: "Who will be responsible for order if worst comes to worst, that is who will remain behind as the last administrative official in the city and see to it that the power of the police is used to prevent mob violence?" To which the marshal, or maybe General Tang, replied: "In such a case the Japanese will have to establish order."

In other words: No administrative official will remain here. No one is going to sacrifice himself for the welfare of hundreds of thousands of inhabitants! What a prospect! Good God, if only Hitler would help! The misery that a full-fledged bombardment will bring upon this city is unimaginable.

I also hear from Dr. Rosen that the ambassador is said to have asked from Hankow who the German was that telegraphed the Führer. In the meantime, Dr. Trautmann has likewise received the letter Dr. Rosen wrote him. . . . No mention of the neutral zone on the radio at noon.

Sperling picks me up for the 3 o'clock meeting of the committee at Dr. Smythe's, at which Mr. Fitch is officially named the director and Dr. Han Liwu the Chinese codirector. We agree to take no further steps until we receive official word from the Japanese.

Reverend Mills suggests we attempt as soon as possible to inform the highest Chinese dignitaries—the generalissimo and General Tang—that from a military point of view any defense of Nanking is absurd, and that we ought to consider whether it wouldn't be better to surrender the city peacefully. Dr. Han Liwu replies that this is not the appropriate moment for such an action. We should wait until we have received a positive answer from Japanese officials that a Safety Zone is possible.

We adjourn at 4:30 without having accomplished much, precisely because things are still up in the air. At 6 o'clock, a meeting at the British Cultural Association. Postal Commissioner Ritchie informs us that the post office is officially closed. You can still put letters in the mailbox, which will occasionally be emptied. Mr. Ritchie appears a little nervous. His entire vast staff, which has functioned well up till now, is drifting away.

There is talk that the Japanese are about 40 miles from Wuhu and could be here in three days. Something fishy about that; I'd say it's not possible.

At the meeting we are also given large handbills printed in Chinese that we're to paste on the front door so that we won't be bothered by Chinese soldiers. Soldiers are said to have paid a visit to the house of a German military advisor in the city today. But the problem was quickly resolved.

I had my nameplate and the German flag put up at my new house at Ninhai Lu 5 today. But the palace will be only my token residence. They're now hard at work building the third dugout in my garden.

The second one had to be abandoned because the excavation pit was completely flooded. Wang Kopang, the chief of police, has repeatedly declared that 200,000 Chinese are still living in the city. In response to my question whether he'll be remaining in the city himself, he replied as expected: As long as I can. Which means, he'll decamp!

29 NOVEMBER

Sperling calls to tell me that Wang Kopang has stepped down and that a new man has been named in his place. Dr. Smythe reports that the new man will stay, that he and his police force won't run away. A bit of good news at last. A meeting of the committee at 4 o'clock. We have to make some progress, even if the Japanese don't recognize the neutral zone.

Dr. Rosen calls to say that according to a report from Tokyo the Japanese are still considering whether or not to accept our proposal of a neutral zone.

I have the feeling that perhaps some action has already been taken by Germany in our favor, but that speeches like those of General Tang (saying Nanking must be defended no matter what) only damage our cause. He's a general, of course, and so has to make warlike noises; but it's not appropriate in the present case, especially since the city cannot be effectively defended. Sitting in this crook in the Yangtze is like sitting in a mousetrap.

Straightening things up, I chance on a picture of the Führer, with the following poem by Baldur von Schirach, head of the Reich Youth Organization:

> Our Führer's greatness does not simply lie
> in leading us as hero of each heart,
> but in himself: firm will and steady eye
> are rooted deep within our world, they start
> inside a soul that reaches to the sky.
> And is a man, the same as you and I.

That gave me courage again. I continue to hope that Hitler will help us. *A man of firm will and steady eye—the same as you and I*—has deep sympathy not only for the distress of his own people, but for the anguish of the Chinese as well. There is not a German, or any other foreigner here, who is not convinced that a single word from Hitler, and only from him, would have the greatest possible effect on the Japanese in helping establish our proposed neutral zone, and he will speak that word!

At 6 o'clock the regular meeting at the British Cultural Club. The mayor formally announces the formation of the International Committee. I report that we have the moral support of all embassies, that with the assistance of the American embassy we have already sent two telegrams to the Japanese ambassador in Shanghai, and that I personally have telegraphed both Hitler and Kriebel. I add that no direct answer from Hitler is to be expected, since these matters of high diplomacy are handled in other ways. I state, however, that I am firmly convinced that the Führer will not refuse to help. I ask those gathered to be patient for another day or two, since we ought not yet abandon hope that the Japanese officials will give their permission.

The generalissimo has placed 100,000 dollars at the committee's disposal. I nominate Kröger as treasurer. The others concur and with no hesitation he accepts the job. I've asked Kröger to move into my new house (Ninhai Lu 5), and he has agreed.

Despite a German flag, my truck has been taken over by soldiers guarding the Interior Ministry. I call up Colonel Lung, General Tang's deputy, and get my truck back at eleven p.m.

30 NOVEMBER

I've ordered Mr. Han to move his family in with me. He's living in a few rooms at the school where he had a kitchen and bathroom installed. His friend Sung, the proprietor of the I-Ho-Tung Brick Works and my benefactor, is moving in with me as well. The new dugout is not yet finished. We're working at top speed. In addition to a wall of loose bricks—we have no cement—supported by wooden boards on both sides, we've also used steel plates for the dugout. I don't know who commandeered them. They were suddenly just there, like so many other things. My garden is a sight to behold. I sent the truck to fetch another large water tank because I'm afraid water from the city waterworks will be cut off; we also have a supply of candles. And our coal reserves will last about a month.

Han Hsianglin, John Rabe's able and devoted assistant at Siemens.

Last night I sterilized the reserve instruments for my insulin injections. I always carry with me one set of instruments and three vials of insulin. Chang's wife is still in the hospital, the cook as well, but he's doing a little better. He swallows his Jacopral and thinks it helps because it tastes so awful.

Dr. Brown, who is a physician, and a French monk have arrived from Wuhu. They want to set up a neutral zone in Wuhu as well and are seeking our advice. When we're pretty much out of good ideas ourselves.

I am trying to obtain more precise data about the number of inhabitants left behind. There is now a rumor that the man who wanted to provide me "very precise" data, Mr. Wang Kopang—the ex-chief of police who resigned because he was not a military man and felt unequal to the task—has been arrested.

Dr. Smythe calls to tell me that we have 60,000 sacks of rice in the city and another 34,000 sacks in Hsiakwan. That may well be enough. What we don't have are mats for our temporary housing—thatched huts. The populace must be sheltered from the cold somehow.

Here is an overview of the problems that the International Committee has to tackle:

1. Finances
2. Police
   Control of entrances
   Boundaries
   Number and location
3. Soldiers and Military elements
   Removal orders and inspection
   Anticipation of flight
   Wounded
4. Food
   Quantity
   Location and distribution
5. Transportation
6. Housing
   Survey
   Use and management of buildings
      (a) public
      (b) institutional
      (c) vacant residential
   Mat sheds

7. Utilities
   Water
   Light
   Telephone

8. Sanitation and Health
   Extra latrines: disposal
   Garbage and refuse collection
   Medical

The following is a list of members of the International Committee for the Nanking Safety Zone:

NAME	NATIONALITY	ADDRESS
John Rabe, Chairman	German	Siemens China Co.
Lewis S. C. Smythe, Secretary	American	University of Nanking
P. H. Munro-Faure	British	Asiatic Petroleum Co.
Rev. John Magee	American	American Church Mission
P. R. Shields	*British*	*International Export Co.*
J. M. Hansen	*Danish*	*Texaco*
G. Schultze-Pantin	*German*	*Shingming Trading Co.*
Iver Mackay	*British*	*Butterfield & Swire*
J. V. Pickering	*American*	*Standard Oil Co.*
Eduard Sperling	German	Shanghai Insurance
Dr. M. S. Bates	American	University of Nanking
Rev. W. P. Mills	American	Presbyterian Mission
J. Lean	*British*	*Asiatic Petroleum Co.*
Dr. C. S. Trimmer	American	University of Nanking
Christian Kröger	German	Carlowitz of Nanking
George Fitch	American	YMCA

The gentlemen whose names are in italics left Nanking before the siege.

I DECEMBER

At 9:30 this morning I drive with Kröger and Sperling to the Ping Tsan Hsian, where the committee has gathered. We assign various tasks and put together a list of the people involved. Mayor Ma appears with his staff at the meeting and promises us 30,000 sacks of rice and 10,000 sacks of flour. Unfortunately we have no trucks for delivering these rations to the refugee zone. We can sell the rice and flour, but we have to fix the price. We will set up soup kitchens.

Dugout No. 3 in our garden is finished, with iron plating for a roof and brickwork exits. This afternoon I receive 20,000 dollars from Garrison

John Rabe's house in Nanking

The office or "headquarters" of the International Safety Zone Committee in Nanking, Ninhai Lu 5, formerly the home of Minister Chang Chun, who made the house available to the German embassy, which then turned it over to John Rabe for his committee. The Chinese people in front are waiting for food or small sums of money distributed to the poor.

Members of the International Safety Zone Committee.

Headquarters as the first payment of the generalissimo's promised 100,000-dollar donation. The answer to my question about when I can expect the rest: shrugs.

Messrs. Fitch, Kröger, Dr. Smythe, Wang from the YMCA, and Riggs visit me in my new house at Ninhai Lu 5, where we want to open Committee Headquarters tomorrow. Dr. Smythe is so taken by the beauty of the house and its splendid furnishings, plus a shelter valued at 17,500 dollars, that he says that in the future he plans to call me simply Mr. John H. D. Rabe-Rockefeller.

6 p.m. committee meeting. We will bear a tremendous responsibility if we first order the remaining populace of Nanking into the neutral zone and then later are turned down flat by the Japanese. A vote is taken, revealing that the majority of the members are in favor of going forward. The text of the announcement for people to move into the zone must be very carefully worded. We first want to ask the Chinese news agencies how many inhabitants are still left, meaning, we want to measure the barometric pressure of the Chinese mood.

Dr. Rosen has received news via the Americans that National Group

Leader and Party-Comrade Lahrmann did forward my telegrams to Hitler and Kriebel. Thank God! I'm certain now that help will come. The Führer won't leave me in the lurch.

Dr. Rosen asks the Germans to meet and discuss when people will have to board the *Hulk*. Herr Kröger, Herr Sperling, young Hirschberg, and Hatz, an Austrian engineer, all want to remain here to help me. Those under consideration for the *Hulk* include: Frau Hirschberg and daughter, who are already on board; plus Dr. Rosen, Hürter, and Scharffenberg, all three from the embassy; two sales clerks, Fräulein Neumann and a Russian woman whose name I don't know; and the bookkeeper at Café Kiessling.

Dr. Hirschberg has taken the ailing Chang Chun to Hankow, after I gave him some of my insulin supply. Dr. Hirschberg wants to return by airplane, he says, because we are in urgent need of doctors. I name (our Siemens assistant) Han, along with his friend Sung from the I-Ho-Tung Brick Works, to be food commissioner. Han simply beams: He's never held such a high-ranking job in his whole life.

2 DECEMBER

Through the good offices of Pater Jacquinot[16] we have received the following telegram (in translation) from the Japanese officials:

Telegram to Ambassy[17] Nanking, 1 December 1937

Your November 30th.
Following for Nanking Safety Zone Committee:

Japanese authorities have duly noted request for safety zone but regret cannot grant it. In the event of Chinese forces misbehavior towards civilians and or property cannot assume responsibility, but they themselves will endeavor to respect the district as far as consistent with military necessity.

JACQUINOT

According to radio reports, London regards this reply as a flat-out refusal. We are of a different opinion here. The answer is cleverly couched in diplomatic terms, leaving a backdoor open, but is generally favorable. We certainly do not expect the Japanese to assume responsibility for "misbehavior by Chinese forces." The telegram's last sentence: "The latter will attempt to respect the district . . . etc." is very satisfactory.

The following reply was telegraphed via the American embassy:

Please transmit to Father Jacquinot Shanghai following message from International Committee for Nanking Safety Zone: Cordial thanks for your services. Committee appreciates Japanese assurance of endeavor to respect the district as far as consistent with military necessity. We have secured full agreement from Chinese military authorities for exact compliance with original proposal. Committee is therefore proceeding with work of organization and administration in safety zone and informs you refugees already entering. At proper time and after inspection Committee will formally notify both Chinese and Japanese authorities that Zone is in operation.

Committee would ask you kindly to confer again with Japanese authorities pointing out that direct assurances from them to us would go still further to lessen the anxieties of distressed civilians, and respectfully requesting them to give us early notification to that effect.

JOHN RABE, Chairman

The return from Hankow of the German ambassador, Dr. Trautmann, and Dr. Lautenschlager, the secretary of the legation,[18] is cause for great surprise. When asked, Dr. Rosen explains that it has nothing to do with the work of the committee. In confidence, Dr. Rosen informs me that the ambassador did not fully agree with my telegrams to the Führer and Kriebel: In his opinion they were unnecessary! I will go see Dr. Trautmann tomorrow, since I have no time today. I assume his return has something to do with Germany's attempt to be a mediator.

We're having great difficulty finding vehicles to transport the rice and flour placed at our disposal, some of which is stored outside the Safety Zone without anyone guarding it. We're told that large quantities have already been removed by military authorities. Allegedly only 15,000 sacks of rice are still left of the 30,000 given us.

Mayor Ma denies that the police have been instructed to leave the city with the military, as Dr. Rosen informed me after having overheard some remarks by the embassy police. At 8 p.m. a farewell dinner for Dr. Han Liwu. He is leaving for Hankow this evening with 14,000 crates of curios. He has to leave 1,000 crates behind because of insufficient cargo space. We are very sorry to see him go, for he is an extraordinarily competent man and a great help to us.

3 DECEMBER

Dr. Rosen called on me to extend greetings from Dr. Trautmann, who returned to Hankow yesterday evening on the same customs cruiser that brought him here. The ambassador has in fact been to see the generalissimo with peace proposals, as Dr. Rosen admits after some hesitation. Understandably enough, I cannot get any details of these proposals out of Rosen, and won't attempt to do so again. It suffices for me to know that such steps have indeed been taken. May they lead to good results! Dr. Rosen shows me another telegram that is actually intended for the ambassador, and reads as follows:

> Diplogerma Nanking
> from Hankow 2.12.—to Nanking 3.12.37
>
> Tokyo wires 30. 11. 37: To whatever extent possible, Japanese wish to spare the city, national government, lives, property, foreigners, as well as a peaceful Chinese populace. Japan hopes the Chinese government will act on the advice of the Great Powers and spare its capital the horrors of war. For military reasons a special Safety Zone for Nanking or its fortified area cannot be granted. The Japanese will issue an official explanation in this regard.
>
> SAUKEN

Dr. Rosen has learned that no other embassies here received telegrams with similar contents. It is up to the committee to make use of this information without betraying who sent it. Rosen recommends that we approach Madame Chiang Kai-shek.

Although General Tang, who is in charge of defending the city, promised us that all military personnel and installations would be kept out of the refugee zone, we now learn that three new trenches and/or foundations for antiaircraft batteries are being dug in the Zone. I inform General Tang's emissaries that I will resign my office and disband the International Committee if work is not stopped at once. Written promises to respect my wishes are provided, but I am informed that carrying them out may take some time.

4 DECEMBER

Soldiers continue to build new trenches and install military telephones in-side the Safety Zone. Air raids lasting for hours have begun again. My friend Kröger had business at the airport and was almost killed when several bombs landed not a hundred yards from him.

The refugees have slowly begun to move into the Safety Zone. One small newspaper has repeatedly told the Chinese not to move into the "foreigners" refugee zone. These extortionists write that it's the duty of every Chinese to face the dangers that a bombardment of the city may bring with it.

5 DECEMBER

By 8 a.m. there's already trouble to disturb a lovely bright Sunday. My driver has left me in the lurch; first he has to be fetched, is given a dreadful dressing-down, answers back, is fired, apologizes, and is rehired. I believe this is the twenty-fifth time I've thrown him out and then rehired him!

This pass permitted John Rabe to drive his car through the city.

When I'm finally sitting in the car, the alarm sounds and bombs start dropping, but I have a pass that lets me drive around even after the second alarm. Besides which, there's so much to do that you can hardly worry about bombs. That sounds very heroic, but luckily the bombs kept landing somewhere else.

With the help of the American embassy we have finally received an official answer from Tokyo. The answer is somewhat more detailed, but is not all that much different from the reply wired to us several days ago by Pater Jacquinot, which is to say the Japanese refuse our proposal once again, but promise to respect the Zone if possible.

Together with Dr. Bates and Sperling I pay a call on General Tang, who is in charge of the city's defense, in order to get his consent to have all military personnel and establishments removed from the Zone at once. Imagine our amazement when General Tang tells us that this is quite impossible, that at best it will be another two weeks before the military can vacate the Zone. A nasty blow. It means that the Japanese condition that no Chinese soldiers are to be allowed in the Zone will not be fulfilled. For now at least we cannot even think of claiming to have a "Safety Zone," at most it's a "refugee zone." The matter is discussed at a long committee meeting and a text prepared for release to the press, because if we don't want to see our work destroyed, we dare not let the press learn the whole truth yet. . . .

Meanwhile one bomb after another is falling. When it all gets too noisy, we pull our chairs away from the window. The city gates have been walled up; of the three gates only one half-panel is still open.

We are feverishly trying to get rice and flour into the Zone. Flags marking its borders are being prepared, as well as wall posters intended to explain the Zone to those poor people outside, whose safety we unfortunately cannot guarantee.

Dr. Rosen curses the Chinese military roundly for, as he describes it, having slunk into our Zone, because it's safer next to all those vacant houses with German flags than it is outside the Zone. I can't swear that it's true. But the fact is that General Tang himself received us today in a house inside the refugee zone.

CHAPTER 3

WAITING FOR THE ATTACK

6 DECEMBER

THE LARGEST SHARE of the Americans who stayed behind are boarding an American warship today; the rest are ready to embark at any moment. Only the members of our committee refuse to board. Dr. Rosen has told me in strictest confidence that the peace proposal presented by Ambassador Trautmann has been accepted by Chiang Kai-shek. Dr. Rosen hopes that there will be peace before the Japanese can take Nanking.

I had an interesting conversation with Colonel Huang. He is absolutely against the Safety Zone. In his opinion it demoralizes the troops in Nanking. "Every inch of soil that the Japanese conquer should be fertilized with our blood. Nanking must be defended to the last man. If you had not established your Safety Zone, people now fleeing into the Zone could have helped our soldiers."

What can you say to such monstrous views? And the man is a high official very close to the generalissimo! And so people who had to stay behind because they didn't have the money to flee with their families and a few small possessions, the poorest of the poor, are supposed to pay with their lives for the military's mistakes! Why didn't they force the well-off inhabitants, those 800,000 propertied citizens who fled, to stay? Why is it always the poorest people who must forfeit their lives?

We also got around to talking about the point in time when military personnel and installations are to leave the Safety Zone. At the very last moment and not a minute before, in his view; not until the battle is raging in the streets of Nanking.

If those of us in Nanking want to be truly prepared, we must have rice, flour, salt and fuel, medicine, cooking utensils, and who knows what all besides, inside the Zone before the Japanese arrive. We have to arrange for doctors and nurses, for removal of waste and burials, for police and, if need be, police replacements; for it is highly probable that the police will depart along with the retreating Chinese troops, and then comes the critical moment when mob violence can be expected. Should we follow his example and make preparations for these things only at the last possible moment?

I try to bring Mr. Huang around—to no avail. He is Chinese. What does he care about a few hundred thousand of his countryman? They're poor, and so all they can do is die. We also discuss the problem of defending the city. General von Falkenhausen and all the German advisors have pointed out that this is hopeless. Of course, there must be a line of defense outside it. You can't demand of a general who wants to save face that he simply surrender the city; but a battle at the walls, fighting in the streets, it's insane, just ruthless mass murder! Nothing helps: My powers of persuasion aren't good enough.

Honor, Mr. Huang declares, demands that we fight to the last drop of blood! Well, let's wait and see. Mr. Pai, the manager of electricity works, and Mr. Loh, his first engineer, wanted to hold out in Nanking until the last moment to keep the station running. And it is running. But who's actually responsible, I don't know. Messrs. Pai and Loh bolted long ago.

7 DECEMBER

Last night we heard a great many cars on the move, and at around 5 o'clock this morning a whole host of airplanes passed over just above our house; the generalissimo's farewell salute. Colonel Huang, whom I called on yesterday, has departed as well—on the generalissimo's orders!

Only the very poor are still here, and we few Europeans and Americans who are determined to share our quarters, our so-called Safety Zone, with the poor.

Poor people, with a few household goods and bedding, can be seen fleeing into the Zone from all directions. And they are not even the poorest of the poor, they're the vanguard, the people who still have a little money and can pay for shelter with someone they may know inside the boundaries.

Those who have nothing are yet to arrive. We'll have to open the schools and universities for them, put them in mass shelters and feed them from great soup kitchens. We've been able at best to get a quarter of the food promised us into the Zone, because we don't have enough vehicles, which are constantly being commandeered by the military.

This morning two of our trucks were taken by the military. So far we've only got one of them back; the other, loaded with two tons of salt, has not been returned yet. We're trying to chase it down. Another 20,000 dollars have been paid out by the generalissimo's headquarters. With that we've received a total of 40,000, instead of the 100,000 promised us. We'll just have to make do. The generalissimo probably doesn't know that only part of the donation has been paid out, so you can't really blame him.

The city gates are to be closed tomorrow and the rest of the Americans put on board ship. I sent a telegram to Siemens today asking them to pay up any life insurance premiums that may be due.

Radio Shanghai reports that Dr. Trautmann has returned again to Hankow. His peace proposals have allegedly been turned down by Chiang Kai-shek. As I wrote before, however, according to Dr. Rosen's confidential statement, Dr. Trautmann's peace proposals have already been accepted by the generalissimo, even as final preparations for the defense of the city are being made at this very moment. Every soldier claims that they will fight to the last man.

Houses outside the gates are being burned down. The population from all the suburbs that have been set on fire is being ordered to flee to our Safety Zone, which has quietly been accorded recognition after all. Kröger has just returned from Schmeling's house near the South Gate, which he discovered had been broken into and partially looted. Being a practical man, he ordered the rest of the potables brought back with him.

Mayor Ma was missing at the 6 o'clock press conference, and only about half of the Westerners showed up. The rest have presumably boarded their ships by now.

As a result of a rumor that houses near the gates *inside* the walls are to be burned down as well, panic has broken out among the poor living near the South Gate. Hundreds of families are streaming into our Zone, but now that it's dark they cannot find any shelter. Shivering and weeping, women and children are sitting on their bundles of bedding, waiting for the return of husbands and fathers who are trying to find shelter. We brought 2,117 sacks of rice into the city today. It's doubtful that we'll still be able to get through the gates again tomorrow.

8 DECEMBER

Yesterday afternoon, Chang, our number-one boy, brought his wife home from Kulou Hospital. She still has not recovered, but wants to be near her children in this time of distress. Our coolie is very sad: His family has been left behind, about 40 miles outside the city. He couldn't fetch them, didn't have time, since the cook was sick and he had to take over some of his work. No one said a word to me about it. I thought his family had arrived long ago. It's too late now, unfortunately.

About two years ago, Dr. Trautmann greeted me at a tea party in Peitaiho with the words: "Ah, here comes the mayor of Nanking!" I was deputy local group leader at the time and somewhat offended by his joke. And now his joke has come true in a way. Of course under normal circumstances a European cannot become mayor of a Chinese city. But since Mayor Ma, with whom we have been working closely recently, left Nanking yesterday and since the committee, with his approval, is forced to deal with all the administrative problems and workings of the municipality inside our Safety Zone, I have in fact become something very like an acting mayor. Enough to give you a fit, Rabe!

Thousands of refugees are fleeing into our so-called Safety Zone from all directions; the streets are thronged with more people than in peacetime. The sight of the poorest of the poor wandering aimlessly in the streets is enough to make you weep.

As it grows dark some families, unable to find shelter anywhere, stretch out to sleep in nooks and alcoves of buildings, or simply on the street, despite the cold. We are working feverishly to develop the Zone. Unfortunately we must deal with endless encroachments by the military, who still have not left our Zone and apparently are in no hurry to do so. They're busy burning down houses around the city and sending the refugees to us. I suppose they must think we're terribly stupid for having got involved in relief work on such a grand scale, with no hope of anything in return.

It's the opinion of a few of the foreigners that the entire Chinese opposition is only for show and they will be content with a few mock battles just to save face. I, however, see things differently. I fear that General Tang, who is defending the city, will ruthlessly sacrifice both his soldiers and the civilian population.

I'm going to open an exchange bank, because cash is getting scarce. Two gentlemen from the Chinese government with whom I am friendly are going to help me do it.

We are all close to despair. Chinese military headquarters is our worst problem. Chinese soldiers have removed a whole section of the flags we had just managed to set out around our perimeter. The size of the Zone is to be reduced; they need the reclaimed area for their artillery and fortifications. And with that the whole plan can fall apart, because if the Japanese get wind of it, they'll bombard us without mercy. And that may well turn the Safety Zone into the High Danger Zone. The border is to be checked again tomorrow morning. None of us expected this sort of dirty dealing. The Chinese accepted the Zone definitively on 22 November.

From a Chinese Press Report, the Evening of 8 December 1937:

A week ago yesterday, on 1 December 1937, Mayor Ma approached the International Committee for the Nanking Safety Zone with the demand that they assume full responsibility for the administration of the Safety Zone. The Committee and all its members and staff, with the exception of a few coolies and truck drivers, are doing this work voluntarily and without pay.

9 DECEMBER

We are still busy transporting rice from outside the city. Unfortunately one of our trucks was damaged in the process. One of our transport coolies lost an eye and was taken to the hospital. The committee is seeing to it that he is cared for. The rest of the Americans, along with Dr. Rosen, Scharffenberg, and Hürter, have gone on board the *Hulk*, but if the air is "clear" this evening they want to return to land for our conference.

The crew of another truck arrives back sobbing and weeping. They were at the South Gate, which is being shelled. The guards there didn't want to let the truck out, but were finally talked into it. When the truck returned, of the entire guard unit—about 40 men—not one was still alive.

At 2 o'clock this afternoon I am joined by Dr. Bates, Sperling, Mills, Lung, and a colonel from General Tang's staff to walk the disputed portion of our Safety Zone's border (the southwest section). From the hills we can see the suburbs below wrapped in the smoke and flames of the fires the Chinese have set in order to have a field of operation. We discover a row of antiaircraft batteries within the southwest border of our Zone. During our inspection, three Japanese bombers appear above us and come under heavy fire from the batteries, which are no more than 10 yards ahead of us. We all have to hit the ground. Lying face-up, I was able to follow the flak attack; unfortunately their aim was poor; or let's say, fortunately they missed. I expected bombs to drop on us at any moment. But we were lucky. Since the colonel from the general staff refuses to yield, I threaten to resign and inform him that I will telegraph the Führer that our refugee zone cannot be established because General Tang has broken his word. The colonel and Lung head home in a very pensive mood. Meanwhile we have decided to try a major tactical move, although I put little trust in it. We want to approach Tang once again and try to persuade him to abandon any defense inside the city. To my great amazement, Tang agrees to do so, if we can get the permission of Generalissimo Chiang Kai-shek.

And for that purpose John Rabe, along with two Americans and Chinese, boarded the American gunboat Panay. *They sent two telegrams, one by way of the American ambassador in Hankow to Generalissimo Chiang Kai-shek and another by way of Shanghai to the Japanese military authorities. In the telegram to be forwarded to Chiang Kai-shek by the American ambassador, John Rabe writes that the International Committee hopes to receive assurances from the Japanese military authorities that they will launch no attack against the walled city of Nanking, inside which the committee has established a Safety Zone. If such assurances are forthcoming, the committee requests that for humanitarian reasons the Chinese authorities undertake no military operations within the walled city. The committee proposes a three-day armistice for all forces in the vicinity of Nanking, with the Japanese holding their present position while the Chinese withdraw from the walled city of Nanking. The telegrams are signed:* John Rabe, Chairman.

LATER

Our trip back from the *Panay* through the burning suburb of Hsiakwan is incredible. We arrive home at 7 p.m. just before the conclusion of the press conference. We hear that in the meantime the Japanese have advanced to the gates of Nanking, or just outside them. You can hear thundering cannon and machine-gun fire at the South Gate and across from Goan Hoa Men. The streetlights have been turned off, and in the dark you can make out the wounded dragging themselves over the cobblestones. No one helps them; there are no doctors, no nurses, no medics left. Only Kulou Hospital with its couple of brave American doctors still carries on. The streets of the Safety Zone are flooded with refugees loaded down with bundles. The old Communications Ministry (arsenal) is opened to refugees and in no time fills to the rafters. We cordon off two rooms because our weapons and ammunition are in them. Among the refugees are deserters, who hand over their uniforms and weapons.

10 DECEMBER

The night was very unsettled. Thunder of cannons, rifle and machine-gun fire from 8 o'clock yesterday evening until about 4 this morning. I've heard that the Japanese only barely missed taking the city yesterday morning; they had advanced as far as Goan Hoa Men, which is said to have been almost undefended. A reserve regiment of Chinese had not arrived in time, but this didn't bother the troops waiting to be relieved, who, with the exception of a few companies, retreated anyway. At that same time, the Japanese move in, and the reserve troops, arriving at the last moment, manage painfully to push the enemy back only at considerable cost. We learn this morning that last night the Japanese advanced to a point close to the waterworks on the Yangtze. Everyone expects the city to be in the hands of the Japanese by this evening at the latest.

Dr. King, who speaks German, offers the committee his help. He has eight military hospitals under his command, all outside our Zone. Only the lightly wounded are housed in these eight field hospitals, and most of them, or so Dr. King says, have wounded themselves in order to get out of danger. Dr. King would like to place those with self-inflicted wounds inside our Zone. That is in fact contrary to our agreement, but I hope the Japanese won't object when they learn about it, and I refer Dr. King to Dr. Trimmer, the chairman of our medical division at Kulou Hospital. According to King, he's still in charge of 80 Chinese doctors, about whom we knew nothing before now; but we would be very happy if they really do exist and were to join us; the more, the merrier. Over 1,000 people have been wounded in the city over the last two days.

Rev. John Magee wants to open a European section of the Red Cross here, but even though he has money—Colonel Huang gave him 23,000 dollars—he's getting nowhere because he can't get an answer from the Red Cross, and without their consent he apparently doesn't dare move on the matter. What a shame! In his shoes I wouldn't think twice. If you can do some good, why hesitate? Consent is sure to arrive in due course.

We're anxiously awaiting an answer to our telegrams from the Japanese authorities and from Chiang Kai-shek. The fate of the city and 200,000 people are at risk.

The streets of the Zone are packed with refugees. Many of them are still camping in the streets because they couldn't find any suitable shelter. Sadly, we discover over and over that there are still a lot of military personnel in our Zone. We agree to the following terms with Colonel Lung and Colonel Chow:

1. General Tang unconditionally recognizes the southwest border of our Zone.

2. Lung will see to it that construction of a soup kitchen on Wutaishan Hill will no longer be disrupted by soldiers.

3. Three delegates from military headquarters will join three members of our committee for an inspection of the refugee Zone. Any soldier they meet will be ejected from the Zone. Each of the aforementioned three representatives of General Tang must have the authority to give this order and see to it that it is executed. Mr. Han informs us that the soldiers in Hsiakwan want to burn the rest of our rice supplies. Lung promises to intervene. I am given a military pass so that I can pass through the gate to Hsiakwan.

The battle to the east appears to be expanding. You can hear heavy artillery. Air attacks too.

If things don't change soon, we will be subjected to a bombardment of our Zone, which would surely mean a horrible bloodbath because the streets are teeming with people. If only we would receive a positive answer from Japan!

It's a crying shame that the European war reporters who are still here can't tell the whole truth. Certain people should be exposed for not always keeping their promise to rid the Zone of the military.

We are all terribly depressed! News has just arrived from Johnson, the American ambassador in Hankow, that he sent our telegram on to Chiang Kai-shek and personally approves and supports our proposal, but at the same time he sent us a separate confidential telegram telling us that he has been officially informed by the Foreign Ministry in Hankow that our understanding that General Tang agreed to a three-day armistice and the withdrawal of his troops from Nanking is mistaken, and moreover that Chiang Kai-shek has announced that he is not in a position to accept such a proposal. We have checked again here to make sure that we are not mistaken. Lung and Ling, who were present when we sent our telegram, confirm that it was all correct and that in their opinion the generalissimo is surely in agreement. We're not about to give up that quickly! We send another telegram to Chiang Kai-shek, and at the same time I send one to the German ambassador, Dr. Trautmann, in Hankow, asking him to support our proposal as well.

NOON

The city has been bombarded all day. There's the constant rattle of windowpanes. Some houses on Purple Mountain are in flames. The suburbs continue to burn. But people on the streets of our refugee Zone feel so safe and secure that they pay hardly any attention to Japanese planes.

Japanese radio announces that Nanking will fall within 24 hours. The Chinese soldiers are already considerably demoralized. Meanwhile the military has taken over the Metropol Hotel, the city's finest. Soldiers are getting drunk in the bar and lounging in the club chairs—they want to live it up for once, too.

There are a number of people who think it's perfectly possible that the city will fall into Japanese hands tonight. So far it doesn't look that way. Everything is quiet outside. Once again a great number of refugees, including women and children, are sleeping out on the streets.

10:30 P.M.

I lie down on my bed in my clothes. At 2:30 a.m. a massive bombardment begins, accompanied by machine-gun fire. When grenades start whistling eerily right over our house, I order Mr. Han's family and the servants into the dugout. I put on my steel helmet. In the southeast a conflagration erupts, lighting up the area for hours afterward. All the windows rattle constantly, and at regular intervals of a few seconds the house shakes with the boom of shells landing. The Wutaishan antiaircraft battery is fired upon and replies—and my house is in the line of fire. There is gunfire to the south and west as well. Growing somewhat accustomed to the hellish racket, I lie back down to sleep, meaning I doze a little. Sleep is out of the question.

II DECEMBER, 8 A.M.

Water and electricity are off. The bombardment continues. Now and then the noise ebbs a bit, only to break out anew. Our Peter appears to love it. He sings along at full throat. Canaries apparently have better nerves than a Rabe.[19]

The streets of our Zone are packed with people who aren't even bothered by the din of the shelling. These people have more faith in our "Safety Zone" than I do. The Zone is a long way from being *safe;* there are still armed soldiers inside, and all our efforts to get them out have thus far been to no avail. We cannot tell the Japanese, as was our intention, that the Zone is now free of all military.

9 A.M.

The first grenades land in the refugee Zone in front of and behind the Foo Chong Hotel. A total of twelve dead and about twelve wounded. Sperling, who has been running the hotel, is slightly wounded by flying glass. Two cars standing outside the hotel burst into flames. Another grenade was fired into our Zone (at the middle school) and killed 13 people. There is a steady stream of complaints that the Chinese military has still not left the Safety Zone. Outside Kulou Hospital—and on our side of the Zone— trenches are being dug. The officer in charge refuses to work on the other side of the street. Magee and I drive out to see him to settle the matter peaceably. On the way we notice soldiers are also digging in the middle of Shansi Road Circle ("Bavarian Square"). Soldiers are breaking into the houses on one corner of the square where two streets come to a point. I watch as windows and doors are smashed. And why? No one knows.

On Chung Shan Lu, a number of wounded are carried past us. Barricades made of sandbags, uprooted trees, and barbed wire are being thrown up, although they will present no great obstacle to tanks. We speak with the officer outside Kulou Hospital, who politely but forcefully declines to respect our wishes. From Kulou Hospital I telephone Lung, who says he will speak at once with General Tang.

6 P.M.

At the 6 o'clock conference, the only people present besides the press are the members of our committee. The others have sailed upstream, either on the Jardines *Hulk* or on the American gunboat USS *Panay*.

Dr. Smythe announces that the police, who are now nominally under our control, have arrested a "one-item thief" and want to know what to do with him. The incident provokes general amusement, since until now we hadn't even thought about our having to take the place of the courts. We sentence the thief to death, then pardon him and reduce his sentence to 24 hours in jail, and then for lack of a jail, simply let him go.

At 8 o'clock I call Han in and suggest he and his family move to Ninhai Lu No. 5, the headquarters of our Safety Zone, where the shelter is better than ours here. Besides, my house is too near the antiaircraft batteries on Wutaishan, which are now under serious fire from the Japanese. I consider moving there myself, because fierce attacks are expected tonight. Meanwhile, Han says that he doesn't want to leave his home.

CHAPTER 4

THE JAPANESE MARCH IN

The Atrocities Begin

12 DECEMBER

I FULLY EXPECTED the Japanese to have quietly taken the city, but that turns out not to be the case. All over our Zone you still see Chinese troops with yellow armbands and armed to the teeth with rifles, pistols, and hand grenades. Contrary to all agreements, the police are also armed with rifles instead of pistols. It looks as if both the military and the police are no longer obeying General Tang's orders. Under such circumstances, there's no hope of clearing them out of the Zone. At 8 a.m. the bombardment resumes.

At 11 o'clock Lung and Chow arrive and ask us, on behalf of General Tang, to make a last attempt at establishing a three-day armistice.

During these three days the defending forces are to depart, and then the city will be handed over to the Japanese. We put together a new telegram for the American ambassador, then a letter that General Tang must send us before the telegram can be sent, and lastly rules of conduct for the intermediary who, under cover of a white flag, is to deliver a letter concerning the armistice to the commander of the Japanese forces.

Sperling volunteers to play the role of intermediary. We wait all afternoon for the return of Lung and Chow, who are supposed to get the necessary letter from General Tang. Finally, at around 6 o'clock, Lung appears and declares that unfortunately our efforts have been in vain. It's too late for an armistice now, the Japanese are at the gates.

I don't take it too tragically, am not even sad it turned out this way, because I wasn't very pleased with the idea from the start. It's transparently clear that General Tang wanted to conclude an armistice without the generalissimo's consent. Under no circumstances was the word "surrender" to be mentioned in the message to the Japanese. And above all, the proposal for an armistice was to be worded so that it would be viewed as having come from the International Committee. In other words: General Tang wanted to hide behind us, because he anticipated and feared severe censure from the generalissimo or the Foreign Ministry in Hankow. He wanted to put all responsibility on the committee, or perhaps its Chairman Rabe, and I didn't like that in the least!

6:30 P.M.

Uninterrupted artillery fire from Purple Mountain. Thunder and lightning around the hill, and suddenly the whole hill is in flames. They have set fire to some houses and a powder magazine. An old adage says: When Purple Mountain burns, Nanking is lost. To the south, you can see Chinese civilians fleeing through the streets of our Zone, trying to reach their lodgings. They are followed by various units of Chinese soldiers, who claim that the Japanese are hot on their heels. Not true! You only have to watch the way they're running—the last ones are actually strolling casually through the streets—to know that they're not being driven before the enemy.

We determine that the troops at the South Gate or in Goan Hoa Men came under heavy enemy artillery fire, panicked, and ran. The farther they got into the city, the calmer they became, and what was originally a mad flight turned into a casual stroll. But there can no longer be any doubt that the Japanese are at the gates and that the final push is about to start.

Together with Han, I head for home and make emergency preparations there in case we're shelled or bombed—which is to say, I order both my valise with the most necessary toiletries and the indispensable medical bag with my insulin, bandages, etc. taken out to the new dugout, which seems somewhat safer than the old one. I stuff my fur coat with an emergency ration of medicine and instruments in case I have to abandon house and grounds.

I stop to consider for a moment. What else might I take along? I run through the rooms, carefully looking at everything, as if saying goodbye to all this precious stuff. There were a couple of photographs of my little grandchildren—into the bag! So now I'm armed and ready. I am fully aware that there's nothing to laugh about at the moment; but all the same, my gallows humor gains the upper hand.

Shortly before eight o'clock Colonels Lung and Chow arrive (Ling has marched off by now) and ask if they can take shelter in my house. I agree. Before Han and I left for home, these two gentlemen deposited 30,000 dollars in the committee's safe.

8 P.M.

The sky to the south is all in flames. The two dugouts in the garden are now filled to the brim with refugees. There are knocks at both gates to the property. Women and children plead to be let in. Several plucky fellows seeking shelter on my grounds climb over the garden wall behind the German School.

And I can't listen to their wailing any longer, so I open both gates and let everyone in who wants in. Since there's no more room in the dugouts, I allocate people to various sheds and to corners of the house. Most have brought their bedding and lie down in the open. A few very clever sorts spread their beds out under the large German flag we had stretched out in case of air raids. This location is considered especially "bombproof"!

The entire horizon to the south is a sea of flames. And there's one hell of a racket. I put on my steel helmet and press one down over the locks of the good Mr. Han, since neither one of us is about to go into the dugout now. There isn't room for us anyway. I run through the garden like a watchdog, moving from group to group, scolding here and calming there. And in the end they all obey my every word.

Shortly before midnight, there's a dreadful boom at the main gate, and my friend Christian Kröger from Carlowitz & Co. appears.

"Good Lord, Krischan! What are you doing here?"

"Just checking to see how you're doing!"

He reports that the main street is strewn with bits of uniform, hand grenades, and all sorts of other military equipment cast aside by the fleeing Chinese troops.

"Among other things," Krischan says, "someone has just offered me a usable bus for 20 Mex.[20] dollars. Do you think we ought to take it?"

"Lord, Krischan. You can't be serious!"

"Well," Krischan says, "I've told the man to stop by the office tomorrow sometime."

Around midnight the noise abates somewhat, and I lie down to sleep. To the north the splendid Communications Ministry building is burning.

Every joint in my body hurts. I've not been out of these clothes for 48 hours. My guests are settling in for the night as well. Around 30 people are asleep in my office, three in the coal bin, eight women and children in the servant's lavatory, and the rest, over a hundred people, are in the dugouts or out in the open, in the garden, on the cobblestones, everywhere!

At nine o'clock Lung told me in confidence that General Tang had ordered the Chinese retreat for between nine and ten. Later I hear that General Tang actually broke away from his troops at eight o'clock and went by boat to Pukou. At the same time Lung told me that he and Chow have been left behind to care for the wounded. He pleaded with me to help him. The 30,000 dollars in the safe is to be used solely for that. I gladly accept the gift and promise to help him; the agonies of the wounded, who are without any kind of medical help, are indescribable.

13 DECEMBER

The Japanese took control of several city gates last night, but have yet to advance into the center.

Upon arrival at committee headquarters, it takes us ten minutes to found a branch of the International Red Cross, whose board of directors I join. Our good John Magee, who has been mulling over the same idea for weeks now, is chairman.

Three of us committee members drive out to military hospitals that have been opened in the Foreign Ministry, the War Ministry, and the Railway Ministry, and are quickly convinced of the miserable conditions in these hospitals, whose doctors and nurses simply ran away when the shelling got too heavy, leaving the sick behind with nobody to care for them. We get a goodly number of these employees back, because they screw up their courage again when they see the big Red Cross flag—someone quickly located one—flying above the Foreign Ministry hospital.

A main street in Nanking, strewn with the military equipment that fleeing Chinese troops had cast aside when the Japanese entered the city.

The dead and wounded lie side by side in the driveway leading up to the Foreign Ministry. The garden, like the rest of Chung Shan Lu, is strewn with pieces of cast-off military equipment. At the entrance is a wheelbarrow containing a formless mass, ostensibly a corpse, but the feet show signs of life.

We drive very cautiously down the main street. There's a danger you may drive over one of the hand grenades lying about and be blown sky-high. We turn onto Shanghai Lu, where several dead civilians are lying, and drive on toward the advancing Japanese. One Japanese detachment, with a German-speaking doctor, tells us that the Japanese general is not expected for two days yet. Since the Japanese are marching north, we race down side streets to get around them and are able to save three detachments of about 600 Chinese soldiers by disarming them. Some of them don't want to obey the call to throw down their weapons, but then decide it's a good idea when they see the Japanese advancing in the distance. We then quartered these men at the Foreign Ministry and the Supreme Court.

Two of us committee members drive on ahead and near the Railway

Ministry we come across another group of 400 Chinese soldiers, whom we likewise persuade to lay down their weapons.

Shots are fired at us from somewhere. We hear the whistle of bullets, but don't know where they're coming from until we discover a mounted Chinese officer fooling around with his carbine. Maybe he didn't agree with what we were doing. I must admit: From his point of view, perhaps the man was right, but we couldn't do anything else. If it had come to a battle here in the streets bordering the Zone, fleeing Chinese soldiers would no doubt have retreated into the Safety Zone, which would then have been shelled by the Japanese and perhaps even totally destroyed because it was not demilitarized.

And we still had the hope that these fully disarmed troops would face nothing worse than being treated by the Japanese as prisoners of war. I don't know what happened to the officer who shot at us. But I did see our auto mechanic, Herr Hatz, an Austrian, grab his carbine away from him.

Returning to headquarters, I find a great throng at the entrance. Unable to escape by way of the Yangtze, a large number of Chinese soldiers have found their way here while we were gone. They all let us disarm them and then vanish into the Zone. Sperling stands at the main entrance with an earnest, stern look on his face and his Mauser pistol—without any bullets in it, by the way—in his hand and sees to it that the weapons are counted and placed in neat piles, since we plan to hand them over to the Japanese later on.

It is not until we tour the city that we learn the extent of the destruction. We come across corpses every 100 to 200 yards. The bodies of civilians that I examined had bullet holes in their backs. These people had presumably been fleeing and were shot from behind.

The Japanese march through the city in groups of ten to twenty soldiers and loot the shops. If I had not seen it with my own eyes I would not have believed it. They smash open windows and doors and take whatever they like. Allegedly because they're short of rations. I watched with my own eyes as they looted the café of our German baker Herr Kiessling. Hempel's hotel was broken into as well, as was almost every shop on Chung Shang and Taiping Road. Some Japanese soldiers dragged their booty away in crates, others requisitioned rickshas to transport their stolen goods to safety.

Mr. Forster joins us on a visit to his mission's Anglican church on Taiping Road. Two grenades exploded in one of the houses beside the church.

A coolie leading his old, blind mother to safety. Rabe cut this photograph from a newspaper and pasted it into his diary.

The houses themselves have been broken into and looted. Forster surprises some Japanese soldiers who are about to steal his bicycle but vamoose when they spot us. We stop a Japanese patrol, and point out to them that this is American property and ask them to order the looters to leave. They simply smile and leave us standing there.

We run across a group of 200 Chinese workers whom Japanese soldiers have picked up off the streets of the Safety Zone, and after having been tied up, are now being driven out of the city. All protests are in vain.

Of the perhaps one thousand disarmed soldiers that we had quartered at the Ministry of Justice, between 400 and 500 were driven from it with their hands tied. We assume they were shot since we later heard several salvos of machine-gun fire. These events have left us frozen with horror.

We may no longer enter the Foreign Ministry, where we took wounded soldiers. Chinese doctors and nursing personnel are not allowed into the building, either.

We manage quickly to find lodging in some vacant buildings for a group of 125 Chinese refugees, before they fall into the hands of the Japanese military. Mr. Han says that three young girls of about 14 or 15 have been dragged from a house in our neighborhood. Doctor Bates reports that even in the Safety Zone refugees in various houses have been robbed of their few paltry possessions. At various times troops of Japanese soldiers enter my private residence as well, but when I arrive and hold my swastika armband under their noses, they leave. There's no love for the American flag. A car belonging to Mr. Sone, one of our committee members, had its American flag ripped off and was then stolen.

We have been under way without rest since six this morning, trying to gain exact information about these depredations. Han doesn't dare leave the house. The Japanese officers are all more or less polite and correct, but the behavior of some of the rank and file is disastrous. Meanwhile these people are dropping propaganda material from airplanes announcing that the civilian population will be treated humanely in all respects.

Exhausted and despairing, we return to our committee headquarters at Ninhai Lu 5. There are dangerous shortages at several places in the city. We use our own cars to deliver sacks of rice to the Ministry of Justice, where several hundred people have nothing to eat. I have no idea what the people inside the Waichiaopu,[21] with all those wounded, are living off. Seven gravely wounded people have been lying in the headquarters courtyard for hours now and can finally be transported by ambulance to Kulou Hospital, among them a child who was shot in the lower leg: a lad of ten, maybe, who makes not a sound despite his pain.

15 DECEMBER

At 10 a.m. we are paid a visit by naval Lieutenant Sekiguchi. We give him copies of the letters we have sent to the commanders of the Japanese army.

At 11 o'clock we receive Mr. Fukuda, the attaché of the Japanese embassy, with whom we discuss the details of our agenda. Mr. Fukuda agrees that it is obviously both in our interest and that of the Japanese authorities to have the electricity works, waterworks, and telephone system repaired as quickly as possible. And we, or I, can be of help to him.

Mr. Han and I are well acquainted with how these three facilities function, and I have no doubt that we can get engineers and workers to get them running again. At Japanese military headquarters, located in the Bank of Communications, we again meet with Fukuda, who is very helpful as a translator during our meeting with the current commandant.

Since we could not establish contact with the Japanese commandant yesterday, 14 December, we gave Mr. Fukuda a letter addressing the issue of what to do with the disarmed Chinese soldiers. It reads:

> The International Committee for Nanking Safety Zone is very much perplexed by the problem of soldiers who have thrown away their arms. From the beginning the Committee strove to have this Zone entirely free of Chinese soldiers and up to the afternoon of Monday, December 13, had achieved considerable success in this respect. At that time several hundred soldiers approached or entered the Zone through the northern boundary and appealed to us for help. The Committee plainly told the soldiers that it could not protect them. But we told them that if they abandoned their arms and all resistance to the Japanese, we thought the Japanese would give them merciful treatment. . . .
>
> The Committee fully recognizes that identified soldiers are lawful prisoners of war. But in dealing with those disarmed soldiers, the Committee hopes that the Japanese Army will use every precaution not to involve civilians. The Committee further hopes that the Japanese Army will in accordance with the recognized laws of war regarding prisoners and for reasons of humanity exercise mercy toward these former soldiers. They might be used to good advantage as laborers and would be glad to return to civilian life if possible.
>
> Most respectfully yours,
> JOHN RABE, Chairman

In reply to this letter and our letter to the commandant of 14 December, we have now received from the latter the following recorded minutes.

Memorandum

Of Interview with Chief of Special Service Corps (Bank of Communications, noon, December 15, 1937)

Translator: Mr. Fukuda.
Members of Committee present:
Mr. John Rabe, Chairman,
Dr. Smythe, Secretary
Dr. Sperling, Inspector-General

1. Must search the city for Chinese soldiers.
2. Will post guards at entrances to Zone.
3. People should return to their homes as soon as possible; therefore, we must search the Zone.

4. Trust humanitarian attitude of Japanese Army to care for the disarmed Chinese soldiers.

5. Police may patrol within the Zone if they are disarmed excepting for batons.

6. The 10,000 *tan*[22] of rice stored by your committee in the Zone you may use for refugees. But Japanese soldiers need rice, so in the Zone they should be allowed to buy rice. (Answer regarding our stores of rice outside of Zone, not clear.)

7. Telephone, electricity and water must be repaired; so this p.m. will go with Mr. Rabe to inspect and act accordingly.

8. We are anxious to get workers. From tomorrow will begin to clear city. Committee please assist. Will pay. Tomorrow want 100 to 200 workers.

As we were about to say goodbye to the commandant and Mr. Fukuda, General Harata entered and immediately expressed a desire to become acquainted with the Safety Zone, which we show him on a driving tour. We make an appointment for this afternoon to visit the electricity works in Hsiakwan.

Unfortunately I miss our visitors in the afternoon because a column of Japanese soldiers wants to lead away some former Chinese soldiers who have thrown away their weapons and fled into our Zone. I give my word that these refugees will do no more fighting, which is enough to set them free. No sooner am I back in my office at Committee Headquarters, than my boy arrives with bad news—the Japanese have returned and now have 1,300 refugees tied up. Along with Smythe and Mills I try to get these people released, but to no avail. They are surrounded by about 100 Japanese soldiers and, still tied up, are led off to be shot.

Smythe and I drive back to see Fukuda in an attempt to plead for these people. He promises to do his best; but we have scant hope. I point out that I will have difficulty finding workers for the Japanese if people are being executed. Fukuda admits as much and puts me off until tomorrow. I'm in a truly wretched mood. It's hard to see people driven off like animals. But they say that the Chinese shot 2,000 Japanese prisoners in Tsinanfu, too.

We hear by way of the Japanese navy that the gunboat USS *Panay*, on which the officials of the American embassy had sought safety, has been accidentally bombed and sunk by the Japanese. Two passengers are dead: Sandri, an Italian newspaper correspondent, and Charleson, the captain of the *Maypin*. Mr. Paxton of the American embassy was wounded in the knee and shoulder; Squire was likewise wounded in the shoulder; Gassie broke a leg; Lieutenant Andrews is seriously wounded; and Captain Hughes also has broken a leg.

In the meantime a member of the committee has been wounded as well: Krischan Kröger came too close with an open flame to an almost empty gasoline can and has burned both hands. I gave him a good dressing-down. Hempel is bewailing the fact that the Japanese have completely destroyed his hotel. It appears there isn't much left of Kiessling's café, either.

Report of an Address by Mr. Smith (Reuters) in Hankow[23]

By the morning of 13 December, there were still no Japanese soldiers to be seen in the city. The South City was still in Chinese hands. Two serious battles had been fought at the South Gate during the night, and the number of the Chinese dead was put at over 1,000.

By the eve of 13 December, Chinese troops and civilians had begun to loot. Mainly grocery stores were pillaged, but Chinese soldiers were also seen leaving private homes with food. It would be a mistake, however, to claim that Chinese troops were intent on systematic looting.

It is worth describing the scenes that took place outside Chinese clothing stores in South City. Hundreds of soldiers thronged before these shops. Ready-made civilian clothes of every sort sold like hotcakes. Soldiers spent their last cent on these clothes, changed into them out in the street, threw their uniforms away, and vanished as civilians. Several hundred of these civilians gathered later at the Military College and the International Club. It was not until almost noon that Mr. McDaniel spotted the first Japanese patrols in South City. In groups of six to twelve men they cautiously and slowly felt their way forward along the main streets. Occasional shots could be heard. Here and there one saw dead civilians at the side of the road, who, or so the Japanese said, had been shot while trying to flee. At the sight of the Japanese, a sense of relief seemed to pass through the Chinese civilian population, and they came out ready to accept the Japanese if they would have behaved humanely.

In the so-called Safety Zone about a hundred Chinese had been killed by stray bullets and grenades and several hundreds more wounded. By night Japanese troops had entered the Safety Zone as well. About 7,000 disarmed Chinese soldiers were inside the Zone. They had been quartered at the Military College and other buildings. The police in the Safety Zone had been augmented by several hundred Chinese policemen who had fled to South City.

By the morning of 14 December, the Japanese soldiers had still adopted no hostile attitude toward the Chinese civilian population. By noon, however, in many locations small groups of six to ten Japanese had formed, who then moved from house to house, looting. Whereas the Chinese had restricted their theft primarily to food, nothing was secure from the Japanese. They have looted the city systematically and thoroughly. Until the day I departed, 15 December, by my own observation and that of other Europeans, the houses of the Chinese had without exception been looted, as had most of those belonging to Europeans. European flags flying over these houses were pulled down by the Japanese. Groups of Japanese could be seen departing with various household furnishings, though they appeared to have a special preference for wall clocks.

Flags were first ripped from the few foreign automobiles still remaining in Nanking before they were commandeered. The Japanese commandeered two cars and several trucks from the Safety Zone Committee. Outside the firm of Kiessling & Bader I ran into Herr Rabe, who with the help of the owner threw out several Japanese who had pulled down the flag and were busy looting the shop. In Hsiakwan the Japanese had bound 400 to 500 Chinese and led them away. All attempts by Europeans to reach them were vigorously forbidden by the Japanese. On 15 December the Japanese granted foreign correspondents permission to board a Japanese gunboat leaving Nanking for Shanghai. It later proved possible to take the same journey on an English gunboat. We were told to gather on the pier. When the wait for our departure lasted longer than expected, we used the time to undertake a short investigative walk. We saw how the Japanese had tied up some thousand Chinese out in an open field, and watched as small groups of them were led away to be shot. They were forced to kneel and were then shot in the back of the head. We had observed some 100 such executions, when the Japanese officer in charge noticed us and ordered us to leave at once. What happened to the rest of the Chinese, I cannot say.

Mr. Smith had the highest praise for the work of the Germans remaining in Nanking: Rabe, Kröger, and Sperling who are serving their fellowmen and caring for the welfare of Chinese refugees.

16 DECEMBER

At 8:45 a.m. I receive a note from Mr. Kikuchi, a very modest and charming Japanese translator, that the so-called "Safety Zone" is to be searched for Chinese soldiers.

All the shelling and bombing we have thus far experienced are nothing in comparison to the terror that we are going through now. There is not a single shop outside our Zone that has not been looted, and now pillaging, rape, murder, and mayhem are occurring inside the Zone as well. There is not a vacant house, whether with or without a foreign flag, that has not been broken into and looted. The following letter to Mr. Fukuda provides a general notion of current circumstances and the cases mentioned in the letter are only a few out of a great many that we know about:

Mr. Tokuyashu Fukuda,
Attaché to the Japanese Embassy,
Nanking.

Dear Sir:

Yesterday the continued disorders committed by Japanese soldiers in the Safety Zone increased the state of panic among the refugees. Refugees in large buildings are afraid to even go to nearby soup kitchens to secure the cooked rice. Consequently, we are having to deliver rice to these compounds directly, thereby complicating our problem. We could not even get coolies out to load rice and coal to take to our soup kitchens and therefore this morning thousands of people had to go without their breakfast.

Foreign members of the International Committee are this morning making desperate efforts to get trucks through Japanese patrols so these civilians can be fed. Yesterday foreign members of our Committee had several attempts made to take their personal cars away from them by Japanese soldiers. (A list of cases of disorder is appended.)

Until this state of panic is allayed, it is going to be impossible to get any normal activity started in the city, such as: telephone workers, electric plant workers, probably the water plant workers, shops of all kinds, or even street cleaning. . . .

We refrained from protesting yesterday because we thought when the High Commander arrived order in the city would be restored, but last night was even worse than the night before, so we decided these matters should be called to the attention of the Imperial Japanese Army, which we are sure does not approve of such actions by its soldiers.

Most respectfully yours,
JOHN RABE   LEWIS S. C. SMYTHE
Chairman   Secretary

Almost all the houses of the German military advisors have been looted by Japanese soldiers. No Chinese even dares set foot outside his house! When the gates to my garden are opened to let my car leave the grounds—where I have already taken in over a hundred of the poorest refugees—women and children on the street outside kneel and bang their heads against the ground, pleading to be allowed to camp on my garden grounds. You simply cannot conceive of the misery.

I drive to Hsiakwan with Kikuchi to check on the electricity works and some of what rice remains. The electricity works looks to be intact and could probably be running again within a few days if the workers trusted the Japanese to protect them. I am willing to help, but given the incredible behavior of the Japanese soldiery, prospects are slim that I could drum up the 40 to 45 workers needed. And given the circumstances, neither would I like to risk having the Japanese authorities call one of our German engineers back from Shanghai.

I've just heard that hundreds more disarmed Chinese soldiers have been led out of our Zone to be shot, including 50 of our police who are to be executed for letting soldiers in.

The road to Hsiakwan is nothing but a field of corpses strewn with the remains of military equipment. The Communications Ministry was

Hundreds of Chinese were executed in the open areas of the city.

This gate, Y Chang Men, led to the harbor suburb of Hsiakwan. Only one passage was still open, and in it the bodies of Chinese soldiers were piled high, along with sandbags. People driving to Hsiakwan had to pass them for weeks.

torched by the Chinese, the Y Chang Men Gate has been shelled. There are piles of corpses outside the gate. The Japanese aren't lifting a hand to clear them away, and the Red Swastika Society[24] associated with us has been forbidden to do so.

It may be that the disarmed Chinese will be forced to do the job before they're killed. We Europeans are all paralyzed with horror. There are executions everywhere, some are being carried out with machine guns outside the barracks of the War Ministry.

Katsuo Okazaki, the consul general, who visited us this evening, explained that while it was true that a few soldiers were being shot, the rest were to be interned in a concentration camp on an island in the Yangtze.

Our former school porter is in Kulou Hospital; he's been shot. He had been conscripted to do labor, was given a paper attesting to the work done, and on his way home was shot twice in the back for no reason at all. His old certificate of employment, issued by the German embassy, lies before me drenched with blood.

As I write this, the fists of Japanese soldiers are hammering at the back gate to the garden. Since my boys don't open up, heads appear along the top of the wall. When I suddenly show up with my flashlight, they beat a hasty retreat. We open the main gate and walk after them a little distance until they vanish in dark narrow streets, where assorted bodies have been lying in the gutter for three days now. Makes you shudder in revulsion.

All the women and children, their eyes big with terror, are sitting on the grass in the garden, pressed closely together, in part to keep warm, in part to give each other courage. Their one hope is that I, the "foreign devil," will drive these evil spirits away.

17 DECEMBER

Two Japanese soldiers have climbed over the garden wall and are about to break into our house. When I appear they give the excuse that they saw two Chinese soldiers climb over the wall. When I show them my party badge they return the same way they came.

In one of the houses in the narrow street behind my garden wall, a woman was raped, and then wounded in the neck with a bayonet. I manage to get an ambulance so we can take her to Kulou Hospital. There are about 200 refugees in the garden now. They fall to their knees when you walk by, even though in all this misery we barely know up from down ourselves. One of the Americans put it this way: "The Safety Zone has turned into a public house for the Japanese soldiers."

That's very close to the truth. Last night up to 1,000 women and girls are said to have been raped, about 100 girls at Ginling Girls College alone. You hear of nothing but rape. If husbands or brothers intervene, they're shot. What you hear and see on all sides is the brutality and bestiality of the Japanese soldiery.

Herr Hatz, our Austrian auto mechanic, gets into an argument with a Japanese soldier, who reaches for his sidearm but is immediately floored by a well-placed hook to the chin, whereupon he and his two Japanese comrades, all armed to the teeth, take off.

The Japanese consul general, Katsuo Okazaki, demanded yesterday that the refugees leave the Zone for their homes and open their shops again as soon as possible. The Japanese soldiers have saved them the trouble of opening their shops: There's hardly a shop in the city that has not been broken into and looted. Miraculously, the house of the German ambassador, Dr. Trautmann, has been spared.

When Kröger and I arrive back at my house after checking on Trautmann's, Kröger is amazed to find his car again behind my house. Japanese soldiers had taken it away from him yesterday while he was inside the hotel with some Japanese officers. Kröger stands his ground in front of the car until it is returned to him by its three Japanese occupants, one of whom says, "We friend—you go!"

This afternoon during my absence, these same soldiers are back in my garden again and take Lorenz's car instead. I had instructed Han that if he couldn't get rid of such guests, he should get a receipt, no matter what. He got one, too. It reads as follows: "I thank you present! Nippon Army, K. Sato."

That'll make Lorenz happy!

Across from the War Ministry, at the base of a dugout mound, are 30 bodies of Chinese soldiers who were shot there yesterday under martial law. The Japanese are now starting to clean up the city. From Shansi Road Circle ("Bavarian Square") to the War Ministry, everything is tidy already. The corpses are simply tossed into the ditches.

At 6 p.m. I bring 60 straw mats to my refugees in the garden. Great joy! Four Japanese soldiers scramble over the garden wall again. I catch three of them on the spot and chase them off. The fourth works his way through the rows of refugees as far as the main iron gate, where I nab him and politely escort him out the door. No sooner are these fellows outside than they take off at a run. They don't want to tangle with a German.

Bodies were piled into ditches and left there.

Usually all I have to do is shout "Deutsch" and "Hitler" and they turn polite, whereas the Americans have real trouble getting their way. Our letter of protest directed to the Japanese embassy has apparently made a lasting impression on Mr. Kiyoshi Fukui, the 2nd secretary. At any rate he promised that he would pass the letter on at once to the highest level of army command. While Dr. Smythe and I are speaking with Fukui at the Japanese embassy, Mr. Riggs arrives and asks us to return to headquarters, where Mr. Fukuda is waiting for us. The question of getting the electricity works back into operation is discussed. At the request of the Japanese I send the following telegram to Shanghai:

Siemens China Co.
244 Nanking Road, Shanghai

Japanese authorities would like German engineer to come to Nanking to restart the local power plant. No damage to plant apparently was done in last fighting. Please reply through Japanese authorities.

RABE

The Japanese understand that it's in their interest to come to terms with us, although they recognize us only reluctantly. I tell them to give the commandant my regards and to tell him that I have had enough of my post as "mayor" and would be happy to resign.

18 DECEMBER

Our hope that order would return with the arrival of the commandant has unfortunately not been realized; on the contrary, things are worse today than yesterday. I already had to expel soldiers from our garden early this morning. One of them comes at me with his sidearm drawn, but he quickly puts it away.

As long as I am personally at the house, everything is all right. So far these fellows have shown some respect for Europeans, but not for Chinese. I am constantly being called from headquarters by various people in the neighborhood whose houses soldiers have broken into. I drag two Japanese out of a back room in a house that has been totally looted. While we are speaking with a Japanese officer about getting the electricity works running again, one of our cars just outside the door is stolen. We barely manage to get the car back. The soldiers have almost no regard for their officers.

A Chinese man dashes into the room and tells us that his brother was shot because he refused to give his cigarette case to the soldier who had forced his way into the house. When I protest, the Japanese officer with whom we are negotiating about the electricity works provides me with a Japanese pass to be affixed to the front door. We drive home to paste it on right away.

Just as we arrive we catch a soldier trying to break in. He is driven off by the officer. At the same moment one of my Chinese neighbors arrives and tells us that four soldiers have broken into his house and that one of them is about to violate his wife. The Japanese officer and I storm into the neighbor's house and prevent the worst; the soldier gets a slap on each cheek by the officer, and is then allowed to go.

Just as we are about to drive off again, Han arrives and reports that he has been robbed by one of the soldiers who broke in during my absence. That was too much for me. I got out of the car and told the Japanese officer to drive back without me. All these dreadful events had left me feeling physically ill.

But the Japanese colonel wouldn't hear of it. He apologized and declared quite candidly that after seeing what he had seen today, he was convinced that we had not been exaggerating and would do his best to put an end to this state of affairs.

6:00 P.M.

I arrive home just in time to meet up with a pair of Japanese soldiers who had entered by way of the garden wall. One of the two has already taken off his uniform and sidearm and is about to violate one of the girls among the refugees, when I come up and demand that he return at once the same way he came. The other fellow is already sitting astraddle the wall when he spots me and a gentle push sends him on his way.

At 8 o'clock Herr Hatz shows up in a truck with a Japanese police commissioner and a whole battery of gendarmes, who are supposed to guard Ginling College tonight. Our protest at the Japanese embassy already seems to have helped a little.

I open the gate at our Committee Headquarters at Ninhai Lu No. 5 in order to let in a number of women and children who have fled to us. The wailing of these poor women and children echoes in my ears for hours afterward. The 5,500 square feet in my garden and grounds keep filling up with more and more refugees. There must be about 300 people living here with me now. My house is considered the safest spot. When I'm at home that's probably true, for I physically remove each intruder, but when I'm gone the safety doesn't amount to much. Japanese notices pasted on doors do little good. The soldiers pay no attention to them. Most climb over the garden wall anyway. Chang's wife became so ill during the night that we had to take her to Kulou Hospital early this morning. Unfortunately several nurses at Kulou Hospital have been raped as well.

19 DECEMBER

The night passed peacefully at our house. Next to our main office on Ninhai Lu is a house where about 20 women are sheltered, and Japanese soldiers broke in there to rape the women. Hatz springs over the garden wall and chases the scoundrels off. The following plea for help has come from a refugee camp at Canton Road No. 83–85:

> ### To the International Committee of the Nanking Safety Zone, Nanking
>
> There are about 540 refugees crowded in Nos. 83 and 85 on Canton Road. Since 13th inst. up to the 17th those houses have been searched and robbed many many times a day by Japanese soldiers in groups of three to five. Today the soldiers are looting the places mentioned above continually and all the jewelries, money, watches, clothes of any sort are taken away. At present women of younger ages are forced to go with the soldiers every night who send motor trucks to take them and release them the next morning. More than 30 women and girls have been raped. The women and children are crying all night. Conditions inside the compound are worse than we can describe. Please give us help.
>
> Yours truly   ALL THE REFUGEES.
> Nanking, 18 December 1937

We don't know how we can protect these people. The Japanese soldiers are completely out of control. Under such circumstances I can't find the workers needed to get the electricity works running again. When Mr. Kikuchi calls on me about it again today, I point out to him that the workers have run off because they do not believe that they and their families will be protected, particularly since not even we Europeans are spared the bestiality of these soldiers.

Kikuchi answers: "It was no different in Belgium."

6:00 P.M.

Six Japanese climbed over my garden wall and attempted to open the gates from the inside. When I arrive and shine my flashlight in the face of one of the bandits, he reaches for his pistol, but his hand drops quickly enough when I yell at him and hold my swastika armband under his nose. Then, on my orders, all six have to scramble back over the wall. My gates will never be opened to riffraff like that.

There are large fires spreading to the north and the south of my house. Since the waterworks have been destroyed and the firemen have been taken away by the soldiers, there's nothing we can do. In Gou Fo Lu it looks as if a whole block of houses is burning down. The sky is bright as day. The 300 to 400 refugees here in my garden—I no longer know how many there really are—have used straw mats, old doors, and sheets of tin to build huts for a little protection against the snow and cold. Unfortunately they have started to cook inside these huts. I had to forbid it out of fear of fire. I'm so afraid a fire will break out, for there are still 64 large cans of gasoline stored on the grounds. I have ordered that cooking be done in only two places in the garden.

Crowds of refugees thronged Rabe's house and the streets of the Safety Zone.

20 DECEMBER

At our committee's headquarters I find a Japanese officer who asks for 20 workers to clean the Metropol Hotel, which is to be occupied by Japanese staff officers. I give him 16 workers from our committee, whom he personally delivers back to me by truck at noon and to each of whom, moreover, he pays 5 China dollars. This is the first time that we have experienced serious consideration on the part of Japanese military authorities. And it obviously made a good impression on the Chinese.

Returning to Ninhai Lu, I make the acquaintance of Herr Bernhard Arp Sindberg of the Kiangnan Cement Works in Hsi Sha Shan. Sindberg had wanted to bring several wounded Chinese to Nanking, since he had heard on the radio that Nanking was perfectly calm, with its electricity and waterworks as well as its telephone system fully restored. He was not a little amazed to learn about current conditions. About halfway here he had to send the wounded Chinese back to Hsi Sha Shan, since the Japanese wouldn't let him through. He took it into his head, however, that he had to press on to Nanking no matter what and walked a good part of the way before being picked up by a Japanese truck that brought him safely to the North Gate. Now the question is how to get back home.

At 6 o'clock, I was paid a visit from Mr. Moriyama, the correspondent of the *Osaka Asahi Shimbun,* who was introduced to me by Rev. Mills. Moriyama speaks good German and English and interviews me in regular journalistic fashion. I do not keep my opinions to myself, and I ask him to use his influence to see that order is reestablished among the Japanese troops as quickly as possible. He admits that the matter is indeed urgent and crucial, since otherwise the reputation of the Japanese army will suffer.

As I write this a good number of houses are on fire again, some not all that far away, including the YMCA building. One might almost believe that these fires are set with the knowledge, and perhaps even on the order, of the Japanese military authorities.

During my absence, Japanese soldiers tried to break through the main iron-plated gate to my house with their bayonets. They didn't succeed, but several bayonet slashes in the doors and the bent corners of the ironwork attest to their activity. I order the battered doors hammered back into shape as best as possible. The bayonet slashes are to be left as a memento. Kröger and Sindberg come by to borrow a car from Han for Sindberg's trip home. Han unfortunately assents to this; I am not at all in agreement, because Han's car is sure to be a casualty of the trip, or if not the whole car, then most certainly all four tires.

21 DECEMBER

There can no longer be any doubt that the Japanese are burning the city, presumably to erase all traces of their looting and thievery. Yesterday evening the city was on fire in six different places.

I was awakened at 2:30 a.m. by the sound of walls collapsing and roofs crashing. There was now a very great danger that fire would spread to the last row of houses between Chung Shan Lu and my own house, but thank God it didn't come to that. Only flying and drifting sparks presented a threat to the straw roofs of my refugee camp in the garden and to the supply of gasoline stored there, which absolutely has to be moved.

The following telegram gives some idea of the desperate mood among the Americans.

They want to send this telegram by way of the Japanese embassy, since there is no other way to forward a telegram. The text, however, is so transparent that I seriously doubt that the Japanese will even accept the telegram for sending:

> Nanking 20th December 1937
>
> Telegram to American Consulate-General in Shanghai:
> Important questions require immediate presence American diplomatic representatives in Nanking stop Situation daily more urgent stop Please inform ambassador and Department of State stop signed *Magee, Mills, McCallum, Riggs, Smythe, Sone, Trimmer, Vautrin, Wilson* Delivered to Japanese Embassy 20 December, with request for transmission by naval wireless.
>
> BATES

The Americans are indeed in a bad way. While I succeed in making a suitable impression by pompously pointing to my swastika armband and party badge, and at the German flags in my house, the Japanese have no regard whatever for the American flag. Whereas I simply bellowed down the soldiers who stopped my car this morning and after pointing to my flag was allowed to drive on my way, shots were fired at Dr. Trimmer and Mr. McCallum inside Kulou Hospital. Fortunately the shots missed; but the fact that we are being shot at is so monstrous that you can understand why the

Americans, who have given refuge to so many women and girls at their universities, have lost their patience.

How long, Dr. Smythe asked quite rightly yesterday, will we be able to keep up the bluff that we are equal to the situation? If one Chinese man in our refugee camps kills a Japanese soldier for raping his wife or daughter, everything will fall apart; then there'll be a bloodbath inside the Safety Zone.

The news has just arrived that, just as I predicted, the telegram to the American consulate general in Shanghai was not accepted by the Japanese embassy.

I'm having the entire gasoline supply moved this morning from my house and garden to Ninhai Lu, because I'm afraid that a whole row of houses on Chung Shan Lu will be torched. We now know all the signs of an impending fire. If a largish number of trucks assembles in a given spot, the houses are usually looted and torched shortly thereafter.

At 2 this afternoon all the Germans and Americans, etc., meaning the entire foreign colony, assemble outside Kulou Hospital and march in closed ranks to the Japanese embassy. There were 14 Americans, five Germans, two White Russians, and an Austrian. We presented a letter to the Japanese embassy, asking, for humanitarian reasons, that

1. the burning of large parts of the city be stopped;
2. an end be put at once to the disorderly conduct of the Japanese troops; and
3. whatever steps necessary be taken to restore law and order, so that our food and coal supplies can be replenished. All those demonstrating signed the letter.

We are introduced to Commandant Matsui, who shakes hands all round. I assume the role of spokesman at the Japanese embassy and explain to Mr. Tanaka that we infer that the city is to be burned down. Tanaka denies this with a smile, promises however to discuss the first two points in our letter with the military authorities. As to point 3, he refuses even to discuss it. The Japanese themselves are short on rations and are not interested in whether or not we can make do with our supplies.

During our visit at the Japanese embassy, a Japanese naval officer hands me a letter from Dr. Rosen, who is on board the English gunboat *Bee*, which is anchored very close to Nanking but may not dock. They don't want any more witnesses here. I have no idea how Dr. Rosen, Scharffenberg, and Hürter found their way onto the *Bee*. Mr. Fukuda, whom I ask about this, fears that the Jardines *Hulk* has also been shelled and sunk.

Letter from Legation Secretary Rosen to John Rabe

Near Nanking, 19 December 1937
On board the HMS *Bee*

Dear Herr Rabe:

We have been just outside the city since yesterday, but cannot enter it. Please let me know how you all are and whether any German buildings have been damaged. I can wire the ambassador directly from on board ship. We've been through a lot ourselves, more about that in person later. I will attempt to get this letter to you via the Japanese (and hope that your answer will arrive by the same route).

With many greetings and Heil Hitler,
Respectfully,
ROSEN

22 DECEMBER

Two Japanese from Military Police Headquarters pay me a visit and tell me that the Japanese now want to form their own refugee committee. All refugees will have to be registered. The "bad people" (meaning ex-soldiers) are to be put in a special camp. Our help is requested, and I agree to give it.

In the meantime the official arson continues. I am constantly worried that the fires destroying buildings near the Shanghai Com-Sav Bank will spread across to the west side of the main street, which is part of the Zone. If that were to happen my house would also be in danger. While cleaning up the Zone, we find many bodies in the ponds, civilians who have been shot (30 in just one pond), most of them with their hands bound, some with stones tied to their necks.

The number of refugees living with me is still growing. Six people are now sleeping just in my little private office. The floor in the office, the grounds of the garden are thick with sleepers, all of them a blood-red hue from the light of the massive fires. I've just now counted seven different fire locations.

I promised the Japanese to help them look for employees of the electricity works and told them to look, among other places, in Hsiakwan, where 54 electricity plant workers were housed. We now learn that about three or four days ago, 43 of them were tied up and led down to the riverbank and machine-gunned, ostensibly because they were the employees of an enterprise managed by the Chinese government. News of this execution was brought to me by one of the condemned workers, who fell unwounded into the river beneath the bodies of two of the victims and so was able to save himself.

This afternoon Kröger and Hatz saw a Chinese being bayoneted in the neck by a drunken Japanese soldier; when they hurried to his aid, they were themselves attacked. Hatz defended himself with a chair. The Japanese is reported to have succeeded in tying Kröger up, possibly because Kröger's burned left hand is still bandaged. Mr. Fitch and I raced at top speed to their rescue, met up with them as they were heading for home, and returned with them then to investigate the case on the spot. We found the soldier still there, being slapped around by a Japanese general who just happened by. Mr. Tanaka from the Japanese embassy was also present.

The soldier had apparently painted the two Germans' role in a very unfavorable light, but all the same—and luckily for us—he still was given a thrashing that brought tears to his eyes. The affair turned out all right for us once again; but it could have turned out otherwise.

CHAPTER 5

CHRISTMAS.

23 DECEMBER

YESTERDAY EVENING Police Chief Takadama paid me a visit and asked for a list of all damage or loss of property suffered by foreigners here. By today noon, then, a list has to be prepared of all the buildings that are or were occupied by foreigners. Only national embassies can just rattle off that sort of thing. For our committee, it's not an easy job. But we do it. I sit down with Kröger, Sperling, and Hatz, we divide up the various districts and arrive with the list right on time. Going by it, a total of 38 German buildings have been looted and one (Hempel's Hotel) burned down. The Americans have a much longer list of losses. There are about 158 American buildings looted in all.

While I'm waiting for the list to be put in final form, Chang comes running in and tells me that a Japanese soldier has broken in at home, has torn my office apart, and is doing his damnedest to crack my safe, in which there are about 23,000 dollars. Kröger and I race home in the car. The intruder had just absconded. He'd been unable to open the safe by himself.

We sit down for *tiffin*,[25] and here come three more soldiers over the wall, whom we chase back with some choice words. My door is simply no longer open to this criminal pack. Kröger says that he is prepared to house-sit for me this afternoon. Shortly before I drive back to headquarters, six more Japanese bandits scale the wall. These fellows have to scram right back over it as well. In toto, I've probably experienced close to 20 such incursions by now.

This afternoon I inform the chief of police that I am going to keep this pest out of my house no matter what and that I will defend the honor of the German flag even if it means risking my life. This does not appear to move him. A shrug, and the problem has been dealt with as far as he is concerned. Unfortunately there are not enough police troops available, he says to his regret, to keep these bad soldiers in line.

I'm driving home at 6 o'clock this evening and discover a whole row of houses going up in flames on this side of the bridge railing on Chung Shan Lu. Luckily the wind is blowing in our favor, the rain of sparks is drifting north. At the same time another building behind the Shanghai Com-Sav Bank bursts into flames. It is no longer a secret that we are dealing here with systematic arson. The four houses next to the bridge railing are inside our Safety Zone.

My refugees stand tightly pressed together in the rain and mutely watch the lovely horrible inferno. If these flames were to reach our house, these poor people would have no idea where to go. I am their last hope.

Chang has decorated four little kerosene lamps, along with the rest of the candles—our entire lighting system at the moment—with evergreens. He also unpacked the red Advent star and tied red silk ribbons to the candles. Tomorrow is 24 December, Christmas Eve, Gretel's birthday.

My neighbor, the cobbler, has resoled my old boots for Christmas; he also made a leather case for my field glasses. I gave him 10 dollars, but he just pressed the money back into my hand, not saying a word. Chang says that the man could not possibly take money from me; he is far too much in my debt as it is, the poor fellow!

The letter that Herr Sindberg brought today from Hsi Sha Shan (Sindberg drives back and forth with no problem between Nanking and the Kiangnan Cement Works, a good 1½ hours away) also included a petition to the Japanese authorities from 17,000 Chinese refugees in Hsi Sha Shan asking to be mercifully protected from the excesses of the Japanese soldiers, who are causing the same havoc there as here in Nanking.

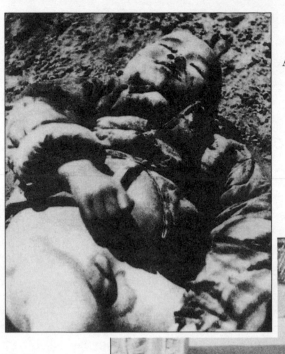

A young boy bayoneted to death.

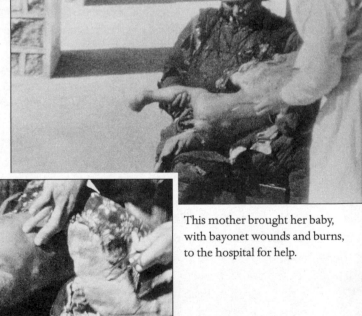

This mother brought her baby,
with bayonet wounds and burns,
to the hospital for help.

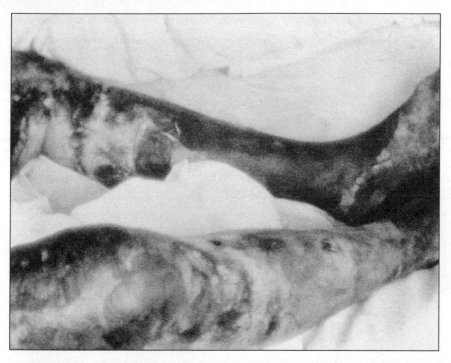

These photographs of burn victims were taken by hospital staff to document
the atrocities.

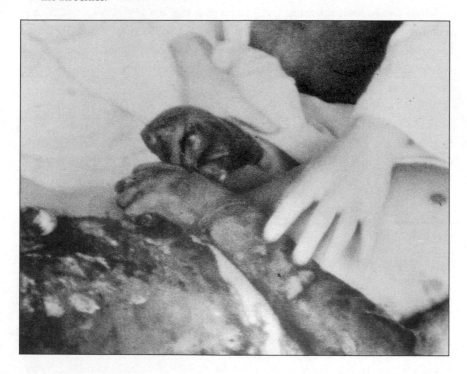

24 DECEMBER

This morning I carefully packed up the red Advent star that we lighted yesterday evening and gave it as a Christmas present, along with a Siemens calendar notebook, to the ladies at Kulou Hospital. Dr. Wilson used the opportunity to show me a few of his patients. The woman who was admitted because of a miscarriage and had the bayonet cuts all over her face is doing fairly well. A sampan owner who was shot in the jaw and burned over most of his body when someone poured gasoline over him and then set him on fire managed to speak a few words, but he will probably die in the course of the day. Almost two-thirds of his skin is burnt. I also went down to the morgue in the basement and had them uncover the bodies that were delivered last night. Among them, a civilian with his eyes burned out and his head totally burned, who had likewise had gasoline poured over him by Japanese soldiers. The body of a little boy, maybe seven years old, had four bayonet wounds in it, one in the belly about as long as your finger. He died two days after being admitted to the hospital without ever once uttering a sound of pain.

I have had to look at so many corpses over the last few weeks that I can keep my nerves in check even when viewing these horrible cases. It really doesn't leave you in a "Christmas" mood; but I wanted to see these atrocities with my own eyes, so that I can speak as an eyewitness later. A man cannot be silent about this kind of cruelty!

While I was at the hospital, Fitch kept watch for me. For now, I cannot leave my house unguarded without running the risk that marauding soldiers will break into it. It was my firm belief that about 350 to 400 refugees had found asylum with me. After an exact head count by Mr. Han, it now turns out that a total of 602 people are camping in my garden (with its 5,500 square feet), my office, etc.: 302 males and 300 females, including 126 children under ten years of age. One child is only two months old. Not included in this census are 14 servants and employees of the firm plus their families, so that the total number probably comes to about 650.

Chang is beaming: His wife was released from the hospital this morning; we've just picked her up in the car. She'll be sleeping from now on in the attic with her children; there's no other place left in the house for them.

Everyone's competing to make this a happy Christmas for me. It's really touching! Chang bought some Christmas roses and has decorated the house with them. He even managed to find a little fir tree that he wants to decorate and he just came in grinning with joy and carrying six very long candles that he rounded up for me somewhere. Everybody likes me suddenly. And it used to be, or so I thought, that no one wanted to have much to do with me, or might I have been wrong there? How strange, my dear Dora, my dear children and grandchildren! I know you're all praying for me today. I feel as if I'm surrounded by loving thoughts. That does a man boundless good after all that I've had to go through these last two weeks. Believe me, I have a prayer in my heart for all of you as well. The terrible crisis that has overtaken us all here has restored our childlike faith. Only a God can protect me from these hordes whose deadly games include rape, murder, and arson.

We've just had news that new troops will be arriving today who will restore the order we've been longing for. From now on, all crimes are to be severely punished at once. Let's hope so! By God it's time there was a turn for the better. We're very near the end of our tether.

I'll close today's entry with this prayer in my heart: May a gracious God keep all of you from ever again having to face a crisis like the one in which we now find ourselves. I do not regret having stayed on here, for my presence has saved many lives, but all the same, my suffering is indescribable.

Letter from the International Committee
to the Japanese Embassy

Nanking, December 25th, 1937.
To the Officers of the Imperial Japanese Embassy, Nanking.

This morning about 10:00, Mr. Riggs found several Japanese soldiers in the house at No. 29 Hankow Road and heard a woman cry. The woman, who was about 25–30 years old, tapped herself and motioned for Mr. Riggs to come. One soldier had her in tow. Other soldiers were in the house. She grabbed Riggs's arm. The other soldiers came out of the house and all of them went on and left the woman with Mr. Riggs. The woman had been out buying things and the soldiers took her. Her husband was taken four days ago and had not returned. She wanted Mr. Riggs to escort her back to the Refugee Camp at the Military College on Hankow Road. So Mr. Riggs escorted her east on Hankow Road and almost to the University Gardens, there they met an inspection officer with two soldiers and an interpreter. The officer grabbed Mr. Riggs hands out of his pockets and grabbed his armband, which had been issued him by the Japanese Embassy. He swatted Mr. Riggs hands when he tried to put them back in his pocket. As near as he could tell, the officer asked Mr.

Riggs who he was, but neither could understand the other. He then hit Mr. Riggs on the chest hard. Mr. Riggs asked him what he meant and that made the officer angry. The officer motioned for his passport but Mr. Riggs did not have it with him. He wanted to know what Riggs was doing. Mr. Riggs told him he was taking this woman home. So the officer hit Riggs again. Mr. Riggs looked to see what armband the officer was wearing and the officer slapped Mr. Riggs in the face hard. The officer then pointed to the ground and grabbed Mr. Riggs' hat so Mr. Riggs thought the officer wanted him to kowtow to him. But Mr. Riggs would not. So the officer gave Mr. Riggs another slap in the face. Then the interpreter explained that the officer wanted a card. Mr. Riggs explained he was taking the woman home because she was afraid. The officer gave an order to the soldiers and they came to either side of Mr. Riggs with guns at attention. Then the interpreter explained that the officer wanted Mr. Riggs to bow to the officer. Mr. Riggs refused because he was an American. The officer finally told Mr. Riggs to go home. Meanwhile, the Chinese woman had been so frightened when she saw Mr. Riggs so treated, she ran off down Hankow Road.

Mr. Riggs explained that he did not touch the officer and simply had his hands in his pockets (of his overcoat) walking down the road, bothering no one. The woman was walking a short distance ahead of him.

We hope that there will speedily be such a restitution of order and discipline among the soldiers that foreign nationals going peacefully about the streets need no longer fear being molested.

Most respectfully yours,
Lewis S. C. Smythe

25 DECEMBER

While I was writing in my diary yesterday afternoon, our number-one boy Chang and several of his Chinese friends secretly decorated the Christmas tree. Chang has often helped do it before. The tree was a faithful copy *en miniature* of our Christmas trees in years past. They even set up the Nativity scene we always enjoyed so much, with the Holy Family and all the animals, higgledy-piggledy, tame or wild side by side, and then when the middle door to the dining room opened and the glow from our few wretched candles filled the room, I really did feel some trace of a Christmas mood come over me after all.

Kröger and Sperling came to see the tree, the only one in all Nanking. Kröger brought along a bottle of white wine that he had "rescued" from the wreckage of the Scharffenberg house. Unfortunately half of it had spilled. After first toasting the health of our dear ones at home, we silently drank a glass.

Then Kröger and Sperling went off to Ping Tsiang Hsian, the residence of some Americans who had invited us for "Xmas dinner." I didn't join them, because I couldn't leave my 602 refugees unguarded. We agreed, however, that some gentlemen of the committee would relieve me from duty during the course of the evening, so that I could spend a quarter of an hour or so together with my American companions in adversity. No sooner had Kröger and Sperling left than I was paid a visit by Mr. Fukui, who is currently top man at the Japanese embassy, to whose staff members I had sent several Siemens calendar notebooks for Christmas. Accompanied by Police Chief Takadama, he gave me a box of Havana cigars in return. A pity I don't smoke. Tobacco products have now become rarities: A tin of cigarettes, that used to cost 85 cents, is not to be had for under $6 now. Both Japanese gentlemen, with whom I shared some wine in celebration of the day, were amazed that I had a Christmas tree and flowers. Since the Japanese are great flower lovers, I shared some of mine with them, which appeared to delight them greatly. I hope to get on something like friendly terms with these gentlemen, in whose hands power now lies, since that may help mitigate the circumstances of my wards.

Once the Japanese departed, we retired to the dining room with its festive candlelight and sat down to Christmas dinner: corned beef and cabbage, which tasted like the finest roast.

Mr. Han came over with his family and received an Advent wreath with four candles as a present, while Mrs. Han and the children were each allowed to pick an ornament from the tree: a colorful ball, an elephant, a little Santa Claus. And with that my bag of gifts was empty; but I had not reckoned with Boy Chang, who now arrived with the biggest surprise of all: four gingerbread hearts! I couldn't believe my eyes; four confectionery hearts that Mutti had decorated with a red ribbon and to which Chang had added a fresh sprig of fir. After having been faithfully kept in storage by the servants for one whole year, they were now immediately and enthusiastically devoured by me and my guests. That is—why should I deny it—a piece got stuck in my throat. It wasn't the cake, which was excellent. It must have been something wrong with my throat.

Mutti, everyone's loving thoughts were of you. One person's eyes were even a little red. Then came Mr. Mills to take over guard duty for me. I drove to the Americans in the black of night, passing many of the corpses that have been lying in our streets unburied for twelve days now.

Corpses of Chinese were left for weeks in the streets.

The Americans were sitting together quiet and pensive. They didn't have a tree; a couple of red banners beside the fireplace were the only sign that the servants had wanted to give their employers some small joy. We spoke about the urgent problem of registering the refugees, about which we are all very worried.

The Japanese have decreed that every refugee must be registered. This has to be completed within the next ten days. No easy matter, what with 200,000 people.

And we're already hearing complaints. A good number of healthy robust civilians have already been "selected," meaning that their fate is either forced labor or execution. And a good number of young girls have also been selected, because the Japanese want to set up a large military bordello. There's no merry Christmas when hard measures like that are being taken.

After only half an hour I drive home through pestilential streets. In my garden camp peace and quiet reign, with only the twelve guards prowling along the walls, whispering to each other—just a few signals, low disjointed cries, so as not to disturb their fellow sufferers. Mills drives home, and I can lie down to rest, though still in my boots and spurs, as always; for I have to be ready to throw out intruders at a moment's notice. But thank God everything is quiet and peaceful. For a long while I listen to the heavy breathing and snoring all about me, broken now and then by the cough of one of the many who are ill.

26 DECEMBER, 5:00 P.M.

I've just received a Christmas present better than any I could have wished. I have been given 600 human lives. The newly founded Japanese committee was here to investigate prior to registering my refugees. Each man was called out individually. They all had to form ranks, women and children on the left, men on the right. There was an awful lot of pushing and shoving; but everything went fine. No one was led away, as happened at nearby Ginling Middle School, where they had to hand over more than 20 men: They were to be shot as suspected ex-Chinese soldiers. My Chinese are all very happy, and I thank my Creator with all my heart that everything went smoothly. Four Japanese soldiers are now filling out passes in the garden. They probably won't finish the job today, but that doesn't mean anything. A Japanese officer has made his decision, and there'll be no altering that.

While I'm busy providing him with cigars and Siemens calendar notebooks, a thick cloud of smoke rises above a building of the Pei-Tze Ting. A shower of ashes falls on my garden. The Japanese officer gazes somewhat thoughtfully at my refugees' endangered straw huts and then ingenuously remarks: *"Il y a des soldats Japonais qui sont très mauvais."*[26] And he's not all wrong there!

LATER

There have been no break-ins here by Japanese soldiers since yesterday. The first time in two weeks. It looks as if things are finally getting better. The registration of my refugees was completed by noon, and they were even generous enough to give a *mingto*[27] to 20 more new people who have smuggled themselves in here.

Liu and one of his children are sick. I drive them to Kulou Hospital to see Dr. Wilson, who is running the whole show there by himself now because Dr. Trimmer has been taken ill as well. Wilson shows me a new instance of the insane brutality of Japanese soldiers: A middle-aged woman who was unable to provide soldiers with young girls was grazed by shots across her abdomen, taking about three handbreadths of flesh with them. She's not expected to recover.

Registration is also being carried out at our Safety Zone headquarters.

It is being done here by Mr. Kikuchi, whom we all like because he's a kind man. The population from other neighborhoods in our Zone is being rounded up by the hundreds and led to the registration offices. About 20,000 people, so I've heard, have been arrested, some of whom are being forced into labor. The rest are to be shot. We shrug in silence at these barbaric measures. But sad to say, we are totally powerless.

I have supplied Police Chief Takadama with a car—a rental! True, he has promised me a receipt, but I don't expect to get the car back.

If only they would remove the corpses from the streets. Ten days ago, just a few steps outside our residence, I found a soldier who had been shot and killed while tied to a bamboo bed, and the body still hasn't been removed. No one dares approach the corpse, not even the Red Swastika Society, because it's that of a Chinese soldier.

Takadama demands that I give him a complete list of all European buildings, together with a list of what has been stolen from them. I decline, because that's a job for the embassies. I have no desire to get my fingers burned on a hot potato like that. I can't even determine whether, and if so, which buildings have in fact been spared.

Today, the second day of Christmas, I've remained at home guarding my refugees; tomorrow, however, I shall have to return to my job at Safety Zone headquarters.

It's getting more and more difficult to feed the 200,000 people in our Zone. Dr. Smythe estimates our rice reserves will last for another week. I'm not that pessimistic.

Our various petitions to Japanese authorities to let us search the city for more stores of rice and then bring them to the Zone have remained unanswered. The Japanese want the Chinese to leave the Zone and return to their homes. In answer to my question as to when train service and shipping between here and Shanghai will be reestablished, all I get from the Japanese are shrugs. They don't know themselves. The river is so full of mines that it will be some time before regular traffic is even thinkable.

I am constantly amazed at how our boys and cooks are still able to find food for us. Especially at my house, it borders on the miraculous. I have three permanent Chinese guests who have been gnawing away at my reserves for two weeks now, and happily there's still enough to go around. Perhaps the refugees, who for now at least have taken me to their hearts, bring items back for me when they go foraging for food. I get fried eggs every day, and there are people who can barely remember what an egg looks like.

Miss Minnie Vautrin, our American Minnie, a proper lady to the core—

I really don't know quite rightly who she is. It would appear that she's a teacher who's now in charge of Ginling Girls College, because at first she fought tooth and nail against allowing male refugees to be housed in the college halls entrusted to her, until someone finally convinced her to let the men be quartered on one floor and the women on another.

And something terrible has happened to our Minnie. She believes in her girls and guards them the way a hen guards her chicks. During the period when Japanese outrages were at their worst, I have seen her with my own eyes leading a procession of 400 female refugees through the Zone on their way to her college camp.

And now the Japanese authorities have come up with the fabulous idea of erecting a military bordello, and with hands clenched in horror, Minnie is forced to watch as authorized underlings force their way into her Girls Assembly Hall filled with hundreds of *gungyangs*.[28] She is not going to hand over even one of them willingly. She would rather die on the spot; but then something unexpected happens. A respectable member of the Red Swastika Society, someone whom we all know, but would never have suspected had any knowledge of the underworld, calls out a few friendly words into the hall—and lo and behold! A considerable number of young refugee girls step forward. Evidently former prostitutes, who are not at all sad to find work in a new bordello. Minnie is speechless!

27 DECEMBER

I've just returned from playing Santa Claus, that is, I tried to give each of the 126 children in my garden a 20-cent piece. It didn't go well. They almost tore me to pieces, and when I saw that fathers holding babies were in danger of being crushed, I had to give up trying to distribute the money. Only about 80 or 90 children received their gift; I'll have to search out the rest of the *xiao haitze*[29] as opportunity arises. I did a little housecleaning at headquarters today. Too many lazy coolies with no business there had made themselves at home. In 20 minutes the whole house was clean and looking respectable again.

A man who had been bayoneted 5 times was admitted to Kulou Hospital today. He reports that he was one of about 200 ex-soldiers who had taken refuge at Ginling Middle College and were then "selected." Instead of being shot, they were all bayoneted. This is now the preferred method, since we foreigners prick up our ears at the sound of machine-gun fire and then inquire about the reason for the shooting.

The Japanese both bayoneted Chinese prisoners and used them as live targets for sword practice.

Chang and Han came today to tell me that at Hsin Chieh Kou (we call it "Potsdamer Platz") a Japanese-Chinese store has opened up where you can buy food of every sort. I immediately drive over with Han to determine if the report is true, and we arrive just in time to witness the building being torched. They want the city in ruins!

28 DECEMBER

Fires are still being set, everywhere, over and over. You feel like a seriously ill patient fearfully watching the hour hand inch forward. All the refugees are afraid of the New Year, because they expect the Japanese soldiers to get drunk and then commit more atrocities. We try to comfort them, but we have only feeble words of comfort. We don't even believe them ourselves.

Someone has been spreading the rumor that today is the last day of registration. As a result, several tens of thousands of people have been thronging the registration office. The streets of the Zone are so overcrowded that you can't even get through on foot. The German flag on my car opens a path, though with great difficulty, through this sea of human bodies. Everyone in the Zone recognizes my car with its swastika flag. They push and shove trying to create a space for the car to slip through. I move slowly toward my goal. The opening instantly closes again behind me. If we should be brought to a halt, I won't easily get out of this crush again, that's certain.

The reports we are hearing from all sides today are so hair-raising that I can hardly bring myself to put them to paper. Before registration began at some of the schools where refugees are camped out, the Japanese first demanded that any former Chinese soldiers in the crowd step forward voluntarily. They were given promises of protection. They were merely to be put into labor crews. At that, a good number of refugees stepped forward. In one case, about 50 people. They were led off at once. As we learned from one of the survivors, they were taken to a vacant house, robbed of all valuables and clothes, and when completely naked, tied up together in groups of five. Then the Japanese built a large bonfire in the courtyard, led the groups out one by one, bayoneted the men and tossed them still alive on the fire. Ten of these men were able to slip free of their ropes, leap over the courtyard wall, and vanish into the crowd, who gladly found clothes for them.

This news has come to us in much the same form from three different sides. Another group, larger than the first, is said to have been bayoneted in the graveyards in the West City. Dr. Bates is at present trying to get more detailed information about these groups. We have to be very careful what we say about such incidents in order not to put the person providing the information at risk.

Mr. Fitch has received a letter from Shanghai in which the Rotary Club informs him that they have collected 35,000 dollars for us. Money is of no use to us. What we need are people, *foreigners,* to come and help us; but the Japanese are letting no one into Nanking.

The officials at the Japanese embassy appear willing to make our situation more tolerable, but they also seem unable to make any headway with their fellow countrymen who happen to be in the military. We have heard that the military command here does not want to recognize the Japanese-Chinese Committee that the Japanese embassy has put together—one similar to our committee for the Safety Zone. It now turns out that Mr. Fukuda was right when on his very first day here he told us: "The military people want to make it very bad for the town, but we, the embassy, will try to avoid it."

The Japanese major Yoshiro Oka in a caricature drawn by
a well-known artist in Shanghai who worked under the
name Sapajou.

Unfortunately neither Mr. Fukuda, nor Mr. Tanaka, nor Mr. Fukui has succeeded in changing the military's mind.

Letter from the Missionary E. H. Forster to George Fitch

Dear George!

In the vicinity of the Sin Ku Sze (a big temple) near #17 Sang Ya Street, are the bodies of about 50 men who have been executed as soldier suspects. They've been there almost two weeks now and are getting into a state where burial is imperative. I have a group of men who are willing to undertake this, but are afraid to act unless they have proper authority to do so. Is the latter necessary? If so, can you get it for me?
Thank you.

LATER

This letter from Forster to Fitch throws the harsh light of day on current conditions here. In addition to the 50 corpses mentioned, there are still more in a pond not far from our headquarters. We have asked on numerous occasions to be allowed to bury the bodies, but have always been refused. How this all will end is a mystery to us, particularly since rain and snow have fallen now, which only accelerates the decomposition.

Dr. Smythe and I had a two-hour discussion at the Japanese embassy with Mr. Fukui and a Japanese Major Oka. The latter informed us that he had been asked by Dr. Trautmann, the German ambassador, to insure our safety. He demands that all Germans—a total of five men—move into one house, where he can then offer better protection. If I disagree with the suggestion, I am to write Mr. Oka a letter declaring I waive all claims to such protection. I was not about to mince words, so I declared that I demanded no other protection for my own person than that which the Japanese army had promised the Chinese here in the city. If I wanted to leave the Chinese in the lurch, I could have joined Dr. Trautmann and the other Germans on board the *Kutwo* long ago.

I have been assigned to safeguard your life, Major Oka declares. If there is proof that property has been stolen or destroyed by Japanese soldiers, it can be compensated for or replaced by the Japanese government. I can only reply that along with a number of American members of our committee I made a tour of the city on 14 December and found, for example, that all German property was intact *after* the fall of Nanking. Only with the entry

John Rabe and the other members of the Safety Committee were refused permission to bury the bodies of victims left floating in ponds and ditches.

of Japanese troops into the city did the looting and arson, the murder, rape, and mayhem begin. We were all prepared to swear to that. The few buildings that had been looted by the retreating Chinese troops were on Taiping Lu. No houses belonging to foreigners were among them.

At 7:30 p.m. a noncommissioned officer arrives with my guard of honor: two strapping soldiers with bayonets fixed and horribly muddy standard-issue boots, who are ruining all my carpets and are supposed to protect me. They are immediately sent back outside and told to march back and forth in the snow and rain. Actually I feel a little sorry for them because the weather is so rotten.

At 9 o'clock this evening two Japanese soldier-bandits suddenly climb over my back garden wall without anyone noticing, and on my way outside I discover them in the pantry. I try to hold them there. Kröger is sent to fetch the men on guard; but they have both vanished! And when Kröger tells me that, the two intruders hastily swing themselves back up over the wall as well.

Mr. Fukui pleads with me not to write Shanghai anything about Nanking, that is, not to describe facts that the Japanese embassy finds unpleasant. I have promised him. What choice do I have? Since my letters can be forwarded only through the Japanese embassy, if I want them sent at all, I have to comply. One fine day the truth will out. I used the opportunity to ask Mr. Fukuda to see to it that the body of the Chinese soldier shot on 13 December be taken away at last. Fukui promises to deal with the matter.

He also informs me that our Zone has now been surrounded by Japanese guards, who will see to it that no prowling soldiers are allowed into the Zone. I've now had a better look at these guards and discovered that they did not stop and interrogate a single Japanese soldier. I even saw soldiers carrying looted items out of the Zone, and with absolutely no questions asked by the guards. What sort of protection is that?

Letter from John Rabe to His Wife in Shanghai

Nanking, 30 December 1937

My dear Dora,

Yesterday, 29 December, I received by way of the Japanese embassy here your sweet letters from 6, 12, 15, and 22 December. I cannot at present describe to you the details of my experiences here, but I can assure you that we 22 Europeans, as well as Mr. Han and his family, are all right. I still have a supply of insulin. You needn't worry about that. What has become of my baggage on board the *Kutwo?* Do you know anything about it? Let's hope nothing has been lost. All my books are packed up in it, too.

There is much to do here. I would not be at all unhappy if I were soon relieved of my post as "mayor." Physically we are all, as noted, in good shape, but psychologically each of us could probably use a nice vacation. I hope we shall see each other soon.

Greetings and kisses (despite what the censor thinks!)
from Your JOHNY

30 DECEMBER

The newly organized Autonomous Government Committee has ordered lots of flags made displaying five stripes. We're expecting a big public ceremony on 1 January when the new flags are to be waved. This Autonomous Government Committee is to be our replacement. We have nothing against their taking over our work, but it looks to us as if they simply want to take over our money.

I'll not voluntarily hand over anything. I'll yield only under greatest pressure, and then only under loud protest. I've already noticed that the

Japanese diplomats are ashamed of the Japanese army's method of operation. They would love to exonerate themselves of the fact that 40 buildings flying the German flag have been looted and some of them even burned down.

Over the last two nights, here in the straw huts, in the muck and mud of my refugee camp, the so-called Siemens Camp, two children were born, a boy and girl. I am ashamed that I cannot provide these new mothers some other lodging. No doctor, no midwife, no nurse to help. There aren't even any bandages or diapers. A few wretched dirty rags were all that the parents had for their newborn infants. I gave each couple ten dollars. In return, they named the girl "Dora" and the little boy "Johny." Great fun!

I have bought two lovely dwarf pines in shallow porcelain bowls to give as New Year's presents to Mr. Fukui of the Japanese embassy and Major General Sasaki, commandant of the Nanking garrison. The little trees are so pretty that I find it hard to part with them; but the Japanese come first these days. Moreover, I've made some New Year's cards with my own original design: the coat of arms of our Safety Zone and my signature on the front, and the signatures of all 22 Europeans and Americans still in Nanking on the back.

CHAPTER 6

NEW YEAR

31 DECEMBER

TWO OF THE MALE OCCUPANTS of my Siemens Camp who were loitering outside the gate today were abducted by Japanese soldiers and forced to carry looted goods for them. When I returned home at noon, the wife of one of them knelt before me pleading for me to bring the men back, because otherwise they would surely be murdered. I then drove back down Chung Shan Lu with this truly shabby looking woman until we found the men in question. I stood across from about 20 armed Japanese soldiers, who did not want to hand the two Chinese over. It wasn't a pleasant situation; I finally did prevail but was very happy to have the expedition behind me.

I gave these two foolish fellows a stern lecture in front of the assembled residents of the camp. I cannot go running after each of my 630 refugees if the rascals are stupid enough to get themselves caught. Why had they crept in here with me if not to hide? I issued a warning that I would not undertake a rescue like this a second time. It's simply too dangerous over the long haul.

Japanese soldiers are being issued three-day passes for the New Year. There has been a promise that the Zone will be off-limits to strolling soldiers, but I don't trust their peace. Tomorrow, 1 January 1938, the Autonomous Government will be solemnly constituted.

1 JANUARY 1938

At 9:30 yesterday evening, my seven trusty lads, the Americans Fitch, Dr. Smythe, Dr. Wilson, Mills, Dr. Bates, McCallum, and Riggs, came to wish me a "Happy New Year." We emptied the last bottle of red wine and chatted for an hour. Since Dr. Bates, usually one of our liveliest minds, dozed off in his armchair from sheer exhaustion, the party broke up early. And since neither my Chinese guests nor I placed any value on sacrificing a good night's sleep, we were all in bed by eleven o'clock.

Around 7 a.m. our boy Chang appeared to tell me that his wife had suffered a relapse. I quickly got dressed and brought her and Chang to Kulou Hospital for the third time.

When I return home in my car, I am received with a royal salute. The *lao bai xing*,[30] my poor refugees, have formed two long lines and in my honor set off thousands of fireworks they've been given by the Japanese to celebrate the establishment of the new Autonomous Government. Then all my six hundred parishioners surround me and give me a New Year's greeting written in red ink on white wrapping paper. They all bow three times and are very happy when I bow my head in gratitude and fold up the greeting and put it in my pocket. What a shame the paper is so big. There's no possible way I can fit it into this book. One of my Chinese friends translates the greeting as follows:

> For Mr. Rabe,
> with best wishes for
> a happy year.
> Hundreds of millions are close to you!
> The refugees of your camp
> 1938.

I'm still not sure what "hundreds of millions" means. It's probably to be read as "hundreds of millions of good spirits." When I ask number-one boy Chang, he puts it very succinctly: "In German mean just *Prosit Neujahr!*"

After I had finally escaped the shower of sparklers and firecrackers, all the servants and employees appeared in a solemn procession to make their usual New Year's kowtow.

Sperling and Riggs pay me a New Year's visit at noon and each is given a cigar as a present—a princely gift. Cigars now cost from five to seven dollars apiece here. Besides which, Sperling gets a new razor, since his was recently stolen. At 9 in the evening, several Japanese soldiers appear in a truck and demand girls. When we don't open the gate, they finally move on. We watch them drive on to the Middle School, which is constantly harassed. I beef up the night guard in the garden, teams of two with whistles, so that I can be on the spot even faster if intruders honor us with a visit. But everything remains quiet, thank God.

2 JANUARY

Several Japanese soldiers have broken into a building next to Safety Zone Headquarters. Women and girls flee over the wall onto our grounds. Kröger gets up on our dugout and jumps from there over the very high garden wall. I want to follow; a policeman helps me up, and we both lose our balance and fall off the wall. But we land in a fairly heavy stand of bamboo that breaks our fall, so no one is hurt. Meanwhile Kröger has collared the Japanese; they immediately make themselves scarce. Ostensibly they were only inspecting!

The wife of my neighbor, the woman with the bayonet slashes whom I sent to Kulou Hospital, has been released again as cured. Since she has no money and has been in the hospital for ten days at a cost of 80 cents a day, I take care of her bill.

The common people have been plundered and are poorer than ever. Yesterday, while the orators of the new Autonomous Government were speaking of cooperation, several buildings torched by the Japanese were burning to the right and left of Kulou Hospital where the ceremony took place.

Mr. Sun, who is the vice chairmen of the new Autonomous Government and a member of the Red Swastika Society and speaks Japanese, condescendingly informs me that he must speak to me very soon about an important matter. Please do, I've been waiting for this. I have a very good idea of what your intentions are!

The streets of the Zone are still packed with people: Untold thousands just stand around or barter and trade. The sides of the streets are taken over by peddlers, most of them offering food, tobacco, and old clothes.

Everyone is running around with Japanese armbands or flying Japanese flags. In the side streets or on vacant lots between streets, entire villages of the refugees' straw huts have sprung up, just like the one in my garden. There's not a blade of grass left growing in my garden, and the lovely hedges have all been trampled underfoot. It's inevitable with such numbers of people—they simply want to live.

Last night there was another series of atrocities committed by Japanese soldiers, all of which Dr. Smythe has written up. As usual we shall present the list in the form of a protest to the Japanese embassy.

Today we received our first visit from Chinese bombers over Nanking, something we've long been quietly worried about. And they certainly did not come as friends, but as foes! They dropped their bombs just as punctually as the Japanese before them, but so far, thank God, on pretty much the same target, the area around the airport south of the city. Japanese anti-aircraft fire was also in evidence, but only just a little and very weak.

We'll have to wait and see if these air raids remain restricted to the area outside our Zone; but we hope so. If that is not the intention, then the results could be far worse than before. Even Shanghai at noon is not as heavily populated as the streets of our Zone at present. One bomb landing in that bustling throng could cost a thousand lives. The mere thought makes me shudder.

3 JANUARY

At 7 o'clock yesterday evening Dr. Smythe came by with the following note addressed to Mr. Fitch from Dr. Hsü, a physician:

Dear Mr. Fitch:

Liu Pan-kwen, who had attempted to protect his wife from being raped by a Japanese soldier, was shot and killed today by the latter at about 4:30 p.m. this afternoon.

Since the house next door is occupied by Japanese soldiers, our house is now full of women who have fled to us. I have written Mr. Sperling and asked him to come quickly to us and stay here to protect us. If Mr. Sperling is not available, can you perhaps send another foreigner who can stay at Ninhai Lu No. 5 and protect us?

Sincerely yours,
DR. C. Y. HSÜ

While Dr. Smythe went out to look for Sperling, who is to camp out on Ninhai Lu for the night, I drove to the Japanese embassy with John Magee, who has received a full report of this crime, in order to ask Mr. Tanaka to petition the Japanese military authorities to investigate the matter. It's a case of brutal premeditated murder.

Early yesterday morning, the Japanese soldier had tried to rape Liu's wife, the mother of 5 children. The husband came in and with some slaps in the face forced the Japanese to leave. That afternoon the soldier, who had been unarmed in the morning, returned with a gun, looked for and found Liu hiding in the kitchen, and shot him, even though all Liu's neighbors pled for the man's life and one even knelt down before the Japanese soldier.

Tanaka promised to advise the military of the incident at once. I do not doubt that he kept his promise, but we have heard nothing of the matter since. We also have yet to hear of any punishment given any soldier other than a few slaps.

Perhaps as a way of consoling me, Tanaka then tells me a very welcome bit of news, that is, that Dr. Rosen and presumably Hürter and Scharffenberg, who are currently staying in Wuhu, will arrive in Nanking on 5 January, the same day that the gentlemen of the American embassy have announced for their visit.

Meanwhile, Krischan Kröger has been on Purple Mountain. The observatory is in ruins and the path to the top more or less demolished, but still passable. I'm not at all pleased by Kröger's little strolls. He should not place himself in danger so often for no compelling reason—but try and tell him that!

LATER

Water has been restored to the city today, so we now have running water in our bathroom on the second floor. At noon there was even power in a few areas of the Zone, but it was turned off again at around 1 o'clock, probably to keep us from listening to news on the radio.

The reports reviewing our soup kitchens and refugee camps provide an interesting insight into how our committee and its subcommittees have to go about their rather difficult business: Some Chinese are not at all shy about "squeezing." We are in China, and nothing gets done without a "squeeze."

Today in my garden I caught a vegetable peddler demanding cut-throat prices. Some women in the camp were about to buy him out. I was able to stop it and showed the fellow the gate.

4 JANUARY

Unfortunately I live a bit too close to the Safety Zone border. I can't stop worrying about the chance that my house may go up in flames. Yesterday three buildings in the vicinity were torched, and as I write this a new cloud of smoke is rising in the south. The city, by the way, is still dark, although the turbines at Hsiakwan are said to be intact. We keep up a steady stream of protests, but without any visible results. Some improvement in our general situation is apparent now that a troop of military police has been specially charged with guarding the Safety Zone, but even among these *shen bings*[31] there are some dubious elements who either close both eyes at once or participate in atrocities themselves.

5 JANUARY

In the review of the individual refugee camps, the Siemens Camp did not do very well. Mr. Han has given our refugees a little too much rice. He's a kind man, that's all! The suggestion that some of the refugees be sent to another camp, because the 5,500 square feet in my garden are too small for 602 people, has met with no favor. People feel safe here with me and don't want to leave. So there's really nothing that can be done.

I'm very worried about the sanitation problem. I have no idea what to do about it and can only hope no epidemics break out. We had city water until this morning, but it dried up at noon. We still don't have light. And houses are burning down all around us.

Registration is still not complete. You see tens of thousands of women with babies in their arms standing five abreast in long lines waiting out in the open for up to six hours. How these people endure waiting in the cold like that is a mystery to me.

The Hanchung Men, the gate that was opened yesterday, has been closed again today. Kröger saw about 300 corpses in a dry ditch near the gate: civilians who had been machine-gunned there. They don't want to let Europeans outside the gates. They probably fear that something about conditions here might get published too soon.

CHAPTER 7

THE DIPLOMATS RETURN

6 JANUARY

HURRAH! The three officials from the American embassy, Mr. Allison, Mr. Espey, and Mr. McFadyen, arrived here today aboard the USS *Oahu* from Shanghai by way of Wuhu. They were already outside Nanking once before on 31 December, but were not allowed to land and so went on to Wuhu. Mr. Allison served previously as a diplomat in Tokyo and speaks Japanese.

We can now buy rice and flour from the Japanese military authorities: supplies that the Japanese have captured here. Despite the high price (one sack of rice costs 13 dollars Mex.), we decide to buy rice worth 50,000 dollars Mex. We also have to buy coal worth about 12,000 dollars Mex. The demand for rice, flour, and coal grows daily, since the supplies that the refugees brought with them into the Zone are almost used up.

Mr. Han does not agree with the purchase. He has heard from a rice dealer that the Chinese troops are about to retake Nanking. People claim to have heard the thunder of cannons southwest of the city. If Nanking is retaken, Han says, we'll have rice and flour for free. Unfortunately, I must disabuse him of any such hopes.

At around 10 o'clock a Japanese truck arrived and took about 15 employees from my Siemens Camp to be put to work at the electricity works in Hsiakwan. The coolies left only very reluctantly. Last time, despite all the promises of the Japanese, they were badly taken care of, if they were taken care of at all. Besides which, instead of being sent to the electricity works in Hsiakwan, some of them were put to work clearing trenches outside the city gates.

At 5 o'clock this afternoon, Mr. Fukuda paid me a visit to tell me that by decision of the military authorities our International Committee is to be dissolved and our supplies and moneys are to be taken over by the Autonomous Government Committee. I immediately protest any handing over of our assets and supplies. We have no objection to their taking over our work, but wish to point out that before the city is secure under the rule of law and order, the refugees cannot return to their former homes, which for the most part have been demolished and looted or burned down.

I at once call a meeting of the committee, in which my answer to Mr. Fukuda is discussed and a proposal prepared outlining how we envision the restoration of law and order. I have the feeling that the Autonomous Government hasn't the vaguest idea how to tackle these problems, even though they are being advised by the Japanese. All that interests them are our assets. Their claim is: "You received the money from the Chinese government, and so now it belongs to us!"

We are most decidedly of a different opinion and will leave no stone unturned in the defense of our opinion, for which we expect strong support from both the American and German embassies, although as yet we do not know what their viewpoints really are.

From a Report of Ambassador Trautmann
to the Foreign Ministry

Hankow, 6 January 1938

Re: Taking of Nanking, Plundering by Japanese troops

The activity of the International Committee, headed by Herr Rabe, an agent of Siemens, has received highest commendation from all sides. Minister Kung[32] has asked me to express his particular thanks to Herr Rabe. I would like to reserve the right to request that Herr Rabe be awarded a decoration later.

TRAUTMANN

7 JANUARY

I presented Mr. Fukuda a letter in which the standpoint of the International Committee is clearly laid out. He told me that strict instructions have come from Tokyo stating that order absolutely must be restored in Nanking imme diately. At the same time, however, all administrative tasks (including those of Mayor Rabe?) must be handled by the Autonomous Government Committee and not by us Westerners. "We Westerners" certainly have no objection there. We only hope the Autonomous Committee is up to the task.

I once again call Fukuda's attention to the danger to which we are all exposed as long as perhaps a thousand corpses are lying about the city unburied. These corpses have been partially eaten by dogs. At the same time, however, dog meat is being sold by the Chinese in the streets. For 26 days now, I have been asking for permission to have these bodies buried, but always to no avail. Fukuda promised to petition the military yet again to give the Red Swastika Society permission to bury the corpses.

During my absence this morning, at about 10 o'clock, a Japanese soldier broke into my servants' quarters. The women and girls ran screaming to my rooms, were pursued up to the attic by the soldier, when a Japanese officer and interpreter who happened to call upon me found them and ordered him out. The incident is a good measure of what sort of safety is to be found in European houses at present, 26 days after Nanking was taken.

Mr. Riggs brings me the following report from his inspection tour today: A woman is wandering the streets with glazed eyes. She is taken to the hospital, where they learn she is the sole survivor of a family of eighteen. Her 17 relatives have been shot and bayoneted. She lived near the South Gate. Another woman from the same area, who has been living in our camp along with her brother, lost her parents and three children, all of them shot by the Japanese. With what little she had left, she bought a coffin so she could at least bury her father. Hearing news of this, Japanese soldiers ripped the lid from the coffin and dumped the body onto the street. Chinese don't need to be buried, was their explanation.

8 JANUARY

Mr. Fukui brings me news that Dr. Rosen, Hürter, and Scharffenberg will be arriving tomorrow with two gentlemen from the British embassy. Dr.

Corpses left unburied were mauled and eaten by dogs.

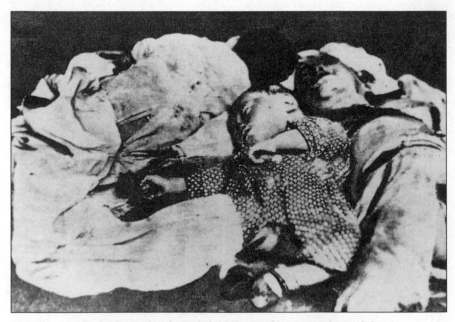

The Japanese slaughtered children as indiscriminately as adults.

Rosen's and Hürter's houses are in good shape, as is the German embassy. All that was stolen at Dr. Rosen's were his automobile, a bicycle, and various bottles of liquor. I don't know how things look at the Englishmen's homes. Scharffenberg's house, which lies outside the Zone, has been badly looted. Scharffenberg will have to live at Hürter's. The unpleasant part is that neither of these houses has water or electricity. I wrote Fukui another letter to that effect. I've heard that the gentlemen from the American embassy are also without water or light. They're all freezing, sitting around a large fireplace at the embassy. It's beyond me why they don't simply demand that the Japanese provide water and power.

I've already received Fukui's assurance that the Japanese embassy will allow new automobiles to be brought from Japan for the gentlemen at our embassy, and presumably at other embassies as well, to replace the cars that were stolen.

The rumor has spread among the Chinese again today that Chinese soldiers are about to retake the city. In fact, the claim is that Chinese soldiers have already been spotted inside the city. The first result of this was that all the many little Japanese flags decorating the huts and houses inside the Zone vanished; even the Japanese armbands that all Chinese wear disappeared, and as Mills has just told me, a sizable group of refugees has come up with the idea of attacking the Japanese embassy.

The least insurrection on the part of any Chinese will be punished by death. We're happy that thus far our Zone has remained perfectly quiet and can only hope that we are spared such tragic events.

LATER

In a Japanese newspaper lent me by Dr. Bates, I found the following article:

The Tokyo Nichi Nichi of 17 December 1937

Returning Normalcy.
Chinese Merchants Prepare for Business:

Nanking, Dec. 15. With the city of Nanking having been cleared of the Chinese looters, an early return to normalcy is expected as the Chinese merchants, now back from the refugee zone, are busy preparing for reopening their shops. Peace and order in the city is maintained by the Japanese Gendarmerie authorities, who posted guards at the important

Chinese government structures including the Executive and Legislative Yuans, the Finance Ministry, the Central Military Academy, and the Central Aviation School.

9 JANUARY

10 a.m.: discussion with Wang ("Jimmy"), a member of the Autonomous Government Committee, who tells us that a few days ago the Japanese were planning to close down our committee by force. But then they thought better of it. We're not allowed to sell any more rice to the refugees, however. We have no objection to that, if the Autonomous Government wants to take over the sale itself.

I visit the houses of Dr. Rosen and Hürter, and the German embassy, and find everything in order, but no electricity or water.

Kröger and Hatz arrive at our Zone headquarters at 11 o'clock and report that there's been a "small" execution that they were forced to witness. A Japanese officer and two soldiers drove a Chinese civilian out into one of the ponds on Shansi Road. When the man was standing hip-deep in the water, one of the soldiers made himself comfortable behind a nearby sandbag barricade and kept firing until his victim sank into the pond.

Dr. Rosen, Hürter, and Scharffenberg have arrived on the English gunboat *Cricket,* which also brought three officials of the British embassy, Consul Prideaux-Brune, Colonel Lovat-Fraser, and Mr. Walser, an air-force attaché, who, however, was not permitted to land, since the Japanese alleged that they had not been informed of his arrival.

Kröger, Hatz, and I went to the German embassy at 2 o'clock this afternoon and at about 3 the three German officials arrived, accompanied by Mr. Tanaka and Mr. Fukuda of the Japanese embassy, and we welcomed them with a bottle of champagne that Kröger had "commandeered" somewhere. Dr. Rosen was given a splendid Buick on loan from the Japanese to replace his stolen car, as well as a Ford for official use by the German embassy. Rosen swears that he will never give the two vehicles back. We join Scharffenberg on a visit to his house, which is in an indescribable state of disorder from having been looted. Among the many things that were dear to him, *Schalauje*[33] misses his top hat and 40 neckties. As soon as we get to take a vacation in Japan again, we'll keep an eye open to see if we can't catch someone wearing said items. The "shah" is quite cool and collected, by the way. I would have thought he'd fly into a rage, but he maintained the splendid composure acquired from 37 years in China!

This evening at 8 o'clock I had the three gentlemen from the German embassy, along with Kröger, for dinner and some of the wine Kröger rescued from Scharffenberg's, and was told stories of what had happened to the passengers aboard the Jardines *Hulk,* and the fates of the *Bee* and *Panay.*[34]

Hürter read us a report that Rosen had sent to the Foreign Ministry in Berlin. Dr. Rosen says that we 22 foreigners who remained behind here in Nanking have behaved as bravely as the first Christians in Rome who were devoured by lions in the arena; but that these lions simply didn't like us and preferred Chinese flesh. When asked about his view of the Japanese, Rosen replied with a Turkish proverb—he was once part of the legation in Constantinople:[35] "As long as you're on the bridge with the billy goat, you have to say 'uncle'!"

As we were about to set down to dinner at 8, one of the buildings nearby burst into flames. The arrival of the diplomats does not seem to have stopped the Japanese soldiers from carrying out their campaign of arson!

10 JANUARY

Rosen brought me letters, from Mutti in Shanghai, from Gretel and Otto in Munich. And I also got a lovely book, "The Story of Tilman's Sons," two cervelat sausages, two packages of rye wafers, insulin, and two pounds of butter. With it all lying so prettily there around me, I felt like a soldier with his gifts from home.

9 A.M.

Kröger returns from a visit by Major Ishida with news that Japanese don't want to sell us the rice and flour they promised. They'll supply only the Autonomous Government Committee. In compliance with Japanese orders, we stopped selling rice this morning, to the great disappointment of the Chinese refugees, for whom the Autonomous Government Committee has thus far not set up a single outlet. The situation is getting critical.

Dr. Rosen visits us at our committee headquarters. The Japanese have asked him, just as they have asked me, to be somewhat cautious in his reports. He says he told them: I shall report that you have cut off our water and power.

4:00 P.M.

The Autonomous Government Committee has opened an outlet for rice inside the Zone, not far from our headquarters. So for now at least, the worst of the crisis is taken care of. Reverend Mills accompanies me on a visit to the American embassy to introduce me to Mr. Allison, who has promised to continue our work in regard to the protests that we have submitted daily to the Japanese embassy about the endless stream of crimes committed by the Japanese soldiery.

FROM THE FAMILY DIARY

I hear from Hürter that an argument broke out on board the *Kutwo* between P. and v. S. as a result of which P. challenged v. S. to a duel (pistols— 30 paces). Since duels are illegal in Hong Kong, where they were headed, the duel is to take place in Germany. P. and v. S. are now each on board separate ships heading for home. All commentary superfluous! Here we are in peril of our own lives, trying to save human lives, and our fellow countrymen are playing games with theirs!

Report from the Nanking Office of the German Embassy (Rosen) to the Foreign Ministry

15 January 1938

On 9 January, after an interruption of one month, the Nanking office was reopened upon our arrival here after a two-day journey without incident aboard the British gunboat *Cricket*.

According to reports of my German and American informants, when it became known that foreigner representatives were intent on returning to Nanking, feverish operations were begun to remove the corpses lying about the streets—in some places "like herrings"—of civilians, including women and children, slain in a campaign of pointless mass murder.

In a reign of terror lasting several weeks, including massive looting, the Japanese have turned the business section of the city, that is the area along Taiping Street and the entire section south of so-called Potsdamer Platz, into a heap of rubble, in the midst of which a few buildings whose exteriors appear somewhat less damaged are still standing. This arson, organized by the Japanese military, is still going on to this day—a good month after the Japanese occupied the city—as is the abduction and rape of women and girls. In this respect, the Japanese army has erected a monument to its own shameful conduct.

Just within the so-called Safety Zone, which thanks to the Rabe committee has essentially been saved from destruction, there have been hundreds of cases of bestial rape, all incontrovertibly documented by Germans, Americans, and their Chinese coworkers. The file of letters that the committee has sent to the Japanese authorities contains a plethora of truly shocking material. As soon as time allows, I shall forward copies, with reference to this report. I would, however, like to note at this point that foreign nationals, and above all Herr Rabe and Herr Kröger, both functionaries of the NSDAP, as well as Herr Sperling, have caught Japanese soldiers in flagranti at such violations and have risked their own lives in scaring them away from their victims.

In many cases, members of Chinese families who attempted to resist these fiends were themselves killed or wounded. Even within the offices of the German embassy, the employee Chao was ordered at gunpoint to hand over any women present on the property. Having previously lived in Dairen, Chao can speak a little Japanese and was able to explain to the Japanese that this was the German embassy and there were no women present. The threats continued even after Chao had explained to them that this was the German embassy.

At the American Mission Hospital women are constantly being admitted, the most recent case occurring only yesterday, who have suffered grave bodily harm from rape committed by packs of men, with the subsequent infliction of bayonet and other wounds. One woman had her throat slit half-open, a wound so severe that Dr. Wilson himself is amazed that she is still alive. A pregnant woman was bayoneted in the belly, killing the unborn child. Many abused girls still in their childhood have likewise been admitted to the hospital, one of whom was violated 20 times in succession.

On 12 January, my English colleague, Consul Prideaux-Brune, the English military attaché Lovat-Fraser, and the English air-force attaché Commander Walser visited the house of Mr. Parsons of the British-American Tobacco Company and discovered there the body of a Chinese woman into whose vagina an entire golf club had been forced. There are documented cases in which accomplices have forced the husbands and fathers of victims to witness the violation of their domestic honor. In several instances, officers are known to be accessories, as was the case when Reverend Magee attempted to protect a group of Chinese Christians in the house of an absent German military advisor.

There is no evidence that any action has been taken—or if so, of what sort—by higher authorities against individual perpetrators, since the Japanese are silent about these matters and refuse to understand that a ruthless cauterizing of these offenses would accomplish more than all attempts to cover them up.

It is considered a self-evident matter of honor for the Japanese army to murder without further ado (indeed, there are thousands of such cases) every enemy soldier no longer actively engaged in combat, as well as any man judged to be such by some noncommissioned officer, whose decision cannot be appealed.

Given such a collapse of military discipline and order, it should therefore come as no surprise that no respect is shown the German flag. Thus various German buildings have been deliberately torched, others looted terribly, and almost all of them subjected to more or less minor theft. Given the cult status that the Japanese accord pictures of their emperor, it is perhaps especially remarkable that the looters did not shy from taking pictures of the Führer and Field Marshal General von Hindenburg.

I have left no doubt in the minds of the Japanese that we demand full restitution for all such losses, since there was no military necessity whatever for them and indeed some of them are the deliberate result of Japanese actions taken well after the occupation of the city, and likewise that I regard the term "consolation money" (*solatium*) favored by the Japanese as perhaps one that may sound better to them, but is in no way acceptable as an expression of partial payment.

ROSEN

II JANUARY

I visit the British embassy, where I meet with Mr. Prideaux-Brune, Colonel Lovat-Fraser, Dr. Rosen, Mr. Allison, and Hürter. At our request, the gentlemen from all three embassies declare themselves willing to accept our daily reports listing the offenses of Japanese soldiers and to make use of them by forwarding them both to the Japanese embassy and their own governments. That takes a great weight off our committee. If from now on it's the embassies who are registering the protest, order will soon be restored.

The Japanese have cut off our rice supply today. At noon the transport of rice, which we had undertaken on behalf of the Autonomous Government Committee, was halted.

This afternoon, while I was still at the office, the Japanese police arrived to search our headquarters. They were allegedly looking for a bundle of old clothes that a refugee had stolen. The bundle had been taken away

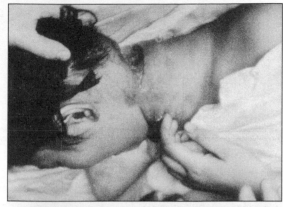

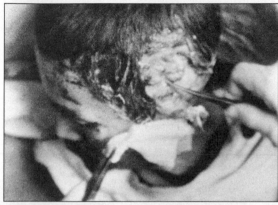

This woman's head was half severed from her body by a sword blow. Another victim's skull was laid open by a bayonet.

Japanese soldiers waiting to take their turns in a makeshift brothel.

from him several days ago and stored at our headquarters in Director Fitch's office. Every room in the building was unlocked this afternoon except Mr. Fitch's, which roused Japanese suspicion. Before they could break down the door, Kröger arrived, sent for a key, and promptly handed over the bundle.

The behavior of the Japanese police was truly mysterious. If they had peaceably asked to be allowed in, the bundle would have been handed over to them just as promptly. There was really no need to surround the entire grounds. Evidently they want to turn this matter I've just described into some kind of "incident," since the clothes were stolen from a Chinese refugee. And now I'll have to contact the embassy to find out precisely how I am to react to this police raid.

12 JANUARY

A month ago today Nanking fell into the hands of the Japanese. The body of that Chinese soldier shot while tied to a bamboo sofa is still lying out in the street not 50 yards from my house.

I visited the German, American, and English embassies and discussed the police search of our headquarters yesterday with Dr. Rosen, Mr. Allison, and Mr. Prideaux-Brune. All are agreed that the Japanese police are not permitted forcibly to enter a building belonging to a European without having first notified the embassy involved or having someone from that embassy with them.

In the meantime, all sales of rice have stopped. Not only can we not bring rice into the Zone, we are forbidden to bring coal in as well. The Japanese have had wall posters put up in the Zone, however, demanding that residents of the Zone return to their homes. The fact that their homes have been burned down or looted is not even considered.

I have come up with a plan for making friends with the Japanese. I shall try to dissolve the Zone Committee and found an International Relief Committee, on which the Japanese will also be represented.

Report from the Nanking Office of the German Embassy (Rosen) to the Foreign Ministry

Upon our entry in Nanking on 9 January, we were greeted by members of the Japanese embassy, by the captain of the gunboat, and by a cavalry Major Hungo from the staff of the garrison commandant. In his wel-

coming speech, which was translated for us, the latter used the unfortunate and less than tactful term "obedience" in describing our relationship
to the occupying power. The English consul did not, of course, mention
this tactlessness in his response, but assured the Japanese of our "cooperation." Then we were brought to the embassy by car, where our countrymen who had remained behind were waiting for us, Herr Rabe at their
head. As I was getting into the car, Major Hungo said goodbye to me
in German, and also questioned me as to why we had arrived together
with the English. I ignored this new bit of tactlessness with a simple
"Why not?"

On 13 January, while driving with Herr Kröger beyond the Chung
Shan Gate in the area around the Sun Yat-sen mausoleum, we twice
encountered officials from the Japanese embassy, accompanied by
Major Hungo and other officers. They stopped me and claimed I had broken my word, inasmuch as I had sworn obedience to the Japanese army!
Also, I had been told that I was not to drive outside the city under any
circumstances.

In my response to these gentlemen, I pointed out that as a German
official I could swear obedience to no other government than my own,
and that indeed I had never done so. I added that despite repeated requests for a pass, I had received none and therefore considered myself
fully justified in relying upon the flag of the Reich when driving my car
outside the city, as I had done on previous occasions without incident.
Major Hungo then expressed his amazement that I was "disobedient" in
light of German-Japanese friendship based on the Anti-Comintern Pact.
At the same time Mr. Hungo and the others pointed photographic equipment at me. Fukuda, the attaché, pulled out pen and paper and composed a confession of guilt that I was then supposed to sign!

I crossed out the words and noted briefly below that, as before, I am
quite willing to offer the Japanese authorities my cooperation, but
nothing else, and most certainly not my subordination. I defended my
right to my own likeness by stating that I did not yet feel quite ready to be
included in a book of mug shots. And in particular I objected to such an
overextended application of the Anti-Comintern Pact. If anyone here
had the right to question German-Japanese friendship, then surely it was
we Germans, given the systematic bombardment of German officials on
neutral ships and, above all, the Japanese military's repeated and flagrant
failure to respect the German flag here in Nanking.

Since this incident, I have twice been visited by Consul General
Okazaki, General Matsui's diplomatic advisor, and, after I had reported
to him the previous tactlessness of Mr. Hungo, he expressed his regret
over these incidents and others about which I also protested (e.g., the
confiscation of a car from the grounds of the Italian embassy only three

days before). On that occasion I told Mr. Okazaki that I would be glad to have an opportunity at some point to speak to him about fundamental questions regarding the status of embassy officials in Nanking, adding that I could be content with treatment no worse than that shown to the members of the Japanese embassy in Berlin.

My only previous experience with this method of first constructing one-sided declarations of subservience and then trying to extort confessions of guilt was its use by the Japanese military mission in northern China; but it is in no way applicable for diplomatic representatives of another normal power, let alone against one on friendly terms with Japan.

During this conversation with Mr. Okazaki, which despite the ticklish subject matter took place in a calm and businesslike atmosphere, I established more precise agreements about our future cooperation. I can therefore only hope that with these unpleasant incidents behind us, the performance of my duties and indeed my personal presence will not be regarded by the military, as it thus far has been, as a disagreeable disturbance and an unwelcome surveillance of current conditions here.

There is no objective basis for restrictions on our freedom of movement, nor for foreigners' currently being prohibited from leaving Nanking itself, but rather these have their basis in the personality of Mr. Hungo, as well as in a desire to cover up atrocities. Nanking is a military base, pure and simple, a conclusion one can draw from the fact that the Japanese have brought along their geishas, whom they apparently view as essential.

The local population is only too glad to speak a candid word with Germans and bewail the fate of family members who have been dragged off. Knowing as I do, on the basis of my experience with the Japanese military in Manchuria, that all-too-easy compliance is regarded as a weakness, I would respectfully ask the Foreign Ministry energetically to support my endeavors.

ROSEN

From a Private Letter of Chancellor Scharffenberg to Legation Councilor Lautenschlager in Hankow [36]

. . . Upon our arrival and then later again as well over dinner at the Japanese embassy, Major Hungo, the son of a field marshal, a polished and sedate cavalry officer, asked him [Rosen] why we had arrived together with the English, and he took the question to be tactless, without ever inquiring why it was asked. I assume that Hungo had something special in mind for us Germans.

It is not Hungo who is tactless, but rather H. R. [Herr Rosen], who in every meeting with the Japanese keeps harping, usually in an offensive tone, on the same old things: the bombardment of Nanking, the artillery shelling of the *Whangpu,* the dive bombings on 12 December, etc.

The second confrontation at the Sun Yat-sen mausoleum could have been avoided if he had listened to the advice of first engineer Ch. Kröger and driven back into the city after receiving his first warning from Japanese officials and Hungo at the Ming graves. Like a spoiled child, however, he angrily refused to do so and instead obstinately insisted that they drive to the golf course. Kröger gave in, unfortunately, although he knew that over dinner Hungo had politely but clearly stated that we were not allowed to leave the city without special permission.

And so a nasty encounter resulted, in which H. R., already furious because of the first warning, carried on like a raving maniac, recited his whole long list of sins committed by the Japanese army, navy, and air force, and attempted to assert his total freedom of movement, in particular his right to drive about without any gendarme along, to visit Lotus Lake, or to leave the city if he liked. Kröger was shocked.

CHAPTER 8

Closing Down the Siemens Nanking Branch

13 January

THE OTHER COMMITTEE MEMBERS do not agree with my suggestion that the Zone Committee be transformed into an International Relief Committee for Nanking. In their opinion, the Japanese have given our Zone Committee de facto recognition, and they're afraid that if we voluntarily dissolve the old committee, they could simply ignore us completely. And of course I accede to the majority, for we must absolutely remain united.

By way of the English navy I receive a telegram from Siemens Shanghai, dated 10 January, telling me to wind up business here and for Han and me to come to Shanghai as soon as possible.[37] I'll reply tomorrow, saying that at present neither foreigners nor Chinese are allowed to leave the city. Kröger has tried on various occasions to get Japanese permission to travel to Shanghai and has thus far been regularly turned down.

Dr. Rosen and Kröger were outside the city wall today to inspect

Schmeling's house near the Veterans' Orphanage and Dr. Eckert's house in the vicinity of Sun Yat-sen Memorial Park. Driving back in Dr. Rosen's embassy car, the two gentlemen were halted by Japanese officers in the company of Fukuda. The exchange between Dr. Rosen and the Japanese grew heated when they wanted to know why he was outside the city wall and asked him, "Why don't you obey the Japanese military regulations?"

Dr. Rosen replied he had never promised to obey orders of the Japanese military. He demanded that he be able to pursue his diplomatic duties, particularly since he was busy determining to what extent German property in Nanking had been destroyed by the Japanese. The Japanese demanded and received a statement to that effect from Dr. Rosen, who reported the incident by telegram to Shanghai. I'm anxious to see what comes of it.

4:00 P.M.

At a meeting of the International Red Cross at Kulou Hospital, with John Magee, McCallum, Kröger, Low, and Pastor Chen attending, it was agreed that in the future McCallum should decide whether patients admitted on the recommendation of the Red Cross should be treated gratis or not. John Magee has been admitting too many free patients of late, including one woman who was admitted as penniless, but when someone was changing her bed, 300 dollars were found in it.

Chang's wife has recovered sufficiently to be discharged from the hospital. We bring her home in the car. Chang has given the hospital his last month's salary of 30 dollars, and I shall pay the rest.

Letter from the Siemens China Co. Central Office to Rabe

Shanghai, 3 January 1938

Dear Herr Rabe:

First, best wishes for the New Year; you have some troubled times behind you, with all sorts of experiences. I hope you are well. We would have liked to have heard from you whether you intend to remain there much longer. I recently spoke with Dr. Baur (of Carlowitz), and he was of the opinion that there is no longer any real point in your staying on.

We intended for you to leave Nanking at the opportune moment, that is before its fall and proceed to Hankow in order to maintain contacts with governmental agencies there. We telegraphed you three times to that effect. Dr. Probst is in Hong Kong at present. I have asked him whether it might be advisable to station you in Hong Kong. As soon as I have a reply, I will try to get word to you. I don't know what your current living conditions are, but I would assume that you have already packed your belongings. Might it not be possible to store your things at the embassy if you haven't already?

As for your trip to Shanghai, that won't be an easy matter, but perhaps it can be arranged sooner or later.

We would like to hear news of you if at all possible.

Best regards,
W. MAIER[38]

Letter from Rabe to Siemens Management, Shanghai (Excerpts)

Nanking, 14 January 1938

Re: Letter from Herr. W. Maier, Director, 3 January 38

This is to confirm receipt today of said letter via the German embassy. Your previous message that I should move on to Hankow came too late. When your telegram arrived, the Germans were already making for Hankow aboard the *Kutwo*. Moreover, I thought it my duty not to desert our Chinese employees, Mr. Han and his family, our fitters, etc., all of whom had fled to join me in the *hong*.[39] As I informed you then in reply to your telegram, I assumed the chairmanship here of an International Committee being organized for establishing a Safety Zone, which would be the last resort for 200,000 Chinese noncombatants. The establishment of the Zone was not easy, particularly since we could not get any clear recognition of the Zone from the Japanese and because high-ranking Chinese military and their staff remained behind until the last moment, that is, remained within the Zone until they fled.

Our committee has thus far succeeded in feeding the city's 200,000 residents packed into our Zone by setting up soup kitchens, distribution centers for rice and flour, etc. An order has now come from the Japanese to close our outlets for selling rice, since care of the refugees is to be taken over by the newly found Autonomous Government Committee. . . . As soon as order is reestablished in the city and I am granted permission by the authorities to leave Nanking, I will join you there. Up till now all such requests have been met with refusal.

I herewith request additional permission to remain here until the Zone Committee is dissolved, since the life and welfare of many people are indeed dependent on a few Europeans. In my house and garden alone, over 600 of the poorest refugees found refuge on the night of 12 December in order to avoid being molested or killed by the unchecked

Japanese soldiery. Most people are housed in straw huts in the garden and live from the daily rice ration doled out to them.

With German greetings,
JOHN RABE

15 JANUARY

As is obvious from the letters that arrived for me yesterday from Shanghai via the German embassy and to which on 14 January I replied to the management of Siemens China Co. in Shanghai, people there have not the vaguest notion of current conditions here.

Memorandum of Chancellor[40] P. Scharffenberg, German Embassy, Nanking Office

Situation in Nanking as of 13 January 1938

There is no telephone, telegraph, or postal service in Nanking, nor are there any buses, taxies, or rickshas. The waterworks are not operating, electric power is to be had only in the embassy buildings, where all windows above the ground floor must be blacked out. The English embassy has no electricity as yet.

There is no traffic in the streets, since the suburbs were burned down almost in their entirety by the Chinese and the center of the city has largely been burned down by the Japanese. No one lives there now. The rest of the population—circa 200,000—is confined to the Safety Zone, formerly a residential area. People vegetate there in various buildings and their adjoining gardens, where up to 600 people live in straw huts, and no one may leave this Zone. The Zone is controlled by sentries.

The streets outside the Zone are deserted, the ruins a desolate sight. Food is dangerously short. Inside the Safety Zone people have been begun to eat horse and dog meat. Hürter managed to get through once again yesterday and was able to procure a pig and a few chickens for us via Dr. Günther at the cement factory in Hsi Sha Shan. (The English embassy was given some, as a thank-you for taking us on board their gunboats.) We cannot buy anything else.

The committee under John Rabe, and which includes several Americans, has done miraculous work. It is not an exaggeration to say that it has saved tens of thousands of lives.

The water problem is also very serious, the water mains are not functioning, and there is no way to wash clothes, since all the ponds are contaminated by the dead bodies that have been thrown into them.

The new city administration, which is supposed to take over duties that are in fact being carried out by the committee, is getting nowhere because of the actions of the Japanese. One of its new members, the well-known auctioneer Jimmy, has at least shown courage and told the Japanese: "If you are against me, then you'd better shoot me here and now!"

It's best not to say anything about the actions of the Japanese since their arrival; it is all too reminiscent of Genghis Khan: Destroy everything! A first lieutenant on the staff told me that during the march from Shanghai to Nanking, the supply columns never once caught up with the troops, and so it is understandable why soldiers went berserk here, grabbing whatever they could. And I'm quite sure that like the Negroes in 1918 they were promised: If you hold out, you'll each get a pretty girl in Nanking.[41] And things have been very, very bad for all the women who remained behind here. It is best not even to discuss the matter with those gentlemen who have witnessed it, they can only shudder at the bestiality of it all.

It is easy to say that the troops got out of hand. But I don't believe that, because Asian warfare is in fact different from war among us. If the sides were reversed, it would probably not have gone any better, especially not with a little incitement.

The harvest in the city and out in the occupied areas of the country is rotting in the fields, because no one from the city is allowed near it and the rural population has either fled or been slain. Vegetables, potatoes, beets, etc. are going to waste, and hunger is rife here.

SCHARFFENBERG

16 JANUARY

Dinner at the Japanese embassy went off without incident. We were 13 people in all. Besides the officials of the Japanese embassy, nine representatives from our committee showed up: Miss Vautrin, Miss Bauer, Dr. Bates, Mills, Smythe, Dr. Trimmer, Kröger, and I. And after we had sat down to eat, John Magee appeared as well, who always tends to bring up the rear, but is otherwise a fine fellow.

On his arrival Kröger received the good news that he may leave for Shanghai. As glad as I am for Kröger, since he plans to get married soon, I am very worried about filling his slot. Kröger is our treasurer and it will not be easy to find a replacement. The food was excellent. Since I needed to be careful about what I said in my after-dinner speech, I brought along the following written text:

Ladies and Gentlemen,

In the name of the International Committee of the Nanking Safety Zone, I would like to express my thanks to our hosts, the officials of the Japanese embassy, for their cordial invitation to join them for dinner. We have, I can assure you, not eaten so well in a long time.

I ask our honored hosts to forgive me for saying a few words about ourselves.

Since most of the members of our committee were active here as missionaries, they felt it was their Christian duty not to desert their Chinese friends in time of war. As a businessman who has lived in this country for 30 years now, I joined them. Having enjoyed the hospitality of this land and its people for so long, I considered it fitting that I not abandon the Chinese in a time of distress.

Those are the reasons that led us who are strangers to this land to remain behind and make some attempt to stand beside those of the poorest Chinese, who in their need lacked the means to leave the city and did not know where to turn.

I do not wish to speak of the work and hardship that we took upon ourselves. They are known to you all.

We appeal to the noble sentiments of the Japanese, to the spirit of the samurai, about whom we foreigners have heard and read so much and who fought so bravely for their land in countless battles, yet never denied clemency to a foe who could not defend himself.

You, the gentlemen of the Japanese embassy, have patiently heard our requests and complaints, and there were many, and have always lent us a willing ear. You have also, to the extent that you could, done your best to help us. And for this much-appreciated help, I would like, in the name of the International Committee, to hereby express my thanks.

I don't know what the Americans thought of my speech. I am aware that I spoke a little against my own conscience, but I thought it useful for our cause and followed the Jesuit principle: "The ends justify the means."

There is no denying that it was the officials of the Japanese embassy who helped us to some extent—were the only ones who could help us by passing on our reports to the Japanese military and interceding for us a bit. That they did not have the success we wished surely lies in the fact that diplomats in Japan must defer to the military, who have the first and last word in the Japanese government. The embassy personnel, Fukui, Tanaka, and Fukuda, could therefore rightly be praised a little if one was to praise at all, which after our bitter experiences was indeed hard enough to do.

Shortly before we left for home, Fukuda also let it be known that the Japanese embassy was very distressed by the "Dr. Rosen affair." It would please him if I would act as a go-between and bring Dr. Rosen to make some sort of conciliatory gesture. Perhaps a visit to the Japanese embassy and a few friendly words—there was no mention of an apology. I shall cautiously feel Dr. Rosen out on this, although I fear that my attempts will meet with no success whatever.

17 JANUARY

As I learned from a conference with Dr. Rosen, Okazaki, the Japanese consul general, has already tried to put the recent altercation to rest. If Berlin and Tokyo demand no other settlement, the file on this dispute can be closed, which I would prefer, since we have to get along peaceably with the Japanese here somehow.

Yesterday I drove through the city on a longer tour with Dr. Rosen, and returned home very depressed. The devastation the Japanese have wreaked here is almost beyond description. To my mind there is no possibility that

The city of Nanking was almost totally destroyed—by both fire and bombardment—by the Japanese army.

the city can be brought back to life anytime soon. Taiping Lu, the pride of Nanking, which was the main business street before and whose lights at night were equal to those on Nanking Road in Shanghai, is totally ruined, everything burned down. There is not one building left intact, just fields of rubble left and right. Fu Tze-Miao, the former amusement district, with its tea houses and big market, is likewise totally destroyed. As far as the eye can see—nothing but rubble! Who's going to rebuild it all? On the way back we visited what fire had left behind of the State Theater and the great bazaar. There, too, everything burned down. I'm afraid I grossly miscalculated when I wrote that a third of the city had been put to the torch by the Japanese. If the East City, which I've not visited to any extent, was dealt with in the same fashion, then more than half the city lies in ruins.

I also have the impression that instead of emptying out as the Japanese have demanded, our Zone is still filling up. You risk your life in the press of people on Shanghai Lu, particularly now that both sides of the street are filled with market booths built of poles and planks, where all sorts of food and clothes and even some stolen curios are peddled. Estimates of the total population of the Zone are now around 250,000. The increase of about 50,000 comes from the ruined parts of the city. People simply don't know where to stay.

18 JANUARY

You can see columns of smoke in several directions. Fires are still merrily being set. At 9 a.m., a meeting of the managers of various refugee camps is to be held at our headquarters. We would not be surprised if the Japanese disrupt the meeting or even forbid it. I've placed sentries outside the walls, who are to inform the German embassy at once if our building is surrounded by the Japanese military police, as happened last time. To my delight, Dr. Rosen, Kröger, and Sperling show up. We are all anxiously waiting to see if the Japanese are going to permit some sort of incursion. But the meeting proceeds normally and calmly.

This afternoon Dr. Smythe and Fitch arrive with news that we may not move rice or any other foodstuff into the city, or fetch it from stores within the city, or import it from Shanghai. It appears the Japanese intend to let the refugees starve. This must be prevented. We therefore send the following telegram to Shanghai:

Boyton, National Christian Council, Shanghai (Excerpt)

Food question more serious because no regular supply available civilian population. . . .

We are feeding fifty thousand daily free rice. Request to truck in rice wheat purchased here and request for necessary passes to ship six hundred tons foodstuffs from Shanghai turned down. Please try negotiations Shanghai. If you can buy Chinese green beans Shanghai get permission to ship one hundred tons as soon as possible. Go ahead raising funds. We will find way to use them.

18 January 1938   FITCH

LATER

The American embassy was able to cable another "incident" to the State Department in Washington. The local American school was looted again today, and in fact they broke a large hole in the outer wall in order to take away the piano. Unfortunately the American officials arrived a little too late to catch the Japanese soldiers at their thievery. You would think it impossible for the Japanese military to compromise itself like that, now that there is an American embassy in the city again.

I'm wracking my brains about how I should go about "winding up business" here as they put it in their telegram. There are no crates to be had at the moment, no craftsmen, and no porters. How I am supposed to pack things? You can't just leave everything lying here—that would be tantamount to losing it all. What would become of my compound here, if I were to just cut and run, meaning go to Shanghai? The Japanese will probably give me a pass to leave at some point; I even have the feeling they would be happy to be rid of me. But what would become of the 650 refugees on the grounds? *What a bitter ending to all our labors!*

19 JANUARY

The radio reports that a Berlin newspaper has warned Japan to refrain from advancing any farther into the interior of China. At the same time the newspaper is said to have recommended that China be offered an honorable peace. That would be "too good to be true." No one here believes that Japan will follow such good advice.

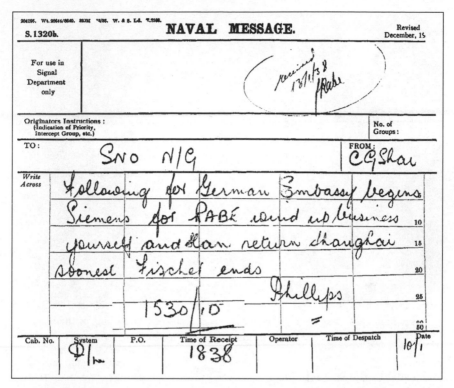

The telegram sent to Rabe via the American naval station: "Following for German Embassy begins Siemens for RABE wind up business yourself and Han return Shanghai soonest Fischer ends Phillips."

There will soon be major battles along the Lunghai Railway. The Chinese army has about 40,000 drawn up there and appears to have regrouped, or so at least the radio report claims. All incompetent officers are said to have been eliminated. We haven't the least hope, sad to say, that China will emerge victorious from those battles.

Meanwhile Tsingtao has been taken by the Japanese, the same goes for Tsinanfu. Word is that the police have revolted and are looting in Cheefoo—according to Japanese reports.

On orders of Chiang Kai-shek, Han Fuchün, the governor of Shandong, and two other generals have been court-martialed for not offering adequate resistance to the enemy. Word is that Han Fuchün put all his cash into Japanese banks. There's little doubt of it, since it's probably the Japanese who are making this claim.

There was also news today that Chang Hsueliang, son of Chang Tsolin

As photographs make clear, the Japanese took pleasure in the killing of their victims. They often posed for snapshots, which were saved as mementos.

and leader of the Sian rebellion, has been shot, the same man who arrested and imprisoned Chiang Kai-shek in Sian about a year ago.[42]

These purges on Hankow's part have all come much too late; people doubt if they will be of any use.

I gave written notice to our Siemens employees today, telling them that on orders from the central office in Shanghai, I am to close our office here; for I see no other possible interpretation of Shanghai's message to "wind up business." I'll pay people their January salaries in full, but no New Year's bonus. That's damned hard, I know, because the Chinese New Year, which begins on 1 February, is at hand and there's been an extraordinary rise in the price of food, that is if you can find any. But hundreds of thousands of people here are just as badly off. The employees all have a roof over their heads as long as I'm still here. And when I run out of money for food, then they'll have to take advantage of the International Committee's soup kitchen, which is already feeding most of the 650 refugees in my house. Two sacks of rice a day.

My landlord's agents have fled, along with the landlord. All the same, I'll write a letter giving him notice, since by contract I can abandon the house if the firm recalls me.

Letter from John Rabe to the Siemens Central Office

19 January 1938

Re: Closing the Nanking Office

This is to inform you that, as per your telegram of 10 January, in which you order me to close the local office, I am giving the local Chinese employees written notice that due to the state of war, they should regard their positions with our firm was terminated as of the end of this month. Could you please inform me if, in addition to their January salary, I can pay them a New Year's bonus or provide some other monetary gratification. Since food prices here have risen considerably and none of our Chinese employees has any savings from which a family could live for any length of time, I would most heartily recommend a positive answer in this matter. In hope of a reply telegraphed to me as quickly as possible, I remain

Very truly yours,
JOHN RABE

John Rabe's Letter of Termination to Han Hsianglin, His Chinese Assistant of Some Years

Nanking, 19 January 1938

Dear Sir,

Since all business has come to a standstill on account of the war, we regret to inform you that following instruction from our head office, the Nanking office of Siemens China Co. has to be closed.

Please note that this will—much to our regret—also terminate your engagement with our firm. We shall be pleased to reengage you after the war, if conditions permit, and ask you to kindly let us know your future address to enable us to keep you informed.

We take this opportunity to express to you our gratitude and appreciation for your faithful service rendered to our firm during the last six years, and beg to remain very truly yours,

JOHN RABE
Representative Nanking, Siemens China Co.

This sequence of photographs records Chinese being beheaded. When the Japanese soldier took the film to be developed, a Chinese boy working in the shop secretly made copies, at the risk of his life, and glued them into a scrapbook documenting the atrocities. He decorated its cover himself and kept it hidden until the end of the war.

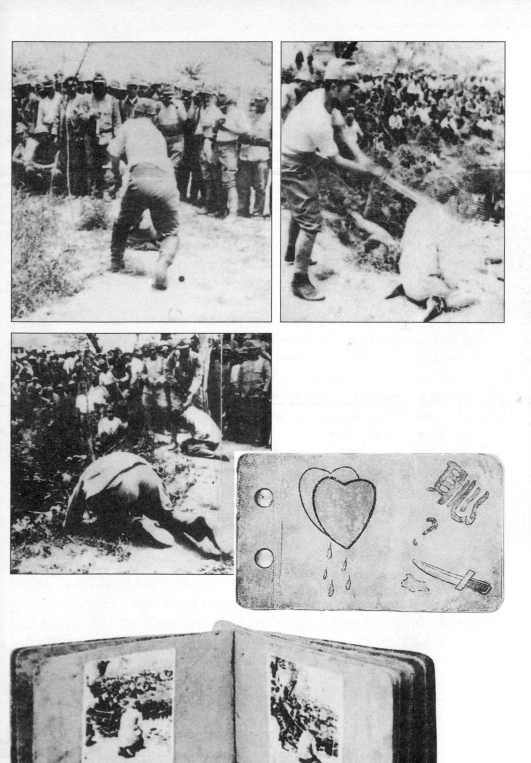

20 JANUARY

Snow storm! The refugees are in an extraordinarily wretched state. You really don't have to be softhearted to feel pity for these poor people here. The camp in my garden has become one huge puddle of mud. Little channels have been dug around the tents and straw huts to let some of the snow water run off. More than once I've just closed my eyes when I've spotted open fires under those low straw roofs. In the driving wind and snow, fires are impossible outside. So if people are to have any warmth at all, we simply have to run the risk. When I look at the misery out in my garden, I'm reminded of two books by Dwinger,[43] *Army behind Barbed Wire* and *Between Red and White.*

Recently we pilfered a few thousand bricks from a half-finished house in the neighborhood and laid narrow footpaths between the tents and huts to keep people from sinking completely into the muck.

We've also built a brick wall around the latrines to make the camp look a bit more respectable. These improvements don't help much, of course. The whole thing is and will remain an incredible swamp. No wonder everyone is coughing and spitting. My worst fear is that an epidemic will break out.

Pastor John Magee, the chairman of our International Red Cross Society, has passed on the report of a Chinese nurse from the Red Cross Hospital for wounded soldiers located in the Foreign Ministry, which we foreigners are forbidden to visit, whereas its staff occasionally receives permission to go out shopping. And they use the opportunity to visit us and tell us things:

One of the wounded Chinese soldiers complained that he was not getting enough to eat. The daily ration, she says, is just three little bowls of rice broth. The patient was beaten, and when he asked, once the beating was over, if they had beaten him because he was hungry, the Japanese took him out into the courtyard and bayoneted him. The nurses watched this execution from the windows.

None of the refugees want to leave the Zone now, not after a number of people who tried to return to their homes were driven off by Japanese soldiers throwing stones or were mistreated even worse. And yet everywhere in the city you find big Japanese posters that proclaim: "Return to your homes! We will provide food. Trust the Japanese army! It will help you!"

From a Report by Christian Kröger,
Treasurer of the Zone Committee (Excerpt)

Nanking, 13 January 1938

On the afternoon of 13 December 1937, I took over the Waichiaopu[44] to use as a hospital. To the shame of the Chinese troops, it must be said that conditions there were beyond description, with wounded men left lying without care for two to three days. All the doctors and staff had run off, no one cared about these wretches. In a most commendable fashion, the Chinese Red Cross took over these wounded men and provided male and female nurses; there were, however, too few doctors, but I hoped things would improve once the city was finally occupied.

By the next afternoon the Japanese attitude had changed entirely. I had persuaded four doctors to come to the hospital. But I was forbidden to enter it. By now the city was completely in Japanese hands, all public buildings were occupied, but we were forbidden to enter any of them, even those in which we had set up large refugee camps. I was told that the Japanese military would take care of the living, and we could bury the dead. To this day, we have been able to get rice into the hospital, but no nurses, no medical supplies, no doctors.

From 14 December on, the situation deteriorated rapidly. Battle-weary Japanese troops, who had been inadequately supplied during their advance, were let loose on the city and behaved in ways no one had thought possible, especially in their treatment of the poorest and most innocent Chinese. They took rice from the refugees, the poorest of the poor, took whatever supplies they could find, warm wool blankets, clothes, watches, bracelets, in short anything that appeared to be of value. Anyone who hesitated to hand something over was immediately slashed with a bayonet, and many people were subjected to such rough treatment for no reason at all. The victims numbered in the thousands, and these brutish soldiers kept coming back to the Zone, its houses packed with refugees, and each time would take what their predecessors had disdained.

Our only defense for protecting our own property and servants was to strike a vigorous pose and point to the German flag, often while being threatened by Japanese officers and soldiers. Once, while I was negotiating with Japanese officers, my car was stolen from the garage, even though both front tires had been removed. Under the threat of bayonets, servants were forced to open doors and hand over everything.

Evidently vehicles of any sort were of special interest, because cars and bicycles were in great demand and stolen everywhere. Where there was no vehicle to be had, the servants or the refugees in a house were forced to carry the looted goods, and you often saw a soldier with weapon in hand driving four coolies before him loaded down with his booty. Children's wagons were used, wheelbarrows, asses, mules, in short, anything that could be found.

This organized robbery lasted for over two weeks, and even now no house is safe from some group on a "commandeering" expedition. When valuables began to run out, carpets, doors, and window frames were next, if only to be burned as fuel. The army had even brought its own safe-crackers, although many a safe was opened simply with a few shots or a hand grenade.

When an individual soldier didn't suffice, units in trucks would appear and under the command of an officer empty a house of anything worth taking and then set it afire. By now, the entire South City has been looted and torched in this fashion.

The systematic burning began 20 December, and there has not been an evening since when the sky has not turned red. They are meticulously returning to buildings that were somehow forgotten or passed over, so that by now I would guess that roughly 50–60 percent of the city has been burned down.

On 14 December, with the city under total occupation, an immediate and rigorous search of the city and especially of the refugee camps began. These searches of the camps were totally arbitrary, and over the course of a few days, although not a single shot was fired by the civilian population and no military courts had been set up, approximately 5,000 people were shot, usually on the riverbank, so that there was no need for burial. That number is probably too low an estimate. Even today, when every person has to be registered, this senseless "selection" continues, even if it is still applied only in individual cases.

On a trip to Hsiakwan on 16 December, I literally drove over bodies in the vicinity of the Navy Office, where rows of executed men lay tied together. It took until 29 December to remove the bodies from the city. Day after day, you had to drive past the dead, who appeared even in my dreams. Three bodies and a dead horse lay outside our house. We were forbidden to clear them away ourselves; I was finally able to arrange only for the horse to be buried, which was still lying there on 9 January. My first trip to Hsi Sha Shan on 28 December came as a shock. We were strictly forbidden to leave the city, but since I needed food, I went in my car anyway. The retreating Chinese army had already burned down villages and farms. The Japanese troops, however, were not to be outdone, and continued to set fire to things on a grand scale, indiscriminately shooting farmers, women, and children out in the fields, all under the motto: "Find the evil Chinese soldiers!" In the fields and beside the high-way lay a lot of dead water buffalo, horses, and mules, already badly eaten by dogs, crows, and magpies. By day the farmers flee to the moun-tains with their few possessions, and only the old women and men re-main behind. Even their lives are in danger: For an hour's drive I did not see a single live human being, not even in the larger villages. Everything has been burned down or is dead or flees the moment a car comes into view. At Thousand Buddha Mountain a large refugee camp had formed with over 10,000 people, all farmers from the vicinity.

The Japanese soldiery doesn't let that stop them, either. Even here they randomly select young boys to be shot, rape the girls, and drunken Japanese soldiers make a sport of using bayonets to skewer or slash whomever they take a dislike to, especially where there is no medical help to be had. Temple images are stolen or destroyed, and even monks are in no way safe from such mistreatment.

Confronted by two Europeans—a German, Dr. Günther, and a Dane—the terror has more or less come to halt outside the cement works. There, too, about 4,000 refuges have settled, bringing what they could carry.

According to Chinese reports, the entire countryside from Shanghai to Nanking and Wuhu has been ravaged in this same fashion. It is hard to see how without so much as a plow or a water buffalo, farmers are going to tend their fields and plant the rice so sorely needed.

From a Report from the Nanking Office of the German Embassy (Rosen) to the Foreign Ministry (Excerpt)

20 January 1938

While we were aboard the British gunboat *Bee*, anchored outside Nanking from 18 to 20 December, the Japanese rear-admiral Kondo de-clared to Holt, the British admiral, that on a large island downstream from Nanking there were still 30,000 Chinese soldiers who would have to be removed. This removal or "mopping up," as it was called in Japanese communiqués, consists of murdering what are now defenseless enemies and is contrary to fundamental principles of humane warfare. Besides mass executions by machine gun fire, other more individual methods of killing were employed as well, such as pouring gasoline over a victim and setting him afire.

Since a large number of Chinese soldiers—some of them disarmed, but in any case defenseless—had fled into the Safety Zone, something that the few policemen were unable to prevent, the Japanese undertook large-scale raids during which any civilian male might be suspected of being a soldier and be dragged off. Generally they looked for some indication of a man's having been a soldier—the circular marking of a helmet on the head, indentations on the shoulder from a weapon or on the back from a kit bag, etc. Foreign eyewitnesses have also attested that the Japanese lured a good number of Chinese soldiers out of the Safety Zone by promising they would not be harmed and even given work, only then to execute them. No trials by military tribunal or anything of that sort were to be seen anywhere, and they would have been out of place amidst practices that made a mockery of all the rules of warfare and civilized behavior. The first Japanese patrols were sighted inside the city on 13 December. They had apparently entered the city from the south, through the Kuanghua Gate. Reports have already been filed concerning the reign of terror which then began and has continued for weeks now, but I would like to add one more example of how the Japanese conducted themselves: e.g., of the 54 workers at the municipal electricity plant who reported for work, 43 were slain by the Japanese, under the pretext that that the plant was a state enterprise!

By some strange arrangement of Nature, wherever the Japanese advance with fire and sword, the popular soul spontaneously erupts in the form of autonomous governments kindly disposed toward the Japanese. And so on New Year's Day, an autonomous government arose in Nanking under the chairmanship of the president of the Red Swastika Society, Tao Hsi-san. This society is a charitable organization similar to the Red Cross. Little is known about the other members of the "government," except that a Dr. Hsü of the same charitable society and a certain Wang Changtien are "advisors" to it. This Wang, who is also known in Nanking under the name Jimmy, is at any rate the most active member of the new system, whose five-colored flag, the old flag of the First Chinese Republic, can be seen flying here and there above buildings in Nanking, but is hardly noticeable for all the Japanese flags.

Among Jimmy's first official acts was the establishment of bordellos, for which he was able to recruit the necessary workers among those females still residing in the old amusement district around the Confucius Temple. It is said that he provided the requisite furniture free of charge from his own inventories, but is demanding payment for furnishing similar institutions that are to be outfitted with Japanese ladies who have been brought in. At any rate Jimmy has done a great service to his fellow Chinese in providing a less perilous means by which to satisfy the amorous needs of the Japanese soldiery, which up until now has employed the Erl-King's method of abducting the honest women of Nanking.

As nearly as I can tell thus far from my conversations with my Japanese colleagues, the new Nanking government is not taken seriously. It is also already having its problems with the Japanese, especially as regards the increasingly grave issue of supplying the population with food.

It is not only in this matter that the greatest confusion about future political arrangements seems to reign, even among the Japanese themselves. It should indeed be clear to the Japanese that even those Chinese of some repute who are well disposed toward Japan will not volunteer to govern without strong reservations and assurances, particularly in view of what like-minded fellow countrymen have experienced in Manchuria. Or does the Japanese military believe that it can continue to depend on the same makeshift imperial policies with which it has begun to corrupt China so successfully in the north: encouragement of smuggling, establishment of numerous Korean bordellos, and support for the narcotics trade emanating from the Japanese concession in Tientsin—all without even bothering to provide much window-dressing? Because of the difficulties of sending mail by way of Hankow, this report is being presented directly to the Foreign Ministry. The ambassador in Hankow, the German general consul in Shanghai, and the German ambassador in Tokyo will be provided carbon copies of this report by secured post.

ROSEN

21 JANUARY

Krischan Kröger must postpone his departure for a few days yet. He may not leave till Sunday, although he may now go by train; in addition to which he will be guarded by some hulk of a soldier, just to make sure he doesn't jump off on the way. I intend to make more vigorous attempts to obtain a pass myself now, because I would like to try to get to Mutti in Shanghai, if only for a visit. And for me there is only one way out: to tell the truth and say that the company "has no more money." They'll probably give me a funny look—I'm a Siemens manager after all—but that won't bother me. I've already had to hit Krischan Kröger up for 500 dollars just to scrape enough together for January salaries.

22 JANUARY

I've written several times in this diary about the body of the Chinese soldier who was shot while tied to his bamboo bed and who is still lying unburied near my house. My protests and pleas to the Japanese embassy finally to get this corpse buried, or give me permission to bury it, have thus far been fruitless. The body is still lying in the same spot as before, except that the ropes have been cut and the bamboo bed is now lying about two yards away. I am totally puzzled by the conduct of the Japanese in this matter. On the one hand, they want to be recognized and treated as a great power on a par with European powers, on the other, they are currently displaying a crudity, brutality, and bestiality that bears no comparison except with the hordes of Genghis Khan. I have stopped trying to get the poor devil buried, but I hereby record that he, though very dead, still lies above the earth!

Pastor John Magee accompanied me this morning, along with Cola, who speaks a little Japanese, to return a call by Dr. Hirai, the chief army surgeon. We used the occasion to ask Dr. Hirai for permission to visit the Red Cross Hospital set up in the Foreign Ministry; we have been delivering rice this whole time, but we have been unable to enter since the fall of Nanking, when the Japanese took over its administration. Dr. Hirai seemed dubious about our request, but he promised to present the matter to the general staff. He appears to be a very kindly, genial old gentleman. When we visited him today, he was sitting in an armchair in full uniform and having his portrait done by a Japanese painter.

Magee has been gathering more ugly reports again. The Japanese soldiers are grabbing up every slaughterable animal they can get hold of. Of

One of the victims referred to by Dr. Rosen in his report of 20 January 1938.

Japanese patrols rounding up Chinese for execution.

late they have been making Chinese boys chase pigs. A couple of the boys who weren't quick enough, or had no success, were bayoneted. The bowels of one of these bayoneted victims are hanging out of his body.

It makes you sick just to hear these sorts of stories from eyewitnesses. One might well believe the Japanese army is made up of ex-convicts. Normal people do not behave this way.

Today we saw a truck full of Chinese soldiers coming from the south and heading toward Hsiakwan. I assume that these were prisoners of war who had been captured between here and Wuhu and were to be executed on the banks of the Yangtze.

Takadama-san paid me a visit. He is the chief of consular police and as such is attached to the Japanese embassy. I got him a car, in the hope of receiving a receipt of requisition in return. Instead of signing the receipt, he stuck it in his pocket without a word, and I was left holding the bag.

Whereas before he has always shown up in a well-fitting blue uniform, he is wearing civilian clothes today. At the moment he's looking for photographs taken of the air war and of Japanese planes that crashed here in Nanking. A good number of the photos were taken by a semiofficial Chinese photo agency. Among the pictures that you could buy from them at a dollar apiece was a photograph of 16 Japanese fliers who had crashed and ended up as prisoners of war, but whom the Chinese took special care of and treated quite well.

Takadama claims he has a friend who was one of these prisoners, none of whose names is known to us. He's evidently greatly interested in the fate of this captured Japanese pilot and would like to learn more about him from us.

We cannot give him any information because we in fact know nothing. And even if we did, we would still be very careful about the information we supplied; for I've already learned from Fukuda-san, the embassy secretary, that a Japanese officer—and there were several among these pilots—is supposed to commit hara-kiri if he is captured. A Japanese officer dare not be a prisoner of war. So I won't offer any help or information, although I wouldn't mind if a goodly number of Japanese who have committed atrocities here were to commit hara-kiri.

Papa Sperling, or better, Mr. Sperling, inspector general of the Committee Police, has noticed that we're all writing reports. That has awakened an ambition that until now only slumbered deep in his heart, and he cannot rest until he, too, has managed to write a report. Sperling—honor to whom honor is due—saved many people's lives and has probably been through more than any of us. But he is a simple soul, and his report reflects as much. None of us is a born author, but there's really something very funny about what Sperling has managed. He showed me the first draft. I didn't have the heart to try to persuade him to leave out the wonderful descriptions. So let him go ahead and report about the babe at its mother's quivering breast and the naked soldier and his girl!

Eduard Sperling's Report

To the German Embassy

Attn.: Dr. Rosen

The undersigned, along with other gentlemen, remained in Nanking at his own peril during this time of war and at the founding of the International Committee was named inspector general for the Nanking Safety Zone. As such and in the course of my tours of inspection, I observed many things with my own eyes, the good as well as the bad, but more of the latter. My field work was not easy, but 650 well-drilled native policemen, plus a well-organized private corps of police stood at my side. We maintained public order, and I must once again state herewith that I have

great regard and respect for the Chinese race, who, as I have often witnessed, are willing to bear their pain and sorrow without complaint or
murmur.

Two hundred thousand refugees, among them many, many women
with small babes at their quivering, nursing breasts, driven from house
and home, saving no more than their bare lives, sought safety and protection there.

Within the Nanking Safety Zone we had two well organized fire
stations. Unfortunately our fire engines and fire trucks were commandeered by the Japanese army on its march into the city, and we were
therefore absolutely powerless against the many fires that broke out day
and night and could offer no help, indeed perhaps our help was not
wanted—sad but true.

With the arrival of Japanese troops, our real troubles began within
the Safety Zone, something it in fact was not, for it offered no absolute
safety. Despite swastika flags and notices posted by the German embassy
in German, English, and Chinese, no regard whatever was paid by the
Japanese soldiers to all our arrangements, which had been so calmly and
peacefully organized. Houseboys from vacated German residences,
which enjoyed the special protection of the German embassy, came to
me daily to report that Japanese soldiers had stolen bedding, money, etc.,
opening locked doors with rifle butts and bayonets or simply battering
them down and thus gaining entry, often to no purpose whatever.

On 17 December, Herr Hürter's automobile was stolen. By chance
Herr Hatz and I happened to be nearby, along with an official of the Japanese consulate, so that we were able to halt the thief at the next street
corner, and with great difficulty and long speeches to regain possession
of the vehicle. —During this incident I noticed how little power Japanese
civil servants have. With many bows and scrapes, the consular official
bade his farewell to these military brigands.

On 21 December, at the behest of Mr. Kikuchi at Japanese headquarters, I arranged for and transported 60 electrical workers in order to put
the electricity works in Hsiakwan back in operation; the workers were
loathe to work for the Japanese, because 50 of their comrades, who had
sought refuge in the International Export Co. in Hsiakwan, had been
shot in cold blood by the Japanese.

In well over 80 cases, I was called by Chinese civilians to drive off Japanese soldiers who had forced their way into houses inside the Safety
Zone and were violating women and young girls in the most dreadful
manner. I did so without any serious difficulties.

On New Year's Day, several Japanese soldiers were making themselves especially comfortable. The mother of a pretty young girl called
upon me and pleaded on her knees amid tears that I help her. I drove with

her to a house in the vicinity of Hankow Road. Upon entering the house, I saw the following: A Japanese soldier lay fully unclothed atop a pretty young girl who was weeping terribly. I yelled at the fellow in dreadful tones and in every conceivable language, wishing him "Happy New Year," and in no time he hastened on his way, trousers in hand.

Reports have been made of all such cases, as well as cases of looting, and are kept among the records of the International Committee and may be reviewed at any time.

With German greetings and Heil Hitler!
EDUARD SPERLING

23 JANUARY

Krischan Kröger did indeed leave for Shanghai at 6 o'clock this morning.

Sindberg is back in town again and has brought me six eggs and twenty live ducks, three of which breathed their last inside the sack where they were forced to stay during my office hours. Cook says: "Not matter—*ke shefan*—can eat!"

Takadama visits me in my office, along with eight policemen who are all very upset. The American embassy has telegraphed Washington that a piano was stolen from the American School eight days ago, and now the police have been ordered by Tokyo to see to it that the piano is put back at once; but nobody knows where the instrument is hiding. Presumably it was turned into firewood a long time ago. I shove the whole bunch out the door. I don't want to be bothered with this!

4:30 P.M.

Church service at the Ping Tsang Hsian. Mr. Mills preaches a very fine sermon in which he makes frequent mention of Germany and the Führer, including his efforts to achieve peace.

6:00 P.M.

Pay a call on Dr. Rosen, who went on a longer excursion outside the gates today and returns with the news that the Golf Club has been burned to the ground.

7:00 P.M.

We celebrate the birthday of our director, Mr. Fitch, with a banquet. My present to Fitch is two live, though very skinny ducks. The poor creatures have not been fed a thing for a long time now.

24 JANUARY

General Gao's houseboy shows up at my door and I give him five dollars, because he claims he has nothing to eat. His master, he says, left for Hankow.

The Zone Committee wants to send a telegram via the Christian Council to Siemens China Co., Shanghai, asking them to allow me to stay here until 1 March. So for now I'm postponing my request to the Japanese embassy for a travel pass to Shanghai.

LATER

We're all degenerating around here. We're becoming spineless, losing our respectability. In *Indiscreet Letters from Peking,* a book about the siege of Peking in 1900, Putnam Wheale reports how he and many other Europeans simply joined in the looting. I don't think we're all that far from it ourselves. My houseboy Chang bought an electric table fan worth 38 dollars for $1.20 today, and expects me to be pleased. A couple of genuine Ming vases, costing one dollar each, gaze at me with reproach from my fireplace mantel.

If I felt like it, I could fill the entire house with cheap curios—meaning stolen and then sold for a song on the black market. Only food is expensive these days: A chicken now costs two dollars, the exact same price as those two Ming vases.

Takadama was back at our headquarters today and brought along some high-ranking police officer who can make himself understood in Chinese. Takadama got caught, by Dr. Bates no less, asking for girls at one of the University refugee camps. He claims now that he was looking for "washerwomen and cooks," which of course no one believes, since it's general knowledge in the Far East that in China you hire men to do the washing and cooking. And so Takadama is demanding that his reputation be restored.

Dr. Smythe, who took down the minutes of the entire discussion, promises him that the various embassies will be notified. That, of course, really rubs Takadama the wrong way, and he departs in great disgruntlement, after first expressly asking that the embassies not be bothered. The entire Safety Zone headquarters is pleased as Punch by his comedown.

John Magee lays a report and a Japanese sidearm on my desk. The report describes how a Japanese soldier threatened a Chinese woman with this same weapon but dropped it and ran when he was surprised by three members of our committee. Smythe beams at the news, which he immediately passes on to the American embassy, since all the eyewitnesses were Americans. Mr. Allison from the American embassy has taken over the task of writing protests for us, which pleases us no end. Allison simply can't get over the way the Japanese are behaving. "Allison in Wonderland" is Dr. Rosen's name for him.

25 JANUARY

John Magee brings two Chinese nurses, a man and a woman, from Waichiaopu Hospital to headquarters, who tell us that a hospital coolie has been stabbed by a Japanese soldier. We listen to our two visitors and record their statements in a confidential file. At the same time we have them tell us all about the hospital at the War Ministry, where conditions are evidently very bad.

There is one case that we don't record: A Chinese worker, who has worked all day for the Japanese, is paid in rice instead of money. He sits down in exhaustion with his family at the table, on which his wife has just placed a bowl of watery rice soup: the humble meal for a family of six. A Japanese soldier passing by plays a little joke and urinates in the half-full rice bowl and laughs as he goes his merry way.

The incident made me think of the poem *"Lewwer duad üs Slaav"*;[45] but one simply can't expect a poor Chinese worker to behave like a free Frisian. The Chinese are far too downtrodden, and they patiently submitted to their fate long ago. It is, as I said, an incident that is given the scantest notice. If every case of rape were revenged with murder, a good portion of the occupying troops would have been wiped out by now.

I've just received some mail by way of the German embassy: Mutti writes that I can leave at once on a furlough to Germany. If I don't leave now, I'll have to wait another five years. Well, it won't be as bad as all that.

I'm still waiting for an answer to the Shanghai Christian Council's request that the company let me stay here until 1 March, although I'm afraid we won't be finished with our work here even then. Personally I'd be very happy to take a vacation now. I am in fact a little weary of China at the moment; but I can't desert the colors now!

10:10 P.M.

Radio Shanghai reports that after a twelve-hour ride in an open railway car, Kröger arrived in Shanghai in good shape on Saturday evening, 23 January.

CHAPTER 9

THE JAPANESE WANT TO CLEAR
THE SAFETY ZONE

26 JANUARY

I AM FORCED TO record once again that the dead Chinese soldier just be-yond my house has still not been buried. How long will such incredible conditions go on here? It's said that a very high-ranking Japanese is on his way, someone not attached to the local military, but answerable directly to Tokyo. He's supposed to restore order. It's high time.

Today a young American arrived by car, accompanied by a Japanese guard. He wants to sell some large timber holdings of an Anglo-American lumber company to the Japanese. This man, who is attached to the British embassy, reports that on his trip from Shanghai they encountered a total of perhaps 60 people in the first 50 miles, and that Nanking is the only city with any number of inhabitants worth mentioning. All the other cities be-tween here and Shanghai are as good as dead.

It's a shock to drive through the deserted streets outside our Zone and

Shanghai Road, the main street of the Safety Zone.

be able to simply walk into any house, since all the doors have been ripped off or just stand wide open, and to witness destruction barbaric beyond all comprehension.

You shake your head and ask yourself why this pointless devastation, particularly since it's been clear for some time from the actions of the Japanese embassy that they're very ashamed of the Japanese military's conduct. They try to cover things up wherever it's even vaguely feasible. And the ban on anyone entering or leaving is one of their ways of keeping the world ignorant of Nanking's present state. Even though that can last only for a short time, because ever since the Germans, Americans, and British restaffed their embassies here, hundreds of letters have been sent to Shanghai describing local conditions in precise detail, not to mention all the embassies' telegraphed reports.

The Safety Zone is the only place in Nanking showing any sign of life. New peddler's booths keep springing up along the streets in its center. Early each morning, usually still in the twilight, the Chinese drag into the Zone anything that they still own amid these ruins and that's still worth trading—or presumed worth trading—and try to find a willing buyer who has a few dollars for something other than food. The crowd presses shoulder to shoulder through this city of booths, this permanent Poverty Fair of indescribable want, where there is a revaluation of every value according to the current price of life's necessities like rice, flour, meat, salt, vegetables— and of its delights, like tobacco!

We are trying to get the German, American, and British embassies to help us in regard to supplies of rice that we still have stored in warehouses that are now the property of the Japanese. But there is little prospect of success.

All three gentlemen shake doubtful heads. We can hardly expect the Japanese to hand over these remaining supplies at some point. On the contrary, they will make every effort to prevent us from bringing in any more food. We are in their way, and the Japanese authorities want to be rid of us. With each new day, we make ourselves more unpopular, and are afraid that one fine day they'll simply pack us all off to Shanghai.

Letter from Siemens China Co., Shanghai, to John Rabe

Shanghai, 14 January 1938

Dear Herr Rabe,

From various reports in the newspapers and above all from your messages that have found their way through to your wife we are very happy to learn that you are all right. We hope that communications will be restored soon, so that we can receive your messages about company concerns, the state of the Capital Electricity Works and other important matters.

Enclosed, a list of the residential and office buildings of Hapro in Nanking, which we have received from Herr Eckert, along with the request that, if possible, you determine the condition of these buildings and pass that information along to him.

We have no clear notion here of what sort of freedom of movement you enjoy there, but, like Herr Eckert, we would be grateful for whatever determinations you can make and inform us about.

As before, our thoughts and best wishes are with you.

With German greetings,
Siemens China Co.
DR. PROBST   MAIER

27 JANUARY

Today is the Kaiser's birthday. And a little commemoration is probably harmless, even for a Nazi. Anyone born under the Kaiser's government has never entirely forgotten him. I long for the return of those days, but not of the Kaiser, because I prefer Hitler; but as I said: you can't shake off the memory, for on this day the ghosts of so many dead rise up, ghosts of those who happily and proudly marched in parade in their colorful uniforms. Dust and ashes now, all of them, or almost all. May they rest easy in their graves!

According to radio reports from Shanghai, the French government has named Pater Jacquinot a Knight of the Legion of Honor. Given all that we have been through here, and the difficulties that our committee here, all 15 men, have overcome only with the greatest of effort, the man (who had only himself) must have accomplished some incredible things and rightly deserves his knighthood.

I drove this morning through the East City with Dr. Rosen. All the buildings have been looted of everything and about a third of them have been burned down.

We've just hear the terrible news that McCallum, who is in charge of Kulou Hospital, has been attacked with a bayonet by two Japanese soldiers who forced their way into the hospital without permission, and has been wounded in the neck. Fortunately, the wound appears not to be life-threatening, but this is a very serious incident and the American and Japanese governments will be informed at once by telegram.

FROM THE FAMILY DIARY

N.N. is a cause of great sorrow and worry again! He bought a wonderful automobile from the servant of Pan-chen Lama for 200 dollars. The new Autonomous Government now wants to buy the car from him, and because they know that N.N. paid only 200 dollars for it, they're offering 600 dollars, instead of the 1,900 dollars N.N. is demanding. Moreover, the Autonomous Government Committee has informed us that the servant of Pan-chen Lama had no right to sell the car, since it was the property of the Chinese government. If N.N. continues his profiteering like this, one of these days the Japanese authorities will expel him from Nanking, heaping curses and shame on his head.

Letter from John Rabe to His Wife in Shanghai

Nanking, 27 January 1938

My Dear Dora,

The English consul, Mr. Prideaux-Brune, will be coming to Shanghai shortly aboard an English gunboat. He will be bringing a lot of mail with him, among which are three thick envelopes for you, containing:

My Diary in Nanking:

Vol. II, part 2

Vol. III, parts 1 and 2

Vol. IV, parts 1 and 2

Vol. V, part 1

Vol. I as well as the first part of Vol. II are either on board the *Kutwo* or in storage in Hankow.

What I am sending you today includes the period from the day the *Kutwo* left Nanking until yesterday—the heart of the matter. These pages were written for you. I'll have them bound later. The first volume is already bound. If you decide to give all or part of these books to anyone to read—that's up to you. But nothing can be published without the permission of the Party. And so Herr Lahrmann[46] in Shanghai will have to be asked first. But I think it's better if you don't have any of it published until I'm there, because I very much doubt that the Reich will give its permission. Besides which, like all my books, it's not really written for the general public, but for you and the rest of the family. I don't know when I can get away from here. I can move about freely inside the city; but I may not leave the city, at least not for now.

My warmest greetings and kisses
Your JOHNY

Letter from John Rabe to His Wife

Nanking, 28 January 1938

My dear Dora,

I forgot to ask you in the letter I enclosed with my diaries yesterday to telegraph me when the books have arrived via the German embassy, which can then forward the telegram via the American consulate general. The American embassy here has a wireless receiver and sender in its building. If you telegraph me the word BUGAN, I'll read it as: *"Bücher gut angekommen."* [Books arrived safely.]

I made some inquiries yet again at the Japanese embassy yesterday. I can get permission to leave, but will not be able then to return to Nanking in the foreseeable future. I'm waiting to hear from the firm whether I should leave or not. If I do leave, I'll have to leave everything— Committee, house, furniture, the employees—behind at loose ends. As I see it, it can be another six months or a whole year before the war is over. So: What to do?

Many warm greetings and kisses
Your JOHNY

Memorandum of Chancellor P. Scharffenberg to the German Embassy in Hankow

The situation in Nanking as of 28 January 1938

The food supply provided by the Japanese is completely inadequate. If we were to rely on them, we would starve. Yesterday Sindberg, the Dane from the cement factory, brought us another little pig, eggs, two ducks. Granted, he was arrested on the way here, but by subsidizing the sentries with a crate of beer he got through under the guard of three men and an officer. We gave some of it to the other Germans and the houseboys and police who live off us. There are no onions to be had, and very few vegetables. So all the foreigners, who are afraid of scurvy on a diet of nothing but rice, are desperate for apples, which are available from Japanese canteens—but only for yen. And so everyone is in pursuit of yen. Our hundred yen are gone, because we gave some to all the Germans and a few foreigners.

The number of Japanese canteens has been increased. They sell mainly beer and sake. It's incredible how much beer the Japanese can down, hundreds of crates from a truckload are sold in no time. The Japanese deliberately killed all domestic animals, e.g., all the water buffalo. Pigs were beheaded and left lying there. Ponies and donkeys have all been confiscated. It's comical to watch the Japanese riding donkeys, they even harness them to the rickshas. More and more Chinese are risking leaving the Safety Zone, but only during the day. Mostly it's just aged women and children, who happily loot while the Japanese watch. My impression is that the Japanese encourage this in order to shift the blame away from themselves.

As before, we can't take one step outside without being accompanied by a gendarme. Like political criminals!

SCHARFFENBERG

28 JANUARY

Mr. Tanaka quite unexpectedly granted Mr. Fitch permission to leave for Shanghai today and return six days later. He's traveling aboard the English gunboat *Bee* and will return in a week on the American gunboat *Oahu*. The whole thing seems a little fishy to me, especially since they've given him nothing in writing, no travel pass or the like.

Yesterday evening, when I asked Fukui to give Fitch permission to leave and return, he brusquely refused. Maybe they are somewhat easier on the Americans today because in the meantime they've had a few unpleasant incidents with the Japanese. Yesterday Mr. Allison, the deputy at the American embassy, was even slapped in the face by a Japanese soldier. The incident was reported to Washington at once and was the latest news today on the radio from London. The Japanese have indeed apologized to Mr. Allison for the slaps, but they insist Allison provoked the soldier by speaking rudely to him in Japanese.

Dr. Rosen has made himself unpopular again, too. Yesterday he accompanied me on a drive through the East City but didn't want to take along the Japanese guard assigned to him. My friendly persuasion accomplished nothing. The incident has been reported to the Japanese embassy, which sent me the following statement today:

"There are still Chinese soldiers in plainclothes in Nanking. Japanese soldiers are instructed to shoot at every suspicious person. That is why embassy officials are given a Japanese guard for protection."

To which one can only say that if there really are any plainclothes Chinese left, they certainly would have nothing against a few foreigners because by now every child knows that we remained behind to protect the Chinese.

We have received news that the Japanese want to close all refugee camps on 4 February. The refugees are supposed to return to the devastated city and it doesn't matter where they live amid the ruins. This could be awful; but we don't know how to avert this calamity. The military has all the power.

29 JANUARY

Mr. Prideaux-Brune, the English consul, and Mr. George Fitch left on the *Bee* this morning at 9 o'clock, and with them my diaries. No one believes that Fitch will return in the foreseeable future. Tension between the Europeans and the Japanese is growing daily. We are seriously considering dissolving the Zone Committee and creating a Relief Committee that would cooperate with the new Autonomous Government Committee.

I keep suggesting that we cooperate with the Japanese, but the Americans are against it, and until I have the approval of the entire committee, I can't approach the Japanese, nor can I be sure that they even will consent. Maybe it's too late already for cooperation of this sort. The favorable moment may very well have passed.

On the other hand, we're as good as paralyzed if, as threatened, the Japanese forcibly close all refugees camps on 4 February and then place the refugees in concentration camps that we are forbidden to enter, just as they've done with the Red Cross hospitals.

I learn that the German embassy has received a letter from the Japanese thanking them for all the help given the refugees and likewise informing them that the refugee camps must be closed down on 4 February. I call a meeting of all committee members, and we decide to have our embassies ascertain the following by official or other means:

1. Can the Japanese remove refugees from a camp that is on foreign property or in a house belonging to a foreigner? A large number of the camps are on American property; my own camp would likewise fit in this category, since it is on the grounds of a German.

2. Can we take more refugees into our camps?

3. We also ask our embassies to refrain from answering Japanese letters about this matter until we have clarified our standpoint.

John Magee found two girls, aged eight and four, whose entire family of eleven had been murdered in the most gruesome fashion. The two girls remained in a room with the body of their mother for 14 days until they were rescued by a neighbor. The older one had fed herself and her sister from small stores of rice that were still in the house. [See pp. 281–282]

30 JANUARY

We have stated our committee's concerns in a letter to Dr. Rosen and have asked him to confer with the Japanese about them. I admit I have no great hope that we will accomplish much; because Dr. Rosen is not exactly persona grata with the Japanese—more like non grata. Nonetheless an attempt must be made to dissuade the Japanese from forcing Chinese refugees out of the Zone on 4 February. Dr. Rosen was chosen for the task, because, since I, a German, am chairman of the committee, it would be best to proceed through the German embassy or its representatives.

Our camp has been transformed into a swamp once again. There were two days of heavy snowfall, and now the snow is melting. With heavy hearts, my 600 refugees are getting accustomed to the idea that they will have to leave the camp on 4 February. Most of these people live not all too far from my house and can quickly return here in an emergency.

Han and I started a private collection for the poorest of the poor, about 100 people. We have collected 100 dollars and so are able to give each of these people one dollar, which made them all very very happy.

What vast misery, and tomorrow is Chinese New Year, the biggest holiday of the poor Chinese people! The committee has given my camp, which is a relatively small one, a special extra grant of five dollars to buy spices to season the New Year's rice—five dollars for 600 people! Sadly, we cannot do more than that, but the money is gratefully accepted all the same. Moreover, everyone is to receive (on the sly) one teacup of rice in addition to their daily very scant ration of two cups.

Hatz, our auto mechanic, appeared today in the office in a new pair of top boots that he "commandeered" from Pinckernelle's room, though with Kröger's permission, or so he says! Well, none of us really objects. Hatz is a poor devil himself, and Pinckernelle has a good heart and by now probably has his long legs under a desk somewhere in lovely Shanghai or Hong Kong.

Report of the Safety Zone Committee, 31 January 1938

On Sunday, January 30, police and a soldier representing the Special Service Corps came to some of the camps and told them that the refugees must move out by February 4 or their belongings would be sealed up in the camp and the buildings sealed.

Meanwhile cases come in which indicate that order is far from complete either inside or especially outside the Safety Zone. But it is encouraging to note in some of the cases on the 30th, military police actually arrested soldiers caught in the act. Hitherto it has usually only been a slap or requirement to salute that has been used for punishment of soldiers.

The following cases are only the ones we have been able to get first hand reports of: (the first two are cases overlooked in typing up previous reports.)

209) On January 24th, at 11:00 p.m., two Japanese soldiers entered the Agricultural Implements Shop at 11 Hu Chia Tsai Yuen. They wore light armbands. They threatened the storekeeper with a gun and searched him. Then they took away a woman, raped her, and released her two hours later. (Note: This case involves forcible and irregular entry, intimidation by military weapons, abduction, rape.) The Japanese proclamation on the house door was torn down. Mr. Riggs and Mr. Bates took the woman in a car to see if she could identify the house. She pointed the way to 32 Hsiao Fen Chao and identified that as the place. It is the district office of the military police. Dr. Bates filed a protest with the American embassy because it occurred on University of Nanking property. On the afternoon of January 26th, two gendarmes, a Japanese interpreter, and Mr. Takadama went with Mr. Riggs and Mr. Allison to investigate at the shop and at the above military police office. Then they took the woman to the Japanese embassy for questioning. She was returned on the night of January 27th at 8:30 after 28 hours in custody with the following report:

Since she had made a mistake in the number of steps from the first floor to the second, in the color of the bed cover, in describing the electric light instead of the oil lamp used, and did not know the time she was taken (others at the shop stated the time as they were all aroused), the rape did not occur in this particular house and therefore it was not the military police but ordinary soldiers and the soldiers involved had been punished. Since it was not the military police office, therefore the statement that it was, was merely anti-Japanese propaganda by the American embassy. (This report was given to Dr. Bates and Mr. Riggs at 3 Ping Tsang Hsiang by Mr. Takadama and his interpreter. *Riggs—Bates*)

210) January 21, night, two Japanese soldiers came to 44 Kao Chia Chiu Kwan and asked for women. Fortunately the women in the family had gone to the University Middle School the day before. The family is very poor. So they went next door and found two women and raped them right there in front of their husbands. On the 22nd the two soldiers came back with two other soldiers and stood in front of the house and laughed. (*Sone*)

211) January 25, afternoon, a Chinese woman came to the University Hospital. She and her husband had moved into the Safety Zone and were living in a straw hut near the Bible Teachers' Training School. On December 13 her husband was taken away by the Japanese soldiers and the wife, this woman, was taken to South City where she has been ever since. She has been raped every day from seven to ten times since but usually was given an opportunity to sleep at night. She has developed all three types of venereal disease in their most virulent forms: Syphilis, Gonor-

rhea, Chancroid. She was let go five days ago probably because of her diseased condition. She returned to the Zone then. (*Wilson*)

212) January 29, in the afternoon a young woman from one of the refugee camps went to Moh Tsou Lu to buy flour and was one of about 20 girls picked up in a truck by Japanese soldiers. They carried her to Fu Tze Miao where she was assigned to a military office according to her account. A Chinese servant took pity on her weeping and suggested a possible means of escape. While the officers were eating, she put her finger in her throat, then gagged, whereupon the officers sent her out of the room. She managed thus to escape and found her way back to the refugee camp the next morning at 2 a.m. (*Bates*)

LATER

At 4 o'clock this afternoon, my car was stopped on Hankow Road by a group of about 50 Chinese, who asked me to rescue a woman whom a Japanese soldier had led away to rape. The soldier had vanished into No. 4 Shue Chia Hsiang, to which I am then led.

I find the house completely looted, the floor covered with all sorts of debris. In one of the open rooms is a coffin on a bier, and in the room adjoining, lying on a floor covered with straw and junk, I see the soldier, who is about to rape the woman.

I manage to pull the soldier out of the room and into the entryway. When he sees all the Chinese and my car, he pulls away and disappears somewhere in the ruins of nearby buildings. The crowd stands at the door, murmuring, but quickly disperses when I tell them to, so as not to attract more Japanese soldiers.

4:30 p.m.: Worship service in the Ping Tsang Hsian.

6:00 p.m.: Smythe and I for tea at Dr. Rosen's.

8:00 p.m.: Dinner with Sperling and Hatz at the home of Scharffenberg and Hürter. We send Dr. Lautenschlager, our local group leader, a telegram on the occasion of the fifth anniversary of Hitler's assumption of power.

FROM THE FAMILY DIARY

What I have always secretly feared has come to pass: rancor and quarrels among the few Germans here. Yesterday at the Scharffenberg-Hürter dinner, Sperling and Hatz got into it. The latter is an Austrian or Hungarian and sometimes not very careful about what he says. As tempers warmed under the influence of alcohol—none of us can really handle alcohol anymore—an argument arose about the ridiculous question as to whether the Japanese were treating us relatively well or badly. Since I'm of the opinion that we are definitely not being treated well, I got involved in the argument, too, and had to oppose Hatz; but we finally did at least part in peace!

Relations between Rosen and Scharffenberg-Hürter are not of the best. This stems primarily from the fact that Dr. Rosen wants to shake his Japanese guards when he goes out for a spin in his car or, if you like, is driving it on official business. Scharffenberg-Hürter, however, are of the opinion—and I agree with them absolutely—that it would be advisable to acquiesce to the instructions of the Japanese military in this regard, but Dr. Rosen will not hear of it. By the by, Dr. Rosen helps out whenever he can, as do Scharffenberg and Hürter. I hope that this discord resolves itself, but disagreement among us few Germans is the worst thing that can happen to us.

CHAPTER 10

THE LIVING BUDDHA

31 JANUARY

CHINESE NEW YEAR'S DAY: formal ceremony of congratulation by servants and employees. The refugees stand lined up in rows in the garden and bow to me three times. There are many young girls among them. They all thank me for the protection I've provided, for saving them, which however is not yet a done deed. They present me with a six-by-nine-foot red silk banner inscribed in Chinese, a statement of gratitude, I presume.

I hand the banner on to my houseboy Chang, who to my dismay solemnly rolls it out across the living room. A number of Chinese guests stand reverently gazing at it, and one of them translates the text into English:

> You are the Living Buddha
> for hundred thousand people.

Until then I had been listening only with one ear, but that was going too far. I gave the speaker a closer look. He was a high official of the former

Chinese government, no special friend of mine, but a man who knew the classics, a scholar. I asked him to translate the Chinese text again, but without any flattering addenda. Yes, he said, what I just read is correct; but one can, of course, translate it more precisely, perhaps like this:

> You have the heart of a Buddha
> and share his bold spirit.
> You have saved thousands of poor people
> from danger and want.
> May the favor of Heaven be granted to you,
> May good luck follow you,
> May God's blessing rest upon you!
>
> The Refugees of Your Camp

If these were not such perilous times, I could almost laugh at this touching dedication. I've not even resigned yet from my post as mayor, and here they are making me a living Buddha for thousands of poor people! But I don't dare take any real delight in this gift, which was brought into the house amid exploding fireworks, because 4 February looms ahead, the day when all these poor people are to be forced from my garden camp. I still hope, however, that by showing my German flag I can prevent the worst. God grant it be so! You grow weary in this constant battle against a demoralized Japanese soldiery!

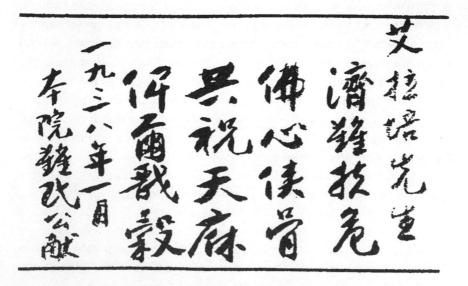

Our houseboy Chang has just arrived with the following report: At 11 o'clock this morning, Wu Hsiu Chen, a girl of twenty-four in my refugee camp, was raped by a Japanese soldier in her old house, Kwang Chou Lu No. 46. She had gone to the house to prepare a midday meal for her uncle, who had returned to the house by order of the Japanese. Bayonet in hand, the soldier demanded she give in to him if she did not want to be killed.

LATER

I was happy to discover that the dead Chinese soldier who has been lying at my door for six weeks now has at last been buried.

1 FEBRUARY

Dr. Rosen protests sending the telegram I mentioned to Dr. Lautenschlager. To keep peace, we yield, because Rosen was in fact not invited to the dinner during which we composed the telegram. So we can't really claim that all the Germans of Nanking were present at the celebration.

Complaints of Chinese families who have returned to their homes are coming in from all sides now, accusing Japanese soldiers of raping their wives and daughters. Many have returned to the Zone for that reason. We don't know what else to do but take them in.

2 FEBRUARY

Some statistics put together by Han show that of the 135 refugee families, who make up the total of over 600 people in my garden, 24 families have no home to which to return, the buildings have been burned down. Several refugees returned home amid tears yesterday. They do not trust the Japanese military, and rightly so. Reports from two camps already show quite clearly that public safety has not yet been established.

General Homma arrived here yesterday from Tokyo vested with special powers to establish order. Almost everyone doubts that he can succeed in the two days he is to remain here. Dr. Rosen spoke with him about the plight of the refugees as described in my letter of 30 January, and Rosen's impression was that we are not to expect much from him to make us smile.

At noon today I joined Dr. Rosen at his house for *tiffin* with Hidaka of the Japanese embassy in Shanghai. We have had to register 88 offenses by Japanese soldiers over the last three days. That is even worse than what we experienced in this regard in December. Hidaka, into whose hand I press our report, apologizes for these "Japanese rascals," but offers as an excuse that such things occasionally happen when troops are being relieved. The old bad troops were ostensibly sent off on 28 January and behaved badly yet again before being sent off.

I've heard this particular excuse before, but we believe we have proof that the rapes, etc. that have been reported were committed by the new troops.

To my question whether the refugees will in fact be removed from the camps in the Zone on 4 February by force, Hidaka replied that as far as he was informed no force whatever would be employed. Those refugees who left the Zone before 4 February would therefore be granted some easing of their conditions on their return home, that is, those refugees whose houses have been burned down are to have other houses made available to them, etc. According to Hidaka's figures, 80,000 refugees have already reported their return to their old homes. I point out to Hidaka that we have pleaded with the refugees on several occasions to return to their homes, especially since we, too, are very interested in seeing the Zone disbanded soon, but that the return of the refugees is dependent solely on public safety in parts of the city outside the Zone. Hidaka asks that we not tell the Chinese that the Japanese will not employ force to disband the Zone, in order not to bog down the process even further. I promise him not to make the news public.

From Dr. Trautmann in Hankow I hear that the Chinese prime minister, H. H. Kung, wishes to express his gratitude for our work. I officially pass the news on to the committee.

3 FEBRUARY

The same spectacle can be seen now in all the refugee camps. In my garden, about 70 girls and women are on their knees, banging their heads against the ground. Their weeping and wailing would melt a heart of stone. They don't want to leave my garden camp, because they are quite rightly afraid that they will be raped by Japanese soldiers. They keep wailing the same thing over and over: "You are our father and our mother. You have protected us till now, don't stop half way! If we are going to be violated and have to die, then we want to die here!"

Impressive language. And one cannot close oneself off to such justifiable laments. I have allowed them to stay on. Only a couple of old people have left.

I hope Hidaka told the truth when he said that the Japanese military will not use force to drive the refugees from the Zone. I have had so many disappointments by now that I am ready for anything. Every member of our committee will be on the alert tomorrow. We have gradually lost all patience with this pack of soldiers, whom Japanese officials politely call rascals, but whom we call a "murderous pack." If these bandits have been given permission by their authorities to force their way into our camps, clashes will be unavoidable.

Chang has just told me that of the seventeen people living in a small house near the end of the street where our old house used to be, six have been killed because they sank to their knees outside the house and begged the Japanese soldiers to spare their daughters. After the old people had been shot, the girls were dragged away and raped. Out of the entire family, only one girl is still left, and she has been taken in by sympathetic neighbors.

You can't breathe for sheer revulsion when you keep finding the bodies of women with bamboo poles thrust up their vaginas. Even old women over 70 are constantly being raped.

I send a letter to Mr. Hidaka asking him to put in writing his promise that the refugees will not be driven from the Zone by force, and at the same time I encourage him to discuss the matter once again with the Japanese military authorities.

Report from the China Press in Shanghai, 25 January (Excerpt)

Claiming that many Chinese army officers and other ranks were seeking refuge in the International Safety Zone established in Nanking following the evacuation of the capital by Chinese troops, Colonel Nagai, army spokesman, announced the report of the Nipponese gendarmerie in Nanking at yesterday's press conference. . . .

It was ascertained, the report claimed, that high officers of the Chinese army were hiding in buildings, foreign embassies and legations after these buildings were evacuated by their staffs. Up to December 28, it said, 23 Chinese officers, 54 non-commissioned officers, and 1,498 privates were seized by the Japanese in the various buildings in the zone. Among them, it was claimed, was the commander of the Nanking peace preservation corps, Wang Hsianglao, "who masqueraded as Chen Mi" and was in command of the fourth branch detachment of the International Safety Zone, Lieutenant General Ma Poushang, former adjutant of the 88th Division, and a high official of the Nanking police, Mi Shinshi.

General Ma, it is claimed, was active in instigating anti-Japanese disorders within the zone, which also sheltered Captain Huan An and 17 rifles, while the report states that Wang Hsianglao and three former sub-ordinates were engaged in looting, intimidating and raping.

In dugouts adjoining foreign embassy and legation quarters evacu-ated by their staffs, were found caches of arms. A search in one dugout disclosed:

> one light artillery gun
> 21 machine guns of Czechoslovakian manufacture with 60 rounds
> three other machine guns
> 10 water-cooled machine guns with 3,000 rounds
> 50 rifles with 420,000 rounds of ammunition
> 7,000 hand grenades
> 2,000 trench mortars shells
> 500 artillery shells

When asked to specify the embassy adjoining the dugout, the spokesman said that that he did not feel he was at liberty to do so. He also evaded a question as to whether anybody was found in the United States legation. Although no official information was available, the spokesman continued, he understood that a number of Chinese army men arrested were executed on charges of looting. When asked whether prisoners would be regarded as prisoners of war or spies, he answered that this was entirely dependent on the circumstances under which they were arrested.

LATER

Dr. Günther's report, passed on to us by Herr Sindberg of the Kiangnan Cement Factory, proves that it is not just Nanking that is suffering at the hands of the Japanese soldiery. The same reports are coming in from all sides about rapes, murder, and mayhem. One might be led to think that the entire criminal population of Japan is in uniform here.

If Dr. Rosen's confidential reports are to be taken seriously, my collec-tion of medals will increase by one very soon, that is, I've been nominated for a German Red Cross medal. Since Kröger and Sperling have been also been similarly threatened, I'll quietly let it all burst over my head.[47]

4 FEBRUARY

I've got to do guard duty today, meaning, I'll have to keep an eye on my own refugee camp, the German school behind my garden with its 600 refugees, and the Middle School with its 5,000. I won't be able to accom-plish much if the Japanese force their way in, but at least I can be there and watch the whole thing so that the world can be told about it.

4 February, which we so feared, is now behind us. Everything was quiet. As regards the Japanese, we were not disturbed. Today is the last day of Chinese New Year. Despite snow and rain, the Chinese are setting off fireworks in the garden and are in a good mood. It's extraordinary how these poor people are so easily satisfied with so little. As long as someone's not trying to kill them, they are content.

Mr. George Fitch showed up on Shanghai Radio yesterday, very much a friend of Japan again. If he knew that between 28 and 31 January there were more rapes, etc. here than in the worst days of December, he might well have spoken otherwise. I have still received no word from Mutti whether my diaries arrived safely in Shanghai. Nor is there any word from the firm about whether they agree with my staying on here until the beginning of March.

5 FEBRUARY

We have 98 more cases of rape to report for 3 February. We have not been harassed here in the camps, thank God; but the enclosed letter of the Chinese director of the Middle School camp, where the number of refugees has climbed from 5,000 to 8,000, speaks volumes:

Letter from the University of Nanking, Middle School, to Rabe

Nanking, 5 February 1938

Dear Dr. Rabe:

Beg to report that there are more refugees coming back to our school for save. They said that they cannot live at home, for day and night the Japs broke in to find girls. They will kill you if you didn't find girls for them. How can they go back under such conditions. Please save these refugees with Christian idea.

Except your friends we have no place to ask save. Will you please consider the matter with the German Embassy and the American Embassy and the Japanese Embassy. They cried to me, but I have no way to save them.

The self-government absolutely has no power to stop them to go in during the day and night. They said no protection except international committee. Now even the wife and the woman servant of the officers of the self-government, they rape as same as the common people. I do not know why they ask the refugees to go back home under such bad and evil conditions.

They can't do that if there is no protection.

How pitiful these refugees are.

I pray God to bless China and save us as soon as possible. Now we are standing in the fire cave, and if you and you friend do not save us, how can we be saved? Please consider with you friend to find any way to save us with love.

My dear teacher. I write this letter with hearty tears. Be God always with you. Please remember us always in your prayers.

> With best wishes I remain very truly yours,
> D. G. GRIMES

2 : 15 P.M.

Chinese pilots are once again drifting through the skies over Nanking; at least the planes carry the Chinese insignia: You can't be certain what nationality the pilots are. Let's hope they aren't Russians, otherwise we won't be all that well-protected under our swastika!

According to the latest reports, the Japanese now want the refuge camps disbanded by 8 February. We move from one state of uproar to another. Thus far about a third of the total number of refugees have emigrated from the Zone, the rest, mainly women and girls, refuse to leave. Today we heard from the doctors at Kulou Hospital that two cases of beriberi have been admitted. Given a diet of nothing but rice, it's no wonder. We have telegraphed to Shanghai for medicine.

We few Germans are quite downcast by the radio report that Blomberg, Fritsch, and various other generals at home have resigned or been removed. Ostensibly it has to do with our foreign policy. We're expectantly waiting for more details. That's all we needed in the midst of this misery here: worrying about peace at home!

Letter from Christian Kröger, Shanghai, to John Rabe

Shanghai, 28 January 1938

Dear Master Rabe,

I am slowly becoming human again, after first warming myself with various grogs in the wake of a rather arduous train trip, nor should I forget to mention a hot bath, and then a week of being able to move about among people who are properly dressed and peaceable, rather than among those beasts of prey in Nanking.

The trip was indeed a mad one, and I must say that my heart was in my throat when I saw the open railway car at the train station. My ridiculous policeman is to blame for that, and I could have boarded the horse car there and then, which I later did in Chinkiang. With a few cigarettes I made it clear to the soldier there that it was my preferred mode of transport, and that worked, despite the protests of my police officer. Luckily he froze even worse than I, and so reason triumphed over a stupid order.

As far as Changchow (Wuchin), it's a devastated and crazy landscape, then all at once things get better, farmers are out in their fields and are already plowing. Apparently mopping-up operations have been completed that far. But there's definitely been the same sort of looting everywhere; because during the whole trip soldiers would board with their heavy bundles, and officers even had soldiers carrying their booty for them. Otherwise there's not much to see. The highway is indeed not quite secure, especially not at night. All the same I would have ten times preferred driving my own car.

I had not seen your dear *taitai*[48] until today. She is very worried, and I'm sure the right thing is for you to show up here in a month at the latest and then leave for Germany. I had a long conversation with Dr. Probst. He's interested in everything. They don't need you to do business, I don't think, but they do want to relieve you and send you home on a vacation that you more than richly deserve. They want to send someone in your place, but I think that's pointless, because no one could really settle in there and there's no business to be done anytime soon. So, see to it that you first get rid of your refugees. The Chinese love to fall to their knees and be protected. But at some point they'll have to take the fresh air, and I think a little consideration for your *taitai* and your own health take precedence here.

One more suggestion. There's a Krupp diesel at my *hong*. Carlowitz & Co. can indeed claim it as theirs, but there'll be no one there who knows how to deal with a diesel. Hatz wanted to drive the car to Shanghai in any case. See to it that you gradually get your things packed up and then have Hatz drive you to Shanghai in it. Surely that will be possible by the middle of March. Let your generous heart take courage, and think of your *taitai*, who otherwise is going to board a Japanese troop train and pay you a visit there. I think she is taking care of pretty much everything for you.

CHAPTER II

FAREWELL

6 FEBRUARY

SINCE IT STRUCK ME that the Chinese pilots all stayed away from the city during the last air raid, I happened to check in passing on various dugouts, and discovered that without exception they are all filled with groundwater. After all the misery the Japanese soldiers have brought us, people have become fully indifferent to the dangers of air raids. The crowd of refugees stands in my garden, silently staring up at the airplanes. A few people don't pay any heed at all, but calmly go about their daily business inside the straw huts.

I presented my request to the Japanese embassy today for a trip to and from Shanghai. In principle, Fukui told me, all such petitions are turned down. He says he will see what he can do nevertheless. Dr. Rosen officially endorsed my request, but that won't help much. As already noted, Rosen is not exactly persona grata among the Japanese, but that goes for me, too, as chairman of the International Committee. But the attempt must be made all the same, for as of today I've not heard one word from the firm telling me that they agree with my staying on here for a while. If I do get permission to leave, however, I would prefer to travel on a foreign gunboat.

From a Report of the Nanking Office of the German Embassy (Rosen) to the Foreign Ministry

On 5 inst. a tea reception was held in the rooms of the Japanese embassy, attended by members of the local foreign legations at the invitation of the newly appointed Japanese garrison commandant, Major General Amaya.

After a rather long delay, we were asked to take our seats, and the general read a long speech from a manuscript, which Attaché Fukuda then translated into halting English.

The general first noted that the Japanese army was famous throughout the world for its discipline. Both in the Russo-Japanese War and in the Manchurian campaign there had been no violations of discipline. But if such things had occurred now in China—and certainly worse would have happened in any other army—then it was the fault of the Chinese. Chiang Kai-shek had called upon not just the army, but the entire populace as well to resist, very much to the embitterment of the Japanese soldiers, for as they advanced they had found no food or other supplies, and had therefore vented their feelings against the populace. The advance on Nanking had proceeded so quickly that it had not been easy for supplies to keep up.

(This was to some extent contradicted by a later remark that the people in the supply columns had had too much free time and for that reason had begun to display the familiar lack of discipline.)

The general berated the Chinese in particular for having marked Japanese officers as a special target, who therefore had had to don the uniforms of the rank and file to avoid notice! And Chinese spies had also set fires, etc. to mark staff headquarters in order to draw artillery and air strikes! As for Nanking itself, the foreigners, especially those from "a certain nation," had presumed to play the role of judge. Without foreign interference, the Sino-Japanese relationship in Nanking would have developed harmoniously! It was foreigners who were provoking the Chinese to resist! He was ready to listen to any criticism pertaining to matters of foreign interest, but he wanted to deal with the Chinese directly himself.

At the conclusion of his speech, the general asked if we had anything to add ourselves. Out of a personal distaste for the strange methods of his "address," I refrained from saying anything in my capacity as senior foreign representative present, but my American colleague, Mr. Allison, asked for a copy of the text of the speech, whereupon all of a sudden the speech was declared to be entirely improvised, the very same speech the general had just read word for word, spectacles perched on his nose and holding his paper to one side now and then for better light, while Attaché Fukuda had stammered his translation from another Japanese copy! During the tea that followed I asked the Japanese deputy general consul, Mr. Fukui, when we might finally be able to count on visiting Dr. Günther, a citizen of the Reich, at the cement works in Kiangnan about 12 miles outside the city. Mr. Fukui replied that according to Major Hungo there were some 3,000 Chinese soldiers in the area; it was therefore too dangerous. I could not refrain from asking whether these 3,000 soldiers were dead or alive.

Of course this was yet another very lame excuse, for that same day Sindberg, a Dane who lives at the cement works with Dr. Günther, arrived in the city without a scratch, as he has often done before. Along with the attempt to prevent us from having a look at what crimes the Japanese troops have committed outside the city, the refusal to allow this official trip may also be connected with the fact that representatives of the Japanese Onoda Cement Works have already expressed some interest in the Kiangnan works, which have only recently been completed, but not yet transferred to a Chinese company. The German engineer and the Dane are therefore currently looking after the interests of the Danish firm that built the plant and the German firm that supplied the equipment.

My American colleague, Mr. Allison, who speaks Japanese, asked the general whether the officers of the American gunboat *Oahu* might be permitted on land to visit the embassy, something that has thus far been denied both them and the English. The general said to Major Hungo and Attaché Fukuda that he could see no reason why that shouldn't be possible, whereupon the two pulled him to one side for whispered conversation, and in the end the decision was that "the military" could not permit it! This example shows how higher Japanese officers defer to younger officers, and also how things are proceeding without any real planning, in matters great and small.

In general, daily life here is made absurdly difficult. Buying coal for the kitchen stove involves bureaucratic stupidity of the sort that in the old days used to be the subject of our humor magazines, and the purchase balloons into a major act of state. I had to provide exact information as to coal yard, truck, route traveled, and required amount of coal. Finally in possession of a large permit, the American embassy truck was able to drive off. Since the designated gate had been closed by Japanese soldiers, the driver wanted to use the next one, but that was impossible without a new permit. Moreover, General Consul Fukui demanded that because this was an American truck, it first be driven back to the American embassy instead of delivering the coal directly to me!

To return to the Major General Amaya's speech, the conclusion to be drawn from it is that Chinese resistance to the Japanese must have rattled them a good deal. Surely it is self-evident to patriots like the Japanese that after years of suffering and constant humiliation, a nation will resist foreign intruders. But in their overweening blindness, the Japanese have never been able to see this. About two years ago, the Japanese assistant foreign minister for Manchukuo, Mr. Ohashi, one of those chiefly to blame for the current war, told me that two Japanese divisions could hold the main Chinese army in check!

The general's admission in regard to the unusual insecurity felt by his officers and even his general staff clearly shows what a very different picture these gentlemen originally had of their stroll through China. Quite out of place was the general's attempt to shift the blame to foreigners for the failure of the Nanking populace to show enthusiasm for the Japanese, especially when one recalls that the foreigners who remained behind in Nanking chose to place a German, indeed a functionary of the NSDAP, at their head, making Herr John H. D. Rabe their leading figure. And though by "a certain nation" the general may have been referring to the Americans, they have worked in close cooperation with those Germans who remained behind. Without the brave intervention of the Germans and Americans, the bloody culpability of the Japanese would have been considerably worse, so that they should have every reason to be most grateful to these foreigners.

A few days ago, Herr Rabe offered Mr. Hidaka of the Japanese embassy his personal assistance and that of his coworkers to find some solutions to all the problems regarding Nanking's civilian population, but the Japanese think they can do everything better by themselves. And yet one can look to the future only with apprehension when one recalls that from 28 January to 8 February Japanese have committed over 170 violent crimes, i.e., mostly rapes and robberies of even paltry amounts of money from the defenseless poor. As I write this, Herr Rabe calls to report that yesterday an old married couple and two other civilians were shot and killed by Japanese soldiers for no plausible reason.

Granted, one can well understand that the Japanese, who until now have been able to keep their actions in this country from the public, are upset that precise details have been revealed here and that these play havoc with their claim of having brought light and order to a chaotic China whose populace could not contain its jubilation over it all. In contradiction to the fears of the foreigners, the Chinese in fact maintained model discipline under the pressure of several air raids a day, followed by actual fighting in the streets, and except for a few isolated incidents respected foreign flags, whereas the Japanese, even long after Nanking had become a quiet military base, swooped down over everything, including German and other foreign property—murdering, burning, violating.

As a result of changes in the leadership of German foreign policy, the Japanese apparently—judging from radio reports—have set great hopes on an endorsement of their China policy; but perhaps they have failed to note that the very man who created the Anti-Comintern Pact might have something to say about how the Japanese have violated its high ideals. Given the poor postal connections with Hankow, I am presenting this report directly to the Foreign Ministry.

ROSEN

7 FEBRUARY

After first gathering up the remnants of discarded uniforms and equipment lying about in the streets, the Japanese have now set fire to all the wrecked cars that are strewn about—having first removed any valuable parts.

Dr. Hsü arrives with news that the Japanese shot and killed four Chinese near Lotus Lake last night. Cause: An old man evidently wanted to fetch a ricksha he had hidden near his house. When his wife and two other relatives hurried out to assist him, they, too, were cut down.

This morning, led by two workers for the Red Swastika Society, Mr. Sone and I visited a somewhat out-of-the-way field in the vicinity of Sikiang Road, where the bodies of 124 Chinese have been fished out of two ponds, all of them shot, about half of them civilians. The victims had all had their hands tied, were then mowed down by machine guns, doused with gasoline, and set on fire. But when the burning took too long, the half-burned bodies were simply tossed into the ponds. Another pond nearby is said to contain 23 corpses, just as all the ponds in Nanking have been similarly contaminated.

Mills and I are joined by the daughter and sisters of the Chinese woman who was shot, and we drive to the scene of the crime, very close to Major Haub's former residence, to verify in person Dr. Hsü's report about the murder of four people.

Out in an open field we found three corpses, that of a woman, lying right beside that of two men, and the body of another man about ten yards away. Between the bodies lay an improvised litter, that is, a plank suspended on ropes from two poles, which the two men—whom the old man's wife had called—intended to use to remove the body of her husband. And once again these are very poor people: farmers, who owned a small plot, part of which they had already plowed. Their wretched clay huts were empty. According to the daughter, the mother had carried circa ten dollars, their en-

The Japanese army attempted to destroy the evidence of the slaughter by wholesale burning of bodies.

Chinese families had meager means with which to transport their injured to the hospital or their dead for burial. This woman is being carried in a basket strung from a pole.

tire fortune, on her person. Nothing was found among her clothes, however. Mills and I were profoundly shocked. I pressed ten dollars into the daughter's hand, who kept bowing but never shed a tear, so that she would at least have the money. Before we drove home, the murdered woman's sisters threw a handful of dirt on each of the bodies.

8 FEBRUARY

At 8 o'clock this morning, the women and girls are all standing in crowded rows along the middle path in our garden. It is the only open spot left in the garden. They wait patiently until I finish breakfast and am about to set out for committee headquarters. As I come outside they all fall to their knees and cannot be persuaded to get up from the cold cement path until I have given the following speech, translated by Liu the chauffeur, whom they trust implicitly.

> The Japanese and the Autonomous Government Committee have publicly announced that you must leave the refugee camps, the Zone, today. I personally have nothing against your remaining here. I shall not chase you away! But what can I, a single foreigner, do if the Japanese soldiers march in here and force you to leave my house and my garden? You must realize that my own power is too small to protect all of you in the long run.
>   Nevertheless, I will try to prevent the Japanese from entering. Please let me go to the German embassy now to speak to its representatives.

"Ta meo banfang," Liu calls out. "There's nothing you can do. He knows no other solution." At that, they all sit down on the ground and let me go.

I had intended to drive to the Japanese embassy this morning with Dr. Bates and take one of the Japanese officials out to the murder site in Pei Tse Ting. When I see about 200 Japanese soldiers deployed not far from my house, I fear that the military intends to clear the Zone by force. So I quickly drive to the American embassy to mobilize all the foreigners to stand guard at the camps and then go see Dr. Rosen at the German embassy, who is more than willing to drive back with me to observe any forcible entry of my grounds and buildings by the Japanese. Thank God nothing happens! The deployment of Japanese troops was for a passing Japanese general!

After a quiet chat at my house, we went to the American embassy to talk with Mr. Allison about how the Japanese had not attacked the Zone,

The corpses of a family slain by a Japanese soldier. The only survivors of this family of thirteen were two girls, aged eight and four, who hid under blankets beside the body of their mother for two weeks and lived from rice crusts left in a pan. (See Pastor Magee's report, p. 281: Document 16, Case No. 5.)

and then five of us—Dr. Rosen, Mr. Smythe, Sperling, Jimmy Wang, and I—drove out to the murder site in Pei Tse Ting. In the meantime, the four bodies had been wrapped in mats and lay ready to be buried on a little nearby hill. Jimmy hunted up a Chinese man from the neighborhood, who gave us the following account of the incident:

The old Chinese man, allegedly trying to rescue his ricksha, had in fact been trying to bring two chairs from a thatch hut to his house. It was on account of these two chairs, looted or bought cheaply somewhere, that the Japanese soldiers shot him. He lay gravely wounded in the field. When his wife (or sister?) came to his aid with two male relatives, hoping to take him away, they were all shot.

9 FEBRUARY

The Japanese embassy invited us to a concert yesterday evening. Dr. Rosen declined flat-out to take part. Our committee made the best of a bad situation!

Military Band Concert at the Japanese Embassy,
3 p.m., 8 February 1938

Programme:
Conductor: S. Ohonuma.

1. Overture:	Light Cavalry.	F. v. Suppé.
2. Danube Waves Waltz.		V. Ivanovici.
3. One Step:	Chinatown My Chinatown.	J. Schwalz.
4. Nagauta:	Oimatu.	arr. S. Ohonuma.
5. Fantasie:	Aida.	Verdi.
6. Overture:	William Tell.	G. Rossini.
7. March:	Varela no Guntai.	Military Band.

It was a tall order to expect men who have been walking in the morning among Chinese murdered by Japanese soldiers to sit that same afternoon among those soldiers and enjoy a concert, but anything is possible in this dishonest world. So as not to lose face that's been lost often enough and for the sake of famous East Asian courtesy, we committee members appeared almost to a man!

Scharffenberg and Hürter, Allison, the American consul, and the English representative Jeffery were also on hand, and he and I patiently let ourselves be photographed with a cute geisha between us for the Domei.[49]

Mr. Fukui asks me to visit him this morning at the Japanese embassy in regard to my request for permission to travel to Shanghai and back. Presumably he wants to lay it upon my soul yet again that in Shanghai I am allowed to report only good things about the Japanese. If he thought I would contradict him, he's got his head screwed on wrong; but he doesn't, anymore than I do. He's sees through me well enough to know that I'll give him all the false promises he wants to hear. Whether I pay them any mind later on is another matter. I'm sure he doesn't believe that himself. To judge from the company's most recent letter, a return here is out of the question, but I'll keep that to myself for now.

And now comes the huge job of closing up shop. Chang, our houseboy, just shook his head dubiously when I said that I would have to go to Germany and needed crates.

"Wooden?" Chang asks. "There's not enough wood even for coffins."

Despite everything, I shall try to drum up a few boards. All our furniture and the office setup will have to remain behind. Nobody knows what will become of it all. I'm saddest about the oil paintings; but what's a man to do?

10 FEBRUARY

Fukui, whom I tried to find at the Japanese embassy to no avail all day yesterday, paid a call on me last night. He actually managed to threaten me: "If the newspapers in Shanghai report bad things, you will have the Japanese army against you," he said.

According to him, Kröger has had some very bad things to say. As proof of Kröger's bad attitude, he specified a long telegram from London that, so it's believed, came from Hong Kong and is being attributed to him.

In reply to my question as to what I then could say in Shanghai, Fukui said, "We leave that to your discretion."

My response: "It looks as if you expect me to say something like this to the reporters: 'The situation in Nanking is improving every day. Please don't print any more atrocity stories about the vile behavior of Japanese soldiers, because then you'll only be pouring oil on a fire of disagreement that already exists between the Japanese and Europeans.' "

"Yes," he said, simply beaming, "that would be splendid!"

"Fine, then give me an opportunity to speak with your General Amaya and Major Hungo, who is said to speak excellent German, so that I may discuss these matters with them in person. I am very much in favor of at last establishing a better relationship and friendly cooperation between the Japanese military and our committee.

"Why do you refuse entry visas to the foreign doctors and nurses that we've asked to help staff Kulou Hospital? Why can't we ship any food here from Shanghai? Why do you forbid us to visit the Red Cross hospital in the Foreign Ministry, for which our committee is providing the food?"

His answer: shrugs and the repeated statement, "If you report bad things, you will annoy the Japanese military and will not be allowed to return to Nanking!"

To my inquiry about whether I might take a Chinese servant with me on the trip, his answer is: "Yes, but he definitely may not return to Nanking!"

From a Report of the Nanking Office of the German Embassy (Rosen) to the Foreign Ministry

10 February 1938

Re: Film documentary of the atrocities of Japanese troops in Nanking

During the Japanese reign of terror in Nanking—which, by the way, continues to this day to a considerable degree—the Reverend John Magee, a member of the American Episcopal Church Mission who has been here for almost a quarter of a century, took motion pictures that eloquently bear witness to the atrocities committed by the Japanese.

Mr. Magee, who has asked that his name be mentioned only in strictest confidence, has worked to find a place for Chinese refugees in the home of a German advisor. He is more open to things German than most of his colleagues are, primarily because his late sister was married to an Austrian diplomat. It is characteristic of his selfless and well-meaning intentions that he is not interested in gaining any commercial advantage from his footage, and that he has offered the embassy a copy of it if we will cover the cost of having it made by the Kodak office in Shanghai, from where it can then be sent by secure mail to the Foreign Ministry. Enclosed is a description, in English, of the events chronicled in various segments of the footage. These present, as does the film itself, such shocking documentary evidence that I would like to request that the film, along with a word-for-word translation of the descriptions, be shown to the Führer and Reich Chancellor.

One will have to wait and see whether the highest officers in the Japanese army succeed, as they have indicated, in stopping the activities of their troops, which continue even today. General Amaya conjures up memories of the Russo-Japanese war, and indeed at that time there was a spirit of true discipline and self-denial in the Japanese officers corps. Troops will always be the image of their officers.

A younger officers corps that has grown up glorifying political murder and for which the geisha trade seems more important than the old virtues of the samurai can demand nothing better of its rank and file than what has taken place here in Nanking. If Japan wishes to bring light to the East, it must first shed light in all the darkest corners of its own nation and do some serious housecleaning.

The expenses associated with the acquiring of this film will be presented by the embassy in Hankow in reference to this report.

ROSEN[50]

11 FEBRUARY

Our coolie Tsian-la set out on a pilgrimage to his home village today. Three hours outside the city. I am very worried whether his family is still alive and what shape he will find them in. Reports say it's been murder and mayhem out there.

We've just got news that a soldier of the Japanese army, famous—as General Amaya put it—for its good discipline, forced his way into a house where a woman and her two daughters were living, intending to rape the daughters. When they resisted, he locked the three women inside the house and set it on fire. One of the daughters burned to death and the mother's face was badly burned. The case is being investigated.

Sindberg arrives bearing an even worse story. This time, however, we're dealing with Chinese bandits, four of them, who suspected one of their countrymen of having hidden some money, so they slowly swung him by his arms and legs back and forth over a fire, roasting him, trying to get him to reveal the hiding-place.

We are indeed in Asia! But homesickness wells up when you hear of too many such atrocities.

Good news from Shanghai. They've shipped us 100 sacks of the green beans we begged for to fight beriberi.

Chang is out looking for wood. I would like to have some crates made that I can pack full with all sorts of odds and ends. Who knows if we'll ever see Nanking again! Carlowitz is said to have an empty crate, which Sperling is going to pilfer for me.

About 1 o'clock: *tiffin* with Dr. Rosen and the officers of the English gunboat *Cricket*. Nice people. What a shame that I've not finished my packing yet. Otherwise I could have boarded the *Cricket* for Shanghai tomorrow.

Reverend John Magee has taken motion pictures of the atrocities. Dr. Rosen is having a copy of the film made in Shanghai, which he then wants to forward to Berlin. I'm supposed to get another copy later, too. I saw some of the casualties (shown in the film) and was able to speak with a few before they died. I was shown the bodies of some of them in the morgue at Kulou Hospital.

Memorandum of Chancellor Scharffenberg
for the Embassy in Hankow

10 February 1938

The Japanese have kept us very busy socially of late. On 3 February all the foreign officials were once again invited to dinner by Embassy Councilor Shinrokuro Hidaka, with no military present, only General Consul Fukui and an attaché. The English came very late.

Since the gendarmes had already knocked off for the evening, the two English officials had to negotiate for a half hour until they were permitted to drive to the Japanese embassy. These officials are calm and cool by temperament, and they saw the incident more from its comic side.

The evening was spent over good food and good wine—the burgundy too chilled, however—a very calm, restrained atmosphere. Councilor Hidaka worked the same phrase into his conversation with the three legation heads—each individually: "Let's not talk about official matters today!"

On 5 February, all officials were again invited to a tea, as guests of garrison commander Major General Amaya. Councilor Hidaka, all the Japanese officials, including Major Hungo, and a few other officers were on hand. We conversed very amiably for a good while, when suddenly it got very quiet and formal, everyone took a seat, put away cigarettes, and Amaya put on his glasses, plucked a paper from his pocket, and gave a speech, which the young, pleasant, and always helpful attaché Fukuda translated sentence by sentence. Unfortunately he was not very well prepared, and so the translation was a bit halting. The upshot was that the general, otherwise a very genial, pudgy gentleman, really pitched into us Westerners. His thesis was: Everything would have gone far better in Nanking without any Westerners. The Chinese had crept in under the Westerners' coattails and by trusting in our intervention, had dared to defy the Japanese. In Yangchow, where he had been the local commander until now, everything had fallen into place wonderfully after a few days, and commercial life had scarcely been interrupted. The high point of his speech was: "Please don't interfere in my dealings with the Chinese!" I think he's right in a certain sense, but he wouldn't hand over a copy of the speech.

The Safety Committee has long been a thorn in the side of the Japanese, but since 4 February a large number of Chinese have in fact left the camps and found shelter somewhere in the city. In my view, Herr Rabe as its chairman has indeed achieved extraordinary things, but he has let himself be lulled far too much by the Americans and is helping promote

American interests and missionaries who are out to catch souls *en gros.* He could have resigned his office on 4 February, the date set for clearing the Safety Zone, and having arrived at the zenith of his excellent work and retiring in a blaze of glory, could have vanished from Nanking. Rabe, here endeth the tale of thy glory!

Rabe realizes as much himself, and is trying to get Japanese permission to go to Shanghai, but he is still actively trying to counter the bloody excesses of Japanese looters, which have unfortunately increased of late. To my mind, this should not concern us Germans, particularly since one can clearly see that the Chinese, once left to depend solely on the Japanese, immediately fraternize. And as for all these excesses, one hears only one side of it, after all.

All the local Germans—with the exception of Rabe—have grasped the fact that Asiatic warfare is simply very different from warfare among us! Since there is no taking of prisoners, savageries necessarily ensue. Much as in the Thirty Years War, looting, etc. is simply a matter of course, and that things are especially bad for women probably has its roots in the massacre at Tungchou: The gruesome murder of Japanese women and children there has to be revenged a thousandfold.

And as sad as things may still be here, one can assume they will improve as soon as the refugees have cleared out of the Safety Zone. General Matsui was here recently to establish order.

But one also observes Amaya's hand in things, particularly since he has had all the wrecks removed from the streets—overturned trucks, buses, and countless vehicles of all sorts, most of them junks, are doused with gasoline and burned, and what's left is hauled away. A good many troops are working in the city, clearing away dangling electrical, telephone, and telegraph wires and stringing new ones.

And so to that extent things have begun to improve. And the Red Swastika Society has received permission to bury the countless corpses still lying about. From one single pond near Dr. Schröder's house, for example, they fished out over 120 bodies, their hands tied behind them with wire. Herr Rabe was there and saw it all. I myself have frequently seen Japanese soldiers fetch water in their cooking pots from these pools. Bon appétit! —One must fear the worst once warmer weather arrives.

At 4:00 p.m. on 8 February, all Westerners were assembled in the now familiar rooms of the Japanese embassy to hear a military concert. The band was seated in the large dining room, all 42 of them, brought here from Tokyo for the occasion; they played well, indeed much better than the grumblers among us had predicted. The conductor, Captain S. Ohonuma, who studied music in Paris, did a very nice job and gratified us with a few encores, some of them compositions of his own.

The foreigners sat in rows in the salon; after we had taken our seats we were first served tea by some of the geishas from the "embassy staff." It was a feast for sore eyes, since the four loveliest had been put into service; and then the concert began. Program enclosed.

After No. 4 there was an intermission, the time filled with a sumptuous buffet set up out on the verandah. The long table sagged under all the cakes, candies, pastries, fruits, etc., like some imperial Russian *zakuska*. Everything for show. The geishas served tea again and as they offered us cigarettes, especially as they lit them, assumed the most charming poses, which were then captured by countless press photographers, so that an astonished world might later behold with its own eyes the cordial relations between the Japanese and Westerners in Nanking. That was the reverse side of the coin. The cloven foot!

Among the many missionaries, etc. I also saw Mr. McCallum, who is Embassy Councilor Fischer's[51] landlord.

P. SCHARFFENBERG

12 FEBRUARY

It really is high time for me to get out of here. At 7 o'clock this morning, Chang brought in Fung, a friend from Tientsin, who is watching the house of an American here and whose wife is expecting a baby, which for three days now has been struggling to see the light of this mournful world, and you really can't blame him. The mother's life is apparently in danger. Birth definitely needs to be induced. And they come to me of all people!

"I'm not a doctor, Chang. And I'm not a *kuei ma*,[52] either. I'm the 'mayor,' and I don't bring other people's children into the world. Get the woman to Kulou Hospital at once!"

"Yes," Chang says, "that all true; but you must come, otherwise won't work, otherwise woman not get into hospital, she die and baby, too. You must come, then everything good. Mother lives and baby, too!"

And that puts an end to that—"Idiots, the whole lot of you!"

And so I had to go along, and who would believe it: As I enter the house, a baby boy is born, and the mother laughs, and the baby cries, and everyone is happy; and Chang, the monkey, has been proved right yet again. And the whole lark cost me ten dollars besides, because I had to bring the poor lad something. If this story gets around, I'm ruined. Just think, there are 250,000 refugees in this city!

5 P.M.

A visit by Chinese pilots. The entire sky is full of airplanes, and the Japanese antiaircraft battalion fires away with everything it's got. But nobody hits a thing! And just as well, since no one bothers to take shelter. The Chinese believe that air raids by their fellow countrymen can't touch them.

Mr. Fitch returns from Shanghai today at noon with "our navy friends," bringing sausage, cheese, insulin, and a lot of letters, among them a picture that Mutti cut out along with an article from a Berlin newspaper, celebrating "Rabe, Mayor of Nanking." Ah, if only I could retire on a mayor's pension!

Shortly before the city was taken by the Japanese, two functionaries of the Chinese government sought and were given refuge in my house. They came equipped with bags full of money and on various occasions gave my servants tips that were far beyond reason.

Since Chiang Kai-shek had promised our committee a donation of 100,000 dollars in toto, of which we were able, with much difficulty, to collect 80,000, I demanded a written statement from these two gentlemen that

Members of the Red Swastika Society (the local branch of the Red Cross) formed details to help with the collection and burial of bodies.

they were in possession of no other moneys for the International Committee of the Nanking Safety Zone.

John Rabe's diary includes the requested statement, in which the two Chinese claim that the government had given them $50,000, which they had then passed on, dividing it between the Safety Zone Committee and the International Committee of the Red Cross in Nanking. They declared that they were in possession of no other moneys for these organizations.

The immediate cause for my making these inquiries is that a bundle of bank notes in the amount of 5,000 dollars suddenly appeared on the desk in my office one day, and with it the following note: "For you honourable deed of saving poor souls."

I immediately put the money into the committee's treasury and gave the two somewhat astounded Chinese an official receipt in that amount.

13 FEBRUARY

In addition, I received the following telegram confirmation, likewise by way of the American embassy.

Siemens China Co.
Hong Kong Branch   Hong Kong, 1.12.37

We received the following telegram from Shanghai with the request to forward it to you: "Not in agreement with measures request immediate departure Hankow to attend to interests of Siemens China Co." Hong Kong Branch

This afternoon a service at the Ping Tsang Hsian, Dr. Bates preached a wonderful sermon about Abraham Lincoln, and much of what Lincoln had to say bears directly on our present time. Lincoln's Proclamation for a Day of Fasting from 1863 was read.

It should be noted in regard to the confirmation of the company's telegram, which is dated 1 December 1937, that I never received it. They did telegraph me to advise me not to put my life at any greater risk and to join the staff of the German embassy if they left Nanking. Ultimately they requested I telegraph them my plans. My answer read:

"Am remaining here as chairman of the International Committee for establishing a refugee zone for over 200,000 noncombatants." And as I now learn from this telegram confirmation, they didn't agree with that. But, as I said, this telegram never reached me.

What a mess! I truly am a "Lame Jack." [53] I went and did the right thing, and now the company doesn't like it!

It can be assumed, however, that the firm probably telegraphed that particular message to me in order to prevent me from putting my life in any danger. On the other hand, it's a good thing I never received it. As a well-disciplined company man, I might very well have changed my decision at the last moment and boarded the Jardines *Hulk*. Moreover, I tend to doubt whether the rest of the employees of Siemens China Co. in Nanking and a few other poor devils would still be alive had I cut and run.

Contrary to expectation, I've managed to come up with some crates. There's a carpenter among my *lao bai xings*, [54] that is, among the refugees in my garden, and through his connections I've been able to round up 20 crates, and not just crates, but straw as well. For the grand sum of two dollars and by pouring rain, several of the refugees carried three cartloads of straw from well beyond the Han Hsi Men city gate, and the carpenter is helping me pack free of charge. You see: The friendship of these poor people is worth something after all, sometimes, as in this case, worth a great deal, for wood has all but vanished from the marketplace.

North China Daily News
Shanghai from 30 Jan. 1938 (Excerpted by John Rabe)

Japanese Envoy Is Skeptical

London, January 29. The Japanese ambassador in London, Mr. Shigeru Yoshida, today said in an interview with the "Daily Sketch" that he "deeply deplored" reports reaching Europe accusing Japanese soldiers of "unspeakable atrocities" and added that it was "unthinkable that our troops would forget their traditions." . . .

"Such conduct is utterly foreign to our noble traditions, and there is nothing in the whole history of Japan which shows any precedent for such conduct. . . . Our army is well disciplined."

14 FEBRUARY

Since we've had a few cases of beriberi here, we had asked Shanghai to ship us 100 tons of green beans, which were expected to arrive today aboard the steamer *Wantung*. The Japanese navy in Shanghai had given permission to ship the beans and likewise to have them unloaded in Hsiakwan. All that was needed was the consent of the Japanese army in Nanking, which then promptly refused it.

At noon today the radio reported the incident from Shanghai and presented the matter as if our International Committee's "lack of cooperation" with the Autonomous Government Committee had caused problems with the shipment, for which only the Autonomous Government Committee can be given authorization.

The Japanese claim that they know of no cases of beriberi in Nanking,

The telegram from Siemens instructing John Rabe to leave Nanking.

which is not at all surprising, since they've showed no concern whatever about public health here.

15 FEBRUARY

Lung and Chow[55] left my house yesterday evening; they intend to leave the city today. I don't know how. They haven't volunteered their plans to me, and I haven't asked. Our friendship has in fact been ruptured. All the same, I wish them a good journey home to Hong Kong. But I have no wish ever to see these people again.

I am now busy packing. It's not an easy task: My health is not up to par, I'm sleeping only about two hours a night. Maybe it has something to do with my diabetes, but so what! You simply do what must be done. Things will turn out all right.

The "green bean problem" is not yet solved. The Japanese demand that we hand the beans over to the Autonomous Committee, no questions asked, otherwise they will not be allowed in. The beans are consigned to Kulou Hospital, which means that the Japanese are trying to prevent the delivery of foodstuffs to a private institution. Mr. Allison is spending all his time trying to bring the Japanese around.

The mass burial mounds dominated the landscape in all directions around Nanking.

A column of women being brought to shelter at the university.

I've just heard that the camp managers have all decided to send a telegram to Siemens in Shanghai, asking the company to allow me to remain on here. I don't like that at all.

My nerves are pretty well shot, and I long for my vacation trip. I'm also afraid that the firm could get the idea that I was behind the telegram (from the camp managers), which, of course, is not the case.

Except for my furniture, I've packed up all the odds and ends and am now sitting in a half-empty house devoid of every comfort. I'll have to leave the large pieces of furniture here under Han's care for now, likewise the crates I've packed.

LATER

What shocks me most about a report by our committee that cannot be made public is the observation that although the Red Swastika Society has thus far been burying about 200 bodies a day, there are still 30,000 to be dealt with, most of them in Hsiakwan. Those numbers tell the story of the last Chinese troops that crowded into Hsiakwan and were unable to escape across the Yangtze.

I'm touched by the way all my American friends, one after the other, have been inviting me to a farewell dinner, when they themselves are short on rations. And now here comes Miss Minnie Vautrin, who wants me to come to a farewell tea. Miss Vautrin won my highest and very special respect in those worst December days when I saw her marching through the city at the head of 400 fleeing women and girls, bringing them to safety at the Ginling University camp.

Mr. Jeffrey, the deputy at the British embassy, promised that he'd speak on my behalf with the British navy, so that I can travel to Shanghai either on the Butterfield & Swire steamer *Wantung* on 22 February or with the English gunboat *Aphis* two days later, together with the servant that the Japanese embassy has allowed me to take along.

16 FEBRUARY

Jimmy Wang, from the Autonomous Government Committee and at the same time a (secret) member of our organization, tells me that the Chinese have decided to buy our headquarters and give the building to the committee as a gift. Very fine idea.

Mr. Allison from the American embassy arrives with news that the "green bean problem" has now been settled. The beans can be imported and distributed both inside and outside the Zone.

From a Memorandum of Chancellor Scharffenberg for the German Embassy in Hankow

Re: Situation in Nanking on 17 February 1938

We were awakened early this morning by the friendly bombs of the Chinese and then a long sequence of flak fire by the Japanese. The sun was so bright, however, that we could not see much.

On 15 inst. we were given permission to drive out to the area of the Sun Yat-sen mausoleum, and we got as far as the swimming pool. The lovely willows along the road near the pagoda have all been chopped down and almost all the villas have been burned. We could not walk in the area because there were still too many corpses, blackened and partially eaten by dogs.

On the trip back we entered the palace of President Lin Sen. The building has not been burned and in time it can probably be restored, despite the great damage to all its façades from the shelling; it looks horrible, and it really is a shame. It's hard to believe, but in the reception room upstairs, there on the splendid marble floor, lay the cadaver of a pony, half decomposed and gnawed away. Which also explained why the marble staircase was in such bad shape.

On our drive through the city some life and movement were to be seen, though mostly just the older generation. The committee claims that about 100,000 are in the city now, that is, they've left the camps. We even saw a ricksha and a horse-drawn wagon. Unfortunately there are cases of beriberi among the refugees now, and the committee acted swiftly to ship beans from Shanghai. I'm very pessimistic about epidemics, especially because of the water supply, and then there's the garbage, and finally still too many bodies lying about. The weather is very changeable at present. When it's as warm as it is today, you can't go out on the street for the stench of corpses. Things will get better only after the Zone has emptied out more. To illustrate conditions in Nanking: The Rev. Forster had reported the theft of a piano to the Japanese; he was then taken to a warehouse in which there was a collection of 17 instruments of all kinds. Was his one of those?

"No!"

Then would he please select a replacement. Forster declined.

Nanking is black as pitch at night, and of course there's no street lighting of any sort.

P. SCHARFFENBERG

17 FEBRUARY

Mr. Ritchie, the postal commissioner, is about to reopen the post office, with the Japanese. Until now he's had no success reopening in any of the destroyed areas.

The farewell tea at Miss Minnie Vautrin's was very nice. Besides Dr. Bates and Fitch, Mr. Ritchie, Mr. Allison, and Dr. Rosen had been invited. There were some very lovely things to eat, but saying goodbye was dreadful!

The refugees at the university—there are still 3,000 women and girls there—besieged the door and demanded that I promise not to leave them in the lurch, that is, not to leave Nanking. They all went down on their knees, weeping and wailing and literally hanging on to my coattails when I tried to depart. I had to leave my car behind, and once I had fought my way to the gate, which was instantly closed behind me, had to return home on foot. This all sounds very exaggerated and lugubrious. But anyone who has witnessed the misery here understands what the protection we've been able to give these poor people really means. It was all so obvious, none of it has anything to do with heroics.

18 FEBRUARY

Committee meeting: The "Green Bean Problem" is finally settled.

My suggestion to name Mr. Mills vice chairman, and/or acting chairman is accepted. I will remain chairman for about two months, and if I have not returned to Nanking by then, presumably Mills will then officially be made chairman. We decide to change the name of the Zone Committee to Nanking International Relief Committee. Mr. Sone is named the successor to Mr. Fitch, who is returning to America. Mr. Smythe will continue to fill the posts of both treasurer and secretary but is to be relieved of one of them later on.

I remain as before a committee member of the International Red Cross in Nanking.

Fukuda pays me a call at headquarters to tell me that my trip to Shanghai has been given final approval. He doesn't know anything about my being allowed to take a servant along, but will make inquiries. Maybe I'll take Tsai with me.

19 FEBRUARY

I receive news from the British embassy that I can leave on the English gunboat *Bee* on Wednesday, 23 February. I gratefully accept. Mr. Jeffery will find out if I can ship my 53 crates of household goods to Shanghai on the *Wantung*. The furniture must remain here in any case, unfortunately all of it still not packed because I couldn't find any crates for it.

20 FEBRUARY

The Chinese on the committee want to hold a large reception in my honor at headquarters tomorrow afternoon. I've got to put together a speech fast. Everyone shall be given their due. The Americans, all of whom have been invited to the reception of course, want to give yet another special reception for all the embassies at eight o'clock tomorrow evening. That pleases me especially: Even the Japanese are invited. It's doubtful if Dr. Rosen will come. He says he doesn't want to spend any more time with these "murderers." For a diplomat, that's going way too far, but it's hard to even approach him about it.

21 FEBRUARY

What a shame I'm so unmusical! Reverend Jas. H. McCallum has composed a choral piece in my honor, entitled *Nanking Nan Ming*, and has also written the text: "We want beans for our breakfast, beans for our lunch." I didn't know the dear old parson, whom the Japanese came close to stabbing to death, had such a sense of humor.

4 : 00 P.M.

Large reception at the headquarters of the Safety Zone Committee. I am given an official letter of thanks in Chinese and English, copies of which are to be sent to Siemens China Co. as well as to Dr. Rosen of the German embassy. I respond to the various speeches in which I am praised more than I merit.

My speech is received enthusiastically, both by the Americans and the Chinese, who ask for the text so that it can be translated into Chinese. The Chinese want my autograph. They have brought along huge sheets of white paper that I'm supposed to fill up somehow. I am embarrassed by my lack of poetical texts, but I manage tolerably enough by taking refuge in the poetry albums of my youth.

7 P.M.

A cozy farewell dinner surrounded by my American friends. Then, at eight o'clock, a reception for the German, American, and Japanese embassies.

The English representative, Mr. Jeffery, could not come because his Japanese guard will not let him out after eight in the evening. Mr. Jeffery has protested at length but is too polite to take energetic action against such nonsense. Dr. Rosen, Scharffenberg, and Hürter were there from the German embassy; Mr. Allison, Espey, and McFadyen came from the American. I had to be careful in formulating my speech because of the Japanese.

22 FEBRUARY

Mr. Loh Fu Hsian, whose real name is Captain Huang Kuanghan, an air force officer and the brother of Colonel Huang of the OMEA (Officers

Moral Endeavor Association), has, with some help from Han, been given a pass for the trip to Shanghai. I will smuggle him aboard the *Bee* as my servant, and that way he can finally escape from danger, because he's been hiding in my house since the fall of Nanking. Capt. Huang, who shot down several Japanese aircraft, was ill when the city was conquered by the Japanese. He attempted to flee, but could no longer get across the Yangtze. While trying to swim one of the arms of the river, he lost his close friend. He, however, managed to get back through the city wall and into the Safety Zone.

I spend the whole morning packing. My *lao bai xing* have dragged in still more wood—all of it pilfered, I'm sure. Some of the planks come directly from a construction site. They're still smeared with cement.

I have received permission from the Japanese embassy to ship my crates to Shanghai on the *Wantung*. And so all that's left is the task of getting them on board, which I'll have to leave to Mr. Han and my American friends here, since I shall have already left for Nanking when the *Wantung* arrives.

1 P.M.

Tiffin with Dr. Rosen and Mills, Dr. Bates, Miss Vautrin, Magee, Forster, Hürter, and Scharffenberg.

8 P.M.

Dinner alone with Dr. Rosen, whose heart is heavy with the problems of his current fate and who tells me some of them.

Radio news at 10 o'clock: Germany has recognized Manchukuo. The report goes on to say that our Ambassador Trautmann, currently in Hankow, has thus been put in a difficult situation vis-à-vis the Chinese government. We're afraid he may very well resign, although nothing is mentioned about that. It's very difficult here to see through the situation at home, but: Right or wrong—my country!

23 FEBRUARY, 8 A.M.

All the Americans come to say goodbye. Sperling, Han, and a few of the Chinese from the electricity works take Captain Huang and me to Hsiakwan.

At 9 o'clock on the dot, Mr. Jeffery and Williams from the British embassy appear, and with their help I am allowed without further ado to

board a launch from the British gunboat *Bee*. On board the *Bee*, lying at anchor about two miles upriver, I am received cordially by the commander,
Captain Armstrong, and his first officer, Mr. Brain-Nicols. The launch is pi-
loted by a young officer, Sub-lieutenant Pearson. The fourth guest in the officers mess is the doctor, Surgeon Lieutenant Colonel Joynt. I'm very happy
there's a doctor on board. I'm not feeling very well, I've caught a cold that
has settled in my bones.

Shortly before departure, Dr. Bates brings me a résumé from the press. I
still have to think about what details I want to make public. In any event, I
don't want to see the committee get into any difficulty because of it.

LATER (ON BOARD THE HMS *BEE*)

HMS *Bee* weighs anchor at 9 a.m. We pass Ching Kiang in the afternoon.
Since by order of the Japanese there can be no traffic on the Yangtze at
night, we anchor this evening near Kou-An.

I am being treated splendidly on board. The cabin, meals, and service
are excellent. The Chinese servants on board are apparently all in a puzzle
over Mr. Huang (or Loh Fu Hsian). It's obvious that he's not a servant, but
we're keeping mum. The *Bee*'s officers think he's my "comprador."[56] I'm
feeling somewhat better.

From a Memorandum of Chancellor Scharffenberg for the German Embassy in Hankow

Re: Situation in Nanking on 4 March 1938

On 23 February Herr John Rabe left Nanking, after being honored by
both Chinese and foreign nationals at several impressive and dignified
gatherings, with many good and stirring farewell speeches expressing
great gratitude for his service on behalf of the Safety Zone. He had to
give a few speeches himself, and especially at the celebration held by the
American missionaries and the foreign nationals he found the right
words to say to Japanese general consul Fukui about the support to be
given the work of the International Relief Committee, as it is now called.

On 27 February, both the Austrian Rupert Hatz and Zaudig the Balt
left town. Richard Hempel, the hotelier, and Eduard Sperling, the "chief
of police" of the Safety Zone, are the only Germans left.

The Safety Zone is now 50 percent cleared. Until night falls, you now
see a good many Chinese in the city. But only an occasional ricksha, no
pony wagons, though now and then a donkey pulling a cart.

Dr. Brady, an American physician, has arrived, and the Relief Committee has assigned him to inspect all 36 refugee camps and inoculate everyone. He has inoculated several thousand people, and Police Chief Sperling has been asked to work with him, to make sure that all the camps are cleaned. Sperling is organizing a kind of "refuse disposal" because you can scarcely imagine how filthy it all is here; the garbage is piled high in vacant lots between buildings in the residential areas, and it's even worse outside.

They are now hard at work removing bodies from the center of the city. The Red Swastika Society has been given permission to bury the 30,000 bodies in Hsiakwan. They manage 600 a day. The bodies are wrapped in lime and straw mats, with only the legs hanging out, then driven back into the city and buried in mass graves also filled with lime. It's said that circa 10,000 have been dealt with.

The garrison commander, Major General Amaya, keeps a tight rein on things, and we no longer hear of atrocities, and order is also being restored in general. All the trees that the Chinese chopped down for barricades against tanks have been removed, so that the roads near the Sun Yat-sen mausoleum are free again. But in that entire area, which is probably as large as the city enclosed by the long city wall, you do not see a single farmer in the fields. The entire harvest there is ruined.

War equipment is being gathered up and taken away as well; it is all piled in Hsiakwan, along a line from the train station to the charred remains of the Bridge Hotel—but we are not allowed there under any circumstances. Thousands of vehicles of every sort, steamrollers, etc. are parked there, waiting to be shipped to Japan, some as scrap metal. But the fire trucks that were also commandeered have been returned to the Chinese.

The Japanese have opened the little movie house on the side street next to the Chinese newspaper offices on Potsdamer Platz as a Chinese theater. The Japanese pay every actor, believe it or not, ten cents a day.

Since 1 March the *Nanking Kung Pao* has been appearing, a small double-column sheet, but very neatly printed, containing Japanese notices put together by Chinese editors. Price: 2 cents.

The number of Japanese canteen owners and petty merchants continues to grow. All in all, conditions here have improved. A major disadvantage, of course, is that the water mains do not yet function very well. The upper stories get only a trickle now and then.

Herr Hempel and Herr Sperling are thinking of reopening the Foo Chong Hotel at some point. They are banking on Japanese officers as hotel guests, and on the banquets that the Chinese on the Autonomous Committee will hold for the Japanese.

The Japanese still make entering and leaving the city difficult, i.e. for Westerners. Attaché Fukuda was in Shanghai again, traveling by car this time; it took eight hours and he claims the road is in good order once more. But we're in a mouse hole here, and the cat is Japanese!

P. SCHARFFENBERG

24 FEBRUARY (ON BOARD THE HMS *BEE*)

Around 11 o'clock we pass the forts at Kian Yin. According to newspaper reports, the devastation should be much worse. You can see Chinese working in the fields along the banks. We pass three wrecked warships. A Japanese gunboat, a Chinese gunboat, and a Chinese cruiser, the *Hai Yin*.

25 FEBRUARY

I radio both the American general consulate to inform Fitch and the German general consulate to inform Siemens China Co. of my arrival. Fitch is leaving for America tomorrow afternoon. I would very much like to speak with him before he departs and give him his mail from Nanking.

28 FEBRUARY

At 2 p.m. yesterday afternoon we arrived in Shanghai. As we passed the *Gneisenau,* which was lying at anchor ready to depart, I heard someone call my name but could not discover from which of the many portholes the call came. Mr. Fitch was on board as well. I wasn't able to get his mail to him because by the time I landed at 3:15, the *Gneisenau* had already pulled out and could no longer be reached. I spotted Mutti waiting for me as we passed the customs jetty. But she didn't recognize me from that distance.

And now I'm sitting nice and cozy in Shanghai, and feel "proud as a Piefke" when the victorious troops marched into Berlin.[57] Everyone thinks I'm a hero, and that can be very annoying; for I can see nothing heroic about me or within me.

With all the hymns of praise being sung in my honor, I'm reminded of the lovely poem that tells of a lad from Hamburg who saves one of his buddies from drowning, and when the father of the rescued lad calls on him that evening to thank him for saving his son's life, the lad says: "Saved his life?—Oh crap!" and rudely rolls over on his other side.

BACK HOME AGAIN AFTER THIRTY YEARS IN CHINA

On 16 March 1938, Mutti and I boarded the *Conte Bianca Mano* for home. Captain Huang, who had preceded us, was waiting for us at the dock in Hong Kong, along with his nineteen-year-old wife and her entire family, who live there and who took touchingly good care of us for three days. The German community had prepared a reception at the German Club in Hong Kong, where I spoke about some of my experiences. Almost the entire community, with Frau von Falkenhausen at their head, came on board to say goodbye.

After an absolutely wonderful trip via Manila and Bombay on the Italian ship, which is fitted out very luxuriously, we landed in Genoa on 12 April 1938.

On 13 April we learned in Munich that Otto, whom we had not seen for seven years, has in the meantime marched into Austria as a soldier. On 15 April we arrived in Berlin.

John and Dora Rabe, 1947.

PART 2

JOHN RABE IN HIS
GERMAN HOMELAND

CHAPTER 12

BETWEEN THE NANKING
AND BERLIN DIARIES

BEFORE RETURNING HOME, John Rabe held a press conference in Shanghai, which was reported in all the newspapers in China and by almost all the large news agencies from around the world. Rabe spoke of his close cooperation with American missionaries, university teachers, and doctors. It had indeed been only these Americans and three Germans, John Rabe, Christian Kröger, and Eduard Sperling, who had remained in the city when the Japanese stood at the gates and whose International Committee had provided 250,000 Chinese relative security inside the Safety Zone. At this press conference Mr. Rabe spoke about the shortage of food in Nanking, about the plight of its citizens, but he said nothing about the excesses of the Japanese soldiers in order not to worsen the relationship between the International Committee and the Japanese army. The *Ostasiatischer Lloyd,* Shanghai's little German newspaper, published some excerpts from his diary, but only those about the Japanese air raids and the shelling of the city of Nanking before it was taken, and nothing of the horrors that everyone was waiting to hear about. Rabe was celebrated as a hero by all the papers and press agencies. He found that amusing.

On 15 April 1938, he and his wife, Dora, arrived in Berlin. The German press took no notice whatever. He was, however, received by Ernst Wilhelm Bohle, the leader of the Nazi party's "district abroad," who was likewise a high official in the Foreign Ministry, where he was the party observer. Bohle awarded John Rabe the medal of the German Red Cross for which he had been nominated by Ambassador Trautmann. The Chinese government presented him with a very prestigious decoration, the star of the Jade Order on a blue, white, and red ribbon, although it was not given to him until some time later. Rabe had himself photographed in tails and wearing both these medals: the splendid photograph, it would appear, of an important diplomat, which would look good in a silver frame atop the grand piano at some diplomatic cocktail party. Yet it bears little resemblance to the John Rabe who waved his swastika armband to intimidate an armed Japanese soldier and thus prevented him from raping Chinese girls.

John Rabe was proud of his decorations. But the German press was not allowed to mention them either. Rabe gave several lectures, the first on 2 May in the Great Festival Hall of Siemens's Schuckert Administration Building in Berlin-Siemensstadt. His American friend, the missionary John Magee, had given him a copy of his film about the victims of the Japanese occupation; it was screened on this occasion. Over the next few days, other lectures followed: one at the foreign policy office of Reich Führer Alfred Rosenberg; another at the Far East Association; a fourth before the SS of the suburb of Siemensstadt, which was attended by one of Himmler's deputies, or so Rabe claimed; and finally a lecture at the War Ministry on Tirpitz Ufer, where only the film was of interest.

He had worked long and hard on the text of his lecture at the Festival Hall in Siemensstadt. His descriptions of events in Nanking are lively and vivid. Rabe illustrates his comments with concrete experiences, some of them drastic and shocking. From the way he occasionally casts his material in an ironic or humorous light, it is obvious how much the British style of storytelling had become part of him after thirty years of living in semicolonial China. He quotes at length from his diaries, and to avoid repetition, the lecture has not been included among the documents at the end of this book.

In this lecture he deftly anticipates certain possible objections and refutes or tries to refute them. For example: It was not his intention to en-

gage in anti-Japanese propaganda in Germany or to give public lectures to
arouse pro-Chinese sentiments. Though very sympathetic to China's suffering, he was first and foremost pro-German and not only did he believe in
the correctness of "the central thrust of our policy," but as an officer of the
party he also stood "one hundred percent behind it."

The Japanese, moreover, had in fact every reason to be grateful to him,
because he had attempted to "blunt the arrow" of the many protests
lodged against the Japanese in Nanking, "precisely because I was a German
and as such both had to and wanted to maintain the friendly relationship
between our embassy and that of our ally Japan." Before sending off their
complaints to the Japanese, his American friends had often asked him to
mix a little honey into the text.

He asks and immediately answers the question of why he remained behind in Nanking, although his company had said he was free to leave the
city with other Germans and officials of the Chinese government. He had
remained behind out of gratitude to China, which had always treated him
well—even during the world war—and in order to protect his Chinese
coworkers and their large extended families. Of course he also wanted to
represent the interests of Siemens China Co.; but he passes over that very
quickly, since with the retreat of the government and the occupation of
Nanking by the Japanese, not a single order had come Siemens's way. How
very much he misjudged the realities of National Socialism can be seen
from his attempt to present his humanitarian efforts in Nanking as simply
those of a National Socialist party member doing his duty.

The conclusion of the lecture is John Rabe all over. He takes up the
cause of Legation Secretary Rosen, who had so energetically represented
German interests against the Japanese. Rabe of course knew just how pre-
carious Rosen's situation was and what difficulties had arisen for him from
Hitler's race laws. Rabe pleads for both Rosen and his sense of right and
wrong, even though he himself had had his reservations about Rosen's
gruff and at times not exactly diplomatic way of dealing with the Japanese.
At the end of his lecture he writes:

> I recall a conversation that he had with a Japanese general. In the course
> of it, Dr. Rosen used the phrase, "Since your troops got out of
> control . . . ," whereupon the Japanese general flew into a rage: "How
> dare you say so! We have the best disciplined troops in the world." To
> which Dr. Rosen replied, "Oh, do you mean to say they did that on
> orders?"

Neither in Rabe's diaries nor in the documents appended here is there any mention of how many Chinese fell victim to the Japanese massacre in Nanking. Indeed, at the time there was no one who compiled statistics or counted how many civilians, prisoners of war, men, women, and children had been murdered. Today people speak of 200,000 to 300,000 victims. In his lecture, John Rabe says:

> We Europeans put the number at about 50,000 to 60,000. According to the Red Swastika Society, which had taken on the task of burying the bodies, but could not bury more than 200 a day, there were about 30,000 bodies still lying unburied in the suburb of Hsiakwan on 22 February 1938, the date I left Nanking.

It is likely that Rabe's estimate is too low, since he could not have had an overview of the entire municipal area during the period of the worst atrocities. Moreover, many troops of captured Chinese soldiers were led out of the city and down to the Yangtze, where they were summarily executed. But, as noted, no one actually counted the dead.

Rabe's most urgent wish was to report personally to his Führer Adolf Hitler about the occupation of Nanking and the suffering of its people. When it became clear that he would not be granted such an audience, he enclosed the lecture he had given to his coworkers at Siemens in a registered letter.

Why did John Rabe want to speak to his Führer? Why did he send him his lecture? In his letter, he answers these questions himself:

> My Führer,
>
> The majority of my friends in China are of the opinion that you have not been provided a detailed report about the actual events in Nanking. In sending you the enclosed copy of a lecture I have given, which however is not intended for the broader public, I am fulfilling a promise made to my friends in China that I would inform you about the sufferings of the Chinese populace. My mission will have been fulfilled if you would be kind enough to let me know that the enclosed copy of my lecture was presented to you.
>
> I have since been notified that I am to abstain from delivering other lectures of this sort or to show any pictures dealing with the subject. I shall obey this order, since it is not my intention to work against German policy and German government offices.
>
> Let me assure you of my allegiance and honest devotion.
>
> JOHN RABE

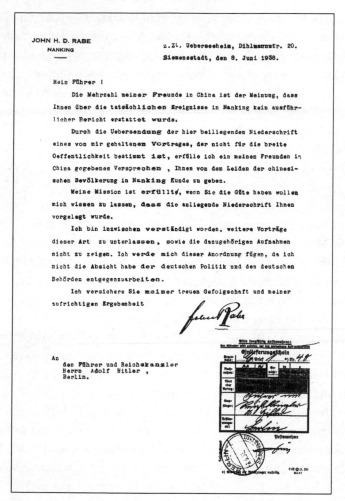

John Rabe's letter to Adolf Hitler.

The majority of his friends in China, Rabe writes, believed that Hitler had not been provided a detailed report about the actual events in Nanking. Who were these friends? Adolf Hitler, to whom the letter is addressed, might have assumed Rabe meant Chinese friends, perhaps even the Americans on the Safety Zone Committee. He had promised them he would inform the Führer about the sufferings of the Chinese people.

Later, however, Rabe would indulge his fantasy a bit at one point and write that he had promised the "Chinese government" that he would tell Hitler what he had seen and experienced in Nanking. That, of course, is out of the question. After the siege of Nanking began, he had no opportunity to speak with representatives of the Chinese government.

Nor did he mean his Chinese or American friends. What he had in mind was the German embassy itself, because the embassy knew that what it said had not been going beyond the Foreign Ministry in Berlin to reach the man who made German policy. Rabe had read Rosen's reports. He sometimes even included them in his diary. He knew exactly what Trautmann's views were, knew of his desire to mediate between the Japanese and the Chinese and of his belief that military advisors should remain in China.

Perhaps John Rabe believed that Hitler would be deeply shocked when he read his report about Japanese war crimes in Nanking, and perhaps even that he would rethink his policies regarding China and Japan. John Rabe probably believed that Hitler, "a man, the same as you and I," would not leave the Chinese to their plight. He had written as much in his diary.

He did not suspect that Hitler didn't give a damn about such bagatelles as the death of hundreds of thousands of Chinese. Hitler thought in the grand categories of world history and was concerned with when and how to take Czechoslovakia in one lightning move.

John Rabe waited for Hitler to reply. In vain.

"Then came the surprise," he writes in a memorandum. "A few days later [after sending the letter to Hitler], I was arrested by the Gestapo, that is, two officials arrived in a car and drove me, along with the six volumes of my diary and the film, to [Prinz] Albrecht Strasse."

Once there, he was interrogated for several hours, but "honorably released," as he wrote. "From then on I could not give any lectures, publish any books, and above all not show the film that had been made by John Magee in Nanking and dealt with the atrocities of the Japanese soldiers. In October 1938, I was given my books back, whereas the police kept the film"—of which, as Rabe surely knew, there were now two copies in Berlin.

It had not been a third-degree interrogation. The Gestapo had seen that John Rabe "stood one hundred percent behind the central thrust of German policy," as he himself had always emphasized, and that he would not cause any trouble. "Right or wrong—my country" was, after all, his motto. John Rabe was glad to fall back on that truly dubious maxim. He followed the Gestapo's orders. He toed the line. He did not make much of a fuss about his brief arrest later, either, when after the war many people were happy to use some minor brush with the Gestapo to turn themselves into resistance fighters.

I first heard the news of Rabe's arrest via the grapevine of German China hands, though in rather dramatized form: Rabe had made a film of the atrocities in Nanking, or so it was said, and had shown it to a small circle of Siemens directors back in Germany. He was then denounced, arrested, and sent to a concentration camp.

In reality the Gestapo had interrogated him because of his letter to Hitler but then left him in peace. According to family tradition, it was Carl-Friedrich von Siemens who then had him sent on a mission to Afghanistan, where he was to look after some Siemens employees who had got into difficulty there.

Which was why I was unable to reach him by telephone at his office and so believed the reports about his being sent to a concentration camp. In reality he soon returned to Berlin. He worked at Siemens as a clerk until the end of the war.

During the war he was responsible for the foreign travel arrangements of Siemens employees. He was also responsible for company employees in Kabul and, later, for those held in detainment camps, especially in India. It was his job to keep connections open with the main office. His son Otto Rabe reports his amazement at how often his father would go to a bookstore and put together large packages of the most varied kinds of literature for the people interned in the camp at Dera Duhn, India.

Rabe kept no diaries after Nanking. He started his last one, his Berlin diary, as the Red Army marched into Siemensstadt on 24 April 1945.

In my autobiography *Mut und Übermut* (1991), I devoted a small chapter to John Rabe. His granddaughter Ursula in Berlin read it and got in contact with me. I learned from her that John Rabe's diaries had not vanished with the Gestapo but that in fact his son Otto Rabe had them stored in the attic of his Black Forest home. The family had never read them; indeed, they had often considered throwing them out or destroying them—after all the cruelties war had brought, they didn't want to read about still more cruelty.

At my request, however, his granddaughter had the diaries sent to her in Berlin, and she provided me with photocopies of all the volumes, about which I was then to write an article. I was so impressed by the diaries, however, that upon completing my article for the *Frankfurter Allgemeine Zeitung*, I decided to publish them as a book. From Rabe's son I also received the manuscript of the Berlin diary that forms the following chapter.

In December 1996, a facsimile set of the diaries was displayed in New York, where they caused quite a sensation. The family's original plan had been to present the diaries to the Chinese, but I persuaded them to give these volumes to the German Federal Archives in Berlin, where they are now to be found and are available to all for research.

CHAPTER 13

JOHN RABE'S BERLIN DIARY

SIEMENSSTADT, 24 APRIL 1945

NONE OF THE RUMORS flying around here yesterday has turned out to be true. It's all just pure rumor. But the bridges in the area close-by have been blown up by our troops. Our antiaircraft is firing away constantly, and the enemy air raids did not stop all night. Even this morning there's whistling and whirring overhead. At three o'clock the water was turned off. But there's water again now, though not much pressure. We've filled all the containers we have in reserve.

8 P.M.

The whole day has been filled with air raid alarms, fighter attacks, and artillery fire. At 11:00 a.m. the house at 11 Harries Strasse was hit. The chimney flew out onto the street, the roof was demolished, but with the exception of bits of broken glass no other damage is visible. It appears to have been an artillery shell.

The Siemens cable works is burning. A huge pitch-black cloud is rising above it. Word is that the Russians occupied part of the works, and so we ourselves then put the torch to the rest. People say we have one division deployed nearby and three divisions that have pulled back from the western front are supposed to be on their way.

Mutti grows braver every day. I have to keep a tight rein on her. She goes out to shop in the midst of the worst air raid and takes cover only from strafers. She worked in our garden today in the middle of severe shelling—planting peas. Pure recklessness!

There's one hell of a racket at the moment. It feels as if we're being encircled. We're surrounded by black clouds of smoke.

25 APRIL

Last night was relatively quiet. This morning, the air raids started again and have continued with no letup.

Yesterday evening at 8:30: two hits—probably flak shells—in the roof of the building directly across from us. During this morning's shelling—there's not much choice, the shelling never stops—I fetched three loaves of bread from Wunicke near the post office, so that we're taken care of for a few days. The next street over, from Riepelt Strasse to the waterworks, is occupied by German soldiers and civilian militia. The bombardment has claimed three victims, slain by flak or bomb shrapnel: one woman, a soldier, and a civilian. According to news I've heard.

At 5:00 p.m. a bomb totally destroyed the building at 13 Riepelt Strasse. Five people are buried inside. By 8:00 o'clock we've managed to dig out four of them, all more or less badly wounded. The fifth, whom we are unable to bring up alive, is dead. Meanwhile the Russians have entered our part of Siemensstadt, but they don't stop our rescue work.

It's been quiet for a good while, and we go down to the cellar to sleep, after first getting some food gratis from the Konsum store (milk, pudding powder, etc.).

26 APRIL

Two armed Russians on patrol came down into the cellar at 4:30 a.m., asked a few questions, and left without bothering us.

8:00 a.m. We go to get some more groceries from the Konsum, where there's no one in charge and the door and windows stand open to anyone. Willi[58] and I haul water over from Riepelt Strasse, since even our garden tap has dried up entirely now.

More Russians appear in our cellar, but then go away. At about 6:00 p.m. heavy bombardment. Word is that the German troops are staging a massive assault. Rumors, of course, with no way of checking on them.

Yesterday evening as some other civilians and I were carrying a critically wounded man through the woods to the first-aid station at 11 Gamme Strasse (Red Cross, Dr. Busch), we saw huge fires off to the right, behind the transformer house (the Röhren works or Osram. Couldn't tell exactly).

12:30 P.M.

A Russian soldier decorated with four medals enters our apartment, comes down into the cellar, and threatens to shoot us unless we hand over our watches and rings. I have to give him a ring and a pocket watch and Mutti's gold watch as well. Then with a handshake the Russian bids us a very friendly farewell. A couple of other Russian solders take a glass of cherry preserves from the cellar and wash them down with a bottle of wine and are in a fine mood. These people don't make a bad impression. They're simply taking what war tosses across their path.

Fighter attack. We keep taking refuge in the cellar. This time from German bombs.

27 APRIL

The first reports of rape are coming in. Frau Kitlaus at 1 Harries Strasse just missed being raped when a neighbor came by and interrupted the Russian. At Nos. 5 and 7, it's reported that two girls, aged 17 and 19, were raped three to four times. Ribbeck tells me that the same thing has happened on Rapp Strasse as well. Ribbeck has left his house on Rapp Strasse, and he and his wife have moved in with friends on Riepelt Strasse. We're very worried about how we're going to protect Irmi[59] and Erika Brechelt.[60]

This morning at 5:00 heavy artillery shelling, machine gun and rifle fire, which has continued until this moment (10:30 a.m.) with only very brief pauses.

The Russian soldiers are making themselves at home in our apartment, but are very amiable—so far. They don't bother us, even offer some of their food, but they're crazy about any kind of alcohol and are unpredictable once they've had too much.

28 APRIL

The night was quiet. No shelling. At 6:30 and 8:30 a.m., brief cannonades from the Russian side aimed into the city. It's horrible to be constantly aware that women are being raped. Frau Freier now admits that the night before last she had to give in to a Russian who threatened to shoot her if she refused. Last night she was able to hide. I'm writing these lines in great haste by the dim light in the room. Russian soldiers are constantly coming and going in our apartment.

The Siemens slaughterhouse (Süd Strasse behind the nursery) has been giving away for free whatever meat was left. A few residents of Siemensstadt walked away with whole quarters of beef. By the time I heard about it, it was too late: nothing left. And we need it so desperately. A Russian soldier, who likewise came away with a quarter, offers it to us—for a gold watch. Sure, if I had one! Both my gold watches have been taken. Frau Becker, our neighbor, is sympathetic and gives Mutti some frozen liver. Mutti is so happy to get it, even though her fingers are numb from preparing it.

Frau Becker brings another bit of sad news. Frau Dr. Orlich killed both her children and herself by injection with poison. I ask a German who lives close-by, but whom I don't know personally, if he knows anything about the incident. He replies: "No. Haven't heard about it. Too bad I don't have any poison, otherwise I'd be happy to take it."

SUNDAY, 29 APRIL

The night was quiet. This morning around 7:30 Russian batteries right outside our windows started firing. Stopped again after fifteen minutes. According to the Russians, Berlin has been surrounded. But in four different pockets, one of which is Tempelhof airport, where German planes are still taking off now and then. The Führer is said to be in Munich.

Our apartment was totally taken over last night by Russian soldiers. Along with the rest of the people in the building, we slept in the bomb cellar.

I've just heard from one of the Russians quartered in our apartment that Himmler is supposed to have capitulated to the Americans and English; i.e., surrendered personally to them, but *not* to the Russians. The man's got it all wrong, the Russian says.

Herr Brechelt went to have a look at his apartment. Now, together with about fifty colleagues, he's being held to work in the pipe mill, but is allowed to visit his family every day.

MONDAY, 30 APRIL

The night was relatively quiet. We, Mutti and I, were able to sleep in the bedroom of our apartment for the first time again; the rooms to the right and left were home to Russians for the night. At the moment there's heavy shelling of Spandau, where they say the Deutsche Werke is still resisting.

Our garden has come through poorly. A Russian truck drove over Mutti's bed of peas. The hedges and garden walls have been partly destroyed, but we can surely endure that. If only we knew what we are to live from! Until now goodhearted neighbors have helped us out with potatoes; and we've been given a little bread and meat by the Russians.

Willi and I are busy hauling water from a pump in the neighborhood. The waterworks haven't been in operation for days, and the Russians want to wash. We hear from various sides that the Russians have chased people right out of their apartments.

TUESDAY, 1 MAY

Our most recent billeted soldiers, a Russian noncom (medical student) and several privates, had to move on yesterday, much to our regret. They were relatively decent fellows [*relatively* inserted as an afterthought], who gave us some of their rations now and then. No sooner were they gone than three Russian soldiers forced their way in, looking for girls. Herr Wagner's calm demeanor—and he speaks fluent Russian—convinced them to leave, after unsuccessfully searching the building and bomb shelter, but without doing any damage, either. The shock still sits in our bones.

All sorts of things have been happening in the neighborhood. A seventeen-year-old girl was raped five times, then shot. The women in a bomb shelter on Quell Weg were raped while their husbands looked on. Herr Gabbert was stopped on the street and had to take off most of his clothes because he claimed he had no jewelry. A ring he had hidden in one shoe was then taken. Only a little shelling overnight, but heavier this morning.

Himmler has shot himself, or so the Russians say. On 28 April the Anglo-American forces were about 20 miles outside of Munich, which they have probably taken by now. These are just oral reports from Russian soldiers.

We're down to our last slices of bread again. How Mutti is going to feed us is a mystery. People sometimes talk about how they would want to share their last crust of bread. *And you want to do it, too!* But none of us ever realized how hard it is. I sit down in a corner of the parlor and read. I'm having a go at an old Gustav Freytag novel—*Debit and Credit*. I'm trying to forget!

Wagner, our neighbor, has poured out all the rest of his alcohol, wines and liqueurs, because he was afraid it would fall into the hands of the Russians, who would get drunk and then get out of control. Who can blame him? But Mutti is crying, she would have so loved one or two bottles. Well, it's too late now. I have other worries: First thing we have to do is replenish our water supply.

5 P.M.

I've just come back from a walk that I took with Willi through Siemensstadt to see if we could scare up food of any kind somewhere. No success. There's nothing more to be had. We visited Fräulein Naumann, who has taken on a little job of some sort in the administration building, in exchange for potatoes or whatever, and who was visiting her mother. She didn't have any suggestions about where to find something to eat. Then we visited Paul Meyer, whose apartment above the pharmacy was horribly damaged during the last air raid and then by a German grenade. One room is ripped wide open. You can look right outside because a wall is missing. The furniture is ruined, and everything is buried under rubble and plaster. But Meyer is as calm and level-headed as always.

"Where are you living, where are you sleeping?" I asked.

"Well, in the bomb shelter. And we cook and eat somewhere together with the rest of the people in the building."

We then joined Meyer to go ask at the waterworks if there was any food to be had there. No go again! There was a food depot there that the Wehrmacht had secretly set up and that no one, not even the directors, knew anything about. What they told us at the waterworks was that directors Bauer and Buol had sworn on oath that there was no food there. When the depot was then found—ostensibly some foreigners were the informers—Buol and Bauer were arrested. There's no way to check the facts, I am only passing on what we were told. The official there also mentioned that a number of local residents had behaved shamelessly when the depot was then cleared. They didn't just take food but used the opportunity to break into offices and steal office supplies, like mechanical pencils and other things stored there, including stuff they could have no use for, like screws and rivets, crates and crates of them. I'm simply recording this incident as well, and the revulsion with which it was described, just to give a feel for the times.

We've heard that street fighting is still going on in the West End and Charlottenburg. I met some refugees who had come from Charlottenburg and were trekking on to Karlshorst. At the east gate, by the war monument, near the T-works and outside the Werner Werk high-rise, are the graves of fallen Russians, decorated with red wooden pyramids bearing the Soviet star.

Frau Freier has just come by with the following news that somebody heard on some foreign broadcast:

1. Himmler's offer of capitulation was not accepted by the Anglo-Americans. Meanwhile, Himmler has been captured and sent off to Moscow.
2. Goebbels has shot himself.
3. Hitler and Göring are in Munich.[61]
4. Of the two tower shelters at the Tiergarten, one has been blown up, while a battle with flamethrowers is raging around the other.

We're told that a German-speaking Russian staff officer is living at 43 Rohr Damm, to whom you can apply for help if you're molested by Russian soldiers. They say the same officer is in charge of getting supplies to the civilian population promptly. That sounds very promising.

SATURDAY, 5 MAY

On Wednesday, 2 May, I went with Willi to the cable works to get some food. The works were in a sorry state, half destroyed, the offices plundered. In the cellar we found some dried vegetables and grain coffee. On the way home, still on the cable works grounds, we were arrested by a Russian officer and locked in a room with other prisoners in apartment No. 368 at 19 Schuckert Damm. Among others, we met Herr Steinberg along with Herr Bücking. We were fed well, and treated well, too.

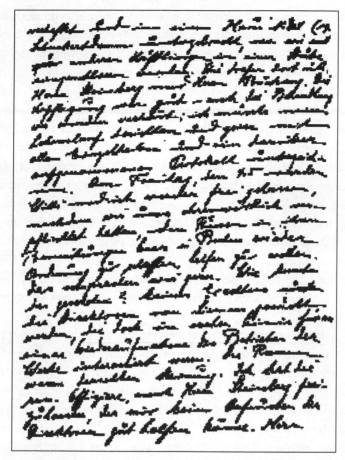

Rabe's entry in his Berlin diary describing his arrest by
the Russians.

We were interrogated, and I had to tell the story of my life, down to the
last detail, and then sign my statement, which they had taken down. On Friday, 4 May, Willi and I were released, after having sworn an oath that we
would help the Russians in their attempts to restore order in Berlin. We
were happy to promise it.

How could that be done? As I see it, the Siemens directors should be located, since after all their primary interest must be to get the operation up
and running again. The Russians shared my view. I asked the Russian
officers to release Herr Steinberg as well, who could help me locate the
directors. Herr Steinberg was then also released.

We then went looking for Herr von Kissling in the administration building, from whom we received a list of the last known addresses of all direc-

tors, which we then gave the Russians. Herr Steinberg is supposed to search for individual directors today by car. In the meantime a certain Herr Brehm from AJ4 has been able to establish contact with directors Bingel and Dr. von Witzleben. When Herr Steinberg and I returned to talk with the Russians at eight that evening, we ran into Herr von Witzleben, who is probably being held under arrest now in the same room where Willi and I spent three days. I'm sorry that Herr von Witzleben has not been spared this discomfort, but without some rigor there is no way to impose a new order.

Herr Director Möller was found shot to death in a garage near his apartment and has already been buried. Herr Hofer is said to have shot himself and his entire family.

The news that Frau Dr. Orlich killed herself and her children has, thank God, turned out not to be true; but Frau Dr. Heyde did take her life with poison.

I have been ordered by the Russians to determine who on our vast staff has ever worked in the Soviet Union. A difficult task. I don't know how I'm going to carry it out.

Mutti was very brave during our arrest, but it was hard on her psychologically. She looked in vain for us everywhere. She wandered around close to distraction in the administration building and at the cable works, too, calling out my name. Words can't describe her happiness when we were able to return home. You have to experience such moments to truly and totally grasp them.

And how are the children doing? Ah, your heart simply overflows and you can't put the words that run through your mind to paper.

SUNDAY, 6 MAY

Yesterday the administration building was occupied by a column of 180 Russian soldiers. On Major Föderoff's orders, Herr von Kissling is rounding up fitters and engineers, most of them from the assembly mill, who previously worked in the Soviet Union. Dr. von Witzleben, with whom I was able to speak for a few minutes as he was getting into a car with a Russian officer to take care of some business or other, asked me to go to Herr Bingel's house where his wife is and tell her that he's all right. Since I have no way of driving there, I asked Herr Steinberg to convey the message, and he said that Frau von Witzleben had already been told.

I'm not feeling well at present. My blood pressure is too high. Yesterday afternoon I was close to collapse but managed to make it home. The Russians apparently had some sympathy with my condition and did not detain me, so that I was able to get back home quickly and immediately crept into bed. I'm doing a bit better this morning. I have to report to Russian Major Förderoff at 9 o'clock.

MONDAY, 7 MAY

I picked up an intestinal infection while I was under arrest, which I'm hoping I can cure with Yatren.

We received the order this morning to clear out of our apartment within three hours. We're moving in with Borowski, 71 Rapp Strasse. I'm storing my model ships, a good number of paintings and bronzes, as well as some Chinese pewter in our and K.'s cellars, since a Russian officer told me that we can lock the cellars. I'm doing so badly this evening that I call on Frau Dr. O. on Riepelt Strasse, who gives me a small package of Tannalbin.

TUESDAY, 8 MAY

I'm feeling a little better this morning, but still very drained, yet I get dressed anyway to be ready for marching orders if need be.

At 10 o'clock, we are ordered to clear out of the apartment that we've only just moved into, and within two hours at that. We drag our bags, mattresses, bedding, and so forth to Richters, 69 Rapp Strasse, 2nd floor. But will we be allowed to stay here? Since we have no coal or wood for the stove, we go to the cellar of our old apartment at 3 Harries Strasse and find the cellar locked on the outside, but all the individual doors inside have been forced open, the contents rifled or simply smashed. A Russian soldier comes into the cellar, sees that we're getting coal and doesn't bother us.

WEDNESDAY, 9 MAY

Orders have come from the Antifascist Central Office that all men must report for work at 7 a.m. Yesterday they had to load stuff from the cable works to be shipped off. Everyone got something to eat (soup and a large piece of bread). This morning Willi went to work as well. I cannot go just yet, since I'm still not over my intestinal flu.

The water has been on again since yesterday, the pressure's low, but there is running water at least.

Some shots this morning, presumably soldiers drilling; then music and hurrahs, down at the end of Rapp Strasse. We're worried whether we can stay on in our present quarters.

NOON

The Russian soldiers are dancing and are all very happy. They say some sort of peace or armistice has been signed between Russia and Germany. No one knows who's in charge on our side, who signed for us (Dönitz?).

Frau Freier comes to see us, very distraught. She had moved into an empty eight-room house with the Brechelts and the Fischers. A Russian commandant also occupied one room, but that night the whole house erupted in tumult. Frau Freier was raped. Frau Fischer and Frau Brechelt were too old and were left alone. The young girls escaped by hiding in the attic. In grappling with the Russians, Herr Brechelt was wounded in the face. And now they've all left the house, are strewn in all directions, and we take Frau Freier in. Part of her belongings are already here with us. The rest are to follow. She went off to get them a good while ago; let's hope nothing else has happened to her!

We have not one bit of bread left in the house. But when need is greatest, God is nearest. A neighbor lady, Frau Kitlaus, brings us a bowl of meat and rice stew. We carefully ladle off the fat. Given my current state, the rice is more than enough for me. Another neighbor, Frau Dr. Hermann, brings us a piece of meat. We've given most of Otto's medicine to Frau Dr. Orlich. Unfortunately she couldn't offer us anything to eat in trade. She doesn't have enough even for herself, and there are patients lying in the Red Cross station at her house, including the man we dug out of the house on Riepelt Strasse on 24 April.

THURSDAY, 10 MAY

From yesterday afternoon until 11:00 p.m., a lot of shooting (in celebration), a great banquet in the garden, with dancing and singing. Since there's a great deal of drinking, too, we fear the worst for the rest of the night. Irmi and Frau Freier hide. Frau Freier was raped four times yesterday. Thank God, the night remains calm. No one dared take off their shoes and clothes.

Willi came home at 5 o'clock yesterday. He brought a quarter of a loaf of bread, and during a break in work he'd been given some broth. He was helping dismantle machines (lathes) at the pipe mill. The dismantling is a bad sign, since the plant cannot return to operation if the machines are all hauled away. Word is that Generals Jodl and von Krosigk[62] signed the armistice.

We all shared Willi's bread, and now there's not a crumb left in the house. And neither do we know where we're supposed to get coal and firewood if the Russians won't let us into our cellar on Harries Strasse. Willi left again for work at 7 this morning. He's still physically strong and if he gets his soup every day from the Russians, he can probably manage the physical labor demanded of him for a good while, despite my illness.

I'm amazed at Mutti. She is brave, never complains or grumbles, and is constantly trying to beg some sort of food for us. God bless her! And along with Irmi she keeps the house in order, to the extent that you can speak of order. We sleep on the floor and hope that no one takes our mattresses away from us, or our bags and clothes, which we've had to drag along on each of our several hasty moves.

And we wonder, how are Gretel and her children and Otto and Eva[63] doing? You don't dare start brooding, it only leads to despair!

FRIDAY, II MAY

Ursi's birthday—dear Ursi, our loving thoughts are with you. May God protect you and your Mutti, Gudrun, and all the others there in Bünde. That is our daily prayer.

Yesterday the Russian soldiers left our building on Harries Strasse. Our apartment and our cellar are in a crazy state. The bed frames are gone, and the couches have vanished as well. They're probably somewhere in the neighborhood and we'll have to go looking for them. We found most of our tables and chairs out in the garden. All the crates in the cellar were broken into, the contents fished out and thrown on the floor. I suppose they were looking for jewelry or the like, which we no longer have. We shall try to put it all back in order a little and thank our Creator that we didn't have to go through worse. I have no idea what state the things are in that we left with Peschke or in our cellar in the city. We'll all pretty exhausted, but composed. I expected nothing different, actually even worse. Let's hope we are spared further surprises.

SATURDAY, 12 MAY

We spent all day yesterday straightening up our apartment on Harries Strasse, and we're still not finished. Willi went to forced labor this morning: shipping off machines and other materials, etc., so that he can get something to eat. I hope to be able to go along on Monday. A man really does want to work, as long as he knows that there is not a constant danger that his apartment will be confiscated while he's gone. And when we do have to move, Mutti can't drag the bags etc. around by herself, and usually we're given a leeway of only 2 to 3 hours.

1 p.m. Willi comes home truly exhausted. His only job today was "shoveling rubble," and he was given nothing to eat. I return from Frau Dr. Orlich, the woman who was mistakenly said to have died along with her children. I wasn't feeling well this morning—dizziness, heart palpitations, etc., symptoms of a weakened body. Her examination revealed: high blood pressure and some weakness in the heart muscle. I had her give me a signed statement that unfortunately I am unable to work.

I'm in a very poor mood. The Fatherland is defeated, vanquished, smashed to smithereens, unconditional surrender! After all the great words and promises of our government: This is the end of their dream of a thousand-year German Reich.

Still no word whatever from the children and grandchildren. Not in the best of health. Tossed out of the apartment twice on short notice, to take refuge with strangers, always worried and afraid that Russian soldiers will force their way in again, always short of our daily bread, for most of which Mutti literally has to go begging to neighbors and good friends, worried about what will become of the firm of Siemens and of us, meaning of Willi and me. Worried about how Eva is doing, who is expecting her first child about now. Want and worry wherever you turn! And yet you have to be happy that you've been spared even worse blows. And there are worse things, I saw more than enough of that in Nanking. But, chin up, even if it's bitterly hard to do! Onward!

SUNDAY, 13 MAY, OTTO'S 28TH BIRTHDAY!

My dear Otto, best wishes! Last night for the first time in a long time I slept in normal pajamas. That's been impossible up to now. We've lain in bed with our boots on to be ready at a moment's notice to clear out or to respond to a military inspection. We don't have our beds anymore, maybe we'll still find them. We sleep on the floor, but we're happy that we could save our mattresses and our bed linens.

MONDAY, 14 MAY

Willi has been called back to work at the cable works. The call comes from the Antifascist Central Office. Today and tomorrow machine and materials are to be dismantled and shipped. Ostensibly the Russians are to pull out of here tomorrow. Nobody knows who or what comes then. The aforementioned Central Office has distributed a number of Russian propaganda fliers, dated from between 1 and 7 May. According to them, Hitler is dead and Mussolini has been hanged by his own countrymen.

Something dreadful—or eerie is going on all around us. Every house door is locked. You can't visit your friends because no one opens to a knock. If you're lucky you run into someone you want to visit on his way home, and after a brief exchange he quickly slips behind the door, which is instantly locked behind him. Why? Because everyone is afraid of Russian soldiers, who try to force their way into homes at every opportunity. Granted, many of them are harmless, but many aren't, and those that just rob you aren't the worst. Above all people are afraid, and rightly so, that they'll rape the girls and women in the house. I wish I could prove that the people who tell stories about these sorts of rapes are liars. But I can't!

Dr. Möhlmann has given us a whole pail full of groats (rye and oats— I'm not much of an expert here), for which I'm very grateful. It's stuff the Russians mix in with their horse feed, but we grind it to flour in our coffee mill, and can make a tasty soup out of that. Now and then we each get a piece of bread, too; last week, half a loaf per person.

I'm a little shaky on my feet at the moment: diabetes, high blood pressure, weak heart, and intestinal problems are all giving me trouble. Frau Dr. Orlich has given me a certificate so that I don't have to take part in the forced labor. So for now all I have to do is live, survive, and I want to do that, because without Mutti and me the children will have difficulty dealing with these new times. Maybe that's only my imagination; but it's what I think, imagined or not, and that should keep us two old folks on our feet!

Mutti lies beside me on the floor and sleeps, and outside the loveliest May weather smiles down on us. The most splendid spring days. The lilac is in full bloom outside our windows. How beautiful the world could be if the war had not been so wretchedly lost and the shadow of the future did not loom ahead so dark and sinister. Cleaning up in the cellar, I found my two model ships, more or less smashed; but I've put them back in their old spot—they've been in "dry dock" once before, i.e., at the Naval History Museum, where a Pole repaired the damage they suffered on the trip from China to Berlin. Who knows, maybe they can be repaired again, although the damage this time is really significant.

We, Mutti and I, tried to get a look at our furniture, etc. in Dr. Selle's apartment, but couldn't find a way into the locked building. Then we visited Frau Meyer, who gave us some sweetener, something we had run out of. On the way we ran into Fräulein Krause, from whom we heard that Siemens employees are all supposed to register at the dynamo works. Before we even get to the dynamo works, we meet Herr Petermann, who tells us there's no point in registering there. He suggested I wait until the administration building is made available again, and then try to get my old job back.

Meanwhile I've found Gretel's iron bedstead at the Reinhardts on Harries Strasse, where the Russians had dragged it. We hauled the bedstead back and also found our furniture in Peschke's apartment, all heaped in a big pile and probably damaged somewhat. The Chinese chest is still there, too. We've just heard that the Russian occupation troops are to withdraw tomorrow and be replaced by the English, with whom we hope we can come to terms better. All the same, the Americans and English are preceded by the reputation of not being as genial as one might have hoped. Wait and see!

TUESDAY, 15 MAY

Willi didn't get home until 7 o'clock yesterday evening. He had to be at the cable works at 6 this morning again. That's 13 hours of work a day, and only a half-hour break to eat: too much for Willi, given how ill he is. As soon as he feels he can't go on, he should report in sick. The food at the cable work consists of a little bread and sweetened tea in the morning. Lunch: watery broth with a few pieces of meat, and a little bread then again in the evening. Not enough for hard labor. The work to be done: dismantling a huge lead press that's to be shipped off. They say that the Russians want to ship off 70 percent of the entire plant's machinery.

I'm still on vacation, involuntary, compulsory vacation, because I'm too old and probably too weak to work in the assembly plant. Just puttering around the house and moving a bit of furniture has left me totally out of breath. There's probably some heart damage from all this toil and trouble. So let's rest up a bit!

If only the thoughts that keep running through your mind would finally give it a rest! The worry and anxiety about the children and grandchildren in Bünde and Munich weigh us down. Frau Freier just told us—she's been living in the front room and saw it all from the window—that a car full of Russians drove past at 10 o'clock last night. The soldiers broke into the cellar of the house across the street and dragged off a sack (of potatoes?). I didn't even notice, since I'd fallen asleep on my mattress on the floor. These nighttime visits are always very upsetting, and dangerous for the women and girls in the building.

Once again at noon today three Russian soldiers force their way into our apartment on Harries Strasse, allegedly searching for radio equipment.

Herr Gutmann and Fräulein Pechtel visited us on Rapp Strasse. What we've been through is harmless compared to what happened to Gutmann. A couple of German sharpshooters were on the roof of his building in Spandau. In such cases, the Russian military generally shot everyone in the building, and Gutmann can well say he was lucky to get out alive. His sister-in-law was wounded during an air raid and lost an eye.

He tells the most hair-raising stories of what went on as the city was being taken. Near Friedrich Strasse there were large numbers of women and children who had sought refuge in the subway tunnel, which the SS decided to use as a defensive position at the last moment. The Russians shelled the tunnel with antitank guns, blowing open a big water main, so that water flooded the tunnel and all the refugees drowned.

A division of soldiers and some civilians were surrounded by the Russians. The women and children were allowed to leave, and so waving white flags, they approached the German lines, but were then mowed down by their own countrymen. The German officer in charge justified his conduct by claiming that Russian soldiers were known to use the trick of crouching behind women in order to creep in closer, etc. etc.

A German-speaking Russian officer gave Herr Gutmann one interesting bit of information: According to him, there haven't been any commissars in Russia since 1941, and as a Russian officer he felt offended if someone addressed him as "commissar."

Gutmann tried to get into the Siemens administration building to visit his office but was warned off and told to give it up because, first, he might be shot by the Russians occupying the building and, second, they're waiting for the whole administration building to be blown sky-high, or so they said.

They didn't say blown up by whom. They let him get only as far as the personnel office. The people who warned him were Germans. The warning seems awfully simpleminded to me. I just heard from Herr Scheichler of the Antifascist Central Office that the Russians intend to pull out in two days. They ought to do it today and make room for the advancing English, who will presumably be quartered in the administrative buildings rather than in private homes.

WEDNESDAY, 16 MAY

Just in case, I had Gutmann give me his address again. Yesterday the Antifascist Central Office (Scheichler) had us all confirm our addresses for the new food distribution. To our great astonishment, we were told that new ration cards are to be given out because the Russians will be supplying us with food on a massive scale—something, as was noted, that the English and Americans cannot do, since they lack food in such tonnage.

Well, we'll be happy to be surprised because so far we've had great difficulty finding food. What have we actually lived on over the past three weeks? The basis of our diet is a pail full of groats, which the Russians use as fodder for their horses and were kind enough to leave behind for us when their first occupying forces left. We then ran these groats through our coffee mill, so that we could use the hulls as well, and that way we've always had some soup. Bread (only rarely) and meat and potatoes were kind gifts that, as noted, Mutti begged from the neighbors, or that Irmi was able to earn by doing some housework for a lady of her acquaintance. Yes, we'd be happy to see some order established in the matter of food.

Another surprise: According to a Russian officer, the Russians aren't even considering shipping the German populace off to Siberia. If that's true, they'll soon have us all on their side! Nothing would bring the Germans into their embrace more quickly than conciliatory policies. Well, somewhere between hope and fear, we'll wait to see to what happens.

And how are the children doing? Do they have food to eat? Are they free? Or captured? Will Otto be allowed to continue to study? What will they live on if he's not allowed to finish his studies? And what about Eva? Is she able to feed her baby? And how are Gretel and Ursi and Gudrun doing in Bünde? Questions that have to remain unanswered and that rob you of your sleep!

It's really pointless to keep jotting down the same complaints; but maybe someone will know what I'm going through when I write that our suffering under this pressure is indescribable, although we keep telling ourselves that hundreds of thousands, indeed millions of Germans have the same, if not worse cares.

Japan, or so I've heard, will capitulate in a few days.[64] And with that, the second and most terrible of all world wars will at last, after six years, have come to a definitive end, meaning: for the others! For us? We'll have to wait and see. After the First World War, which was mild in comparison to this last one, there was a period of hunger and hate. The losers are to blame for everything. Will that be repeated? And what will become now of the Germany that has perished? Berlin has been so completely destroyed that, as I see it, it will be years before they have even cleared away the rubble and demolished buildings. And the rest of Germany's major cities probably came through no better. What I saw last autumn in Munich and Nuremberg was already bad enough.

We're still without gas and electricity, and no trains or subways are running at all.

The Brechelts had an hour and a half to clear out of their emergency quarters on Rohr Damm because the Russians suddenly wanted it, and have now gone back to their old apartment at 3 Harries Strasse. Mutti and I borrowed a wagon from Frau Mützel and helped them move. Presumably we'll be able to move back to our old apartment within the next few days, too.

A section of Harries Strasse is still occupied by the Russians, however, and the street is blocked by a medieval turnpike. While we were helping Frau Brechelt move, we ran into Frau Krüger, who also was being forced to move. I was able to help her a little to clear her apartment. It's a pitiful sight to see all the people in a building suddenly put out on the street with everything they have, except the large pieces of furniture. A fire can't be any worse a catastrophe.

FRIDAY, 18 MAY

We moved back into our old apartment (3 Harries Strasse) yesterday. According to the orders of the Antifascist Central Office, all men between 14 and 65 years of age must report to work. I asked for a deferment on account of my health. At the same time I got myself registered at the Siemens administration building, where let's hope they can soon put me to work doing something. I've heard that Dr. von Witzleben, one of the directors, has been released. Director Bingel is still being detained at the citadel in

Spandau, they say. Director Leiffert shot himself—or so I've been told. There's no way of telling whether it's a fact or just rumor. Some people say that Hitler has fled to Spain and that Himmler is dead. Goebbels, they say, killed himself and his whole family.

I spent the morning shoveling and carting off roof tiles (and other bomb debris) still lying out in front of the house.

The Russians have kept their word. We've been getting food according to the new system (enclosed here). I have been listed as a "worker" and am being given food. Mutti has not yet received her ration cards. Irmi is likewise classified as a "worker." As before, Willi is still working 13-hour days. There will be no Sundays off until the end of May. I've heard that Herr Brendel is being held under arrest. No one could tell me where.

I'm worried about where I'll put our furniture that's stored with Peschke and Dr. Selle when those gentlemen need their apartments again themselves. When I cautiously approach, that is ask, Frau Freier whether there might be some chance of her finding another place to live, she is very offended that I could even think of asking such a question at this point. Mutti also thinks my request is out of place!

Where can I turn with my worries if no one understands me? I don't want to throw Frau Freier out! But it might turn out that she could find lodging elsewhere, which would be a great help to us. But I won't touch the subject again for now. Women's logic and men's logic are two fundamentally different things. Neither side has any insight into the other. The best thing is to hold my peace. Some solution, some way out, will surely come with time.

SATURDAY, 19 MAY

I've just heard from Dr. Möhlmann that Robert von Siemens has been shot and killed. He was in a car with some SS men out on the Avus,[65] when they were surrounded by Russians, and except for one man who escaped all of them were shot, including R. v. S. by accident.

SUNDAY, 20 MAY (PENTECOST)

Mutti and I went into the city on foot today, with a child's wagon and a backpack, to have a look at the cellar on Xantener Strasse. It turned out that there were quite a few things missing, our good china for instance. But a lot of valuable keepsakes are still there, and we will try to salvage them. Today we took the mask of the old man by Michelangelo and the Beethoven mask back home with us, as well as the carved pedestal for the green Kuanyin,[66] the case for medals (pried open at the back) and what medals were still in it; about half were missing, including all the good ones with gemstones and pearls.

We found a Herr Robert living in Dr. Hauser's apartment, who is said to be a prisoner of war. Dr. Hauser's brother, it's claimed, has become mayor of Ruhleben. On the way, we also ran into Herr Marr, who greeted me with these words:

"Well, so where's your 'Heil Hitler'? You should be ashamed of yourself!"

We just left him standing there. The man can't be normal! He's apparently forgotten that he himself was a party member, a commissar for the Ukraine, a civil servant, and I don't know what all, and truly has reason to be ashamed. Maybe he was angry at Frau Goll again, who's still living in their apartment but wasn't there when we called.

After our walk through the devastated city, Xantener Strasse did not come as any big surprise. The Schloss Bridge that leads to Luisen Platz is totally destroyed, evidently blown up by our troops. The Russians have built a provisional footbridge to one side, but no vehicles can cross it. On Wilmersdorfer Strasse we saw women clearing rubble from the street. The tower of the Charlottenburg town hall was badly shelled; it was probably being defended by German troops.

It's a splendid Pentecost Sunday. Willi had to go to work, but is supposed to get double bread rations and sugar. The Russians are still removing lathes and other machines from the Siemens factories and shipping them off. I was actually supposed to report in for the dismantling work, but I can't do that kind of heavy labor. I collapsed yesterday shoveling rubble. My heart just doesn't want to do its job; as much as I hate to admit it, I'll have to dodge the heavy labor. But let's hope we'll soon get some brain work to do at Siemens; otherwise I don't know how I'll feed my family.

There's a rumor that the firm will have to let all former party members go; but I hope that's only a rumor. The most important question is surely whether, and if so, when, the firm can be put back into operation. God grant that some way can be found! Mutti has received a *child's* ration card today, the same goes for Frau Freier. Unfortunately that means a significant reduction in bread, etc. for our household.

No sign thus far of the Americans or English. It looks as if the Russian occupation here will last for a while yet. Maybe that's to our best advantage in terms of diet, since the Russians appear to have enough food, which they say is not the case with the American troops.

MONDAY, 21 MAY

Irmi and I were back on Xantener Strasse this morning and I fetched the following curios from the cellar of our old house: the Borghese fencer, the Goethe mask, the mask of *La belle inconnue de la Seine,* the porcelain laughing Buddha, Napoleon at the Berezina, a collection of Chinese copper coins, and a couple of medals, as well as the balance scale and the Japanese mushroom peddler's basket. We wrapped the really heavy bronze figurines in blankets and pulled them back in the wagon. When we got home, Dora surprised us with the news that three Russians are to be quartered here with us tonight; but, thank God, we can stay in the apartment. Dr. Möhlmann just paid a visit and told me that he has been hired to help in the carpentry shop at the Siemens Schuckert works. The news that Japan surrendered has turned out not to be true, but various large Japanese cities are said to have been destroyed in air raids.

Yesterday we saw a large banner that had just been hung from one of the half-destroyed buildings on Wilmersdorfer Strasse. It read: "Give me 10 years, and you will not recognize Berlin!" And today, when we were about 50 yards away from the same building, it suddenly collapsed with a great crash. On the wall under the arches of the bridge at the Jungfernheide train station is another motto, this one from our recent government: "Let our motto be: Berlin stays free."

Mutti and Irmi have just been told they are to report for work at 7 o'clock tomorrow morning.

TUESDAY, 22 MAY

Mutti was lucky: The grandmothers were allowed to go home without working. Irmi, however, has been ordered off to the waterworks for some kind of task. I met Herr Steinberg, who told me that Dr. Reyss and Herr Brendel, both of them directors, are still being held at Spandau citadel. He couldn't tell me why.

The three Russian officers who were quartered with us last night behaved impeccably, but it's sad to have to constantly hear from the Russian military how badly our troops behaved in Russia. We wouldn't have believed a word of it had we not already heard similar stories from German soldiers who had very bad things to say about their fellow countrymen, and especially party members, the so-called "Golden Pheasants," in the Ukraine. Along with the great misfortune that has come upon our fatherland, comes the feeling that we bear a great deal of guilt, for which we will now have to do bitter penance.

Mutti is indefatigable! I feel so useless by comparison, particularly since in my poor state of health I can't really lend a hand. She's gone to fetch tomato plants. The garden is to be put back into tiptop shape. She's already planted lettuce, but everything takes time; you can't just pull things out of a hat. Crushing the hat is so much easier. One or two army trucks have turned Gretel's lovely parcel into a deeply rutted wasteland. White sand shows through everywhere, but good neighbors will give us some topsoil to spread over the garden and cover the wounds.

A man has just arrived on foot after walking for two weeks, all the way from Minden in Westphalia, and he reports that the American occupation troops in western Germany have not behaved as badly as is generally claimed. The rations doled out to the German populace are no worse than what the occupying forces have. Looters are shot without exception, even when they're Americans. And so the neighborhood is rife with rumors and stories—some good, some bad. People say that the post office is about to be cranked up again, but only in Berlin for now, i.e., inside the city district, which just by itself will be incredibly difficult, since there are no forms of transportation at present. All you see are Russian trucks hauling off dismantled machinery from the Siemens works. It's truly a sad sight and a sad prospect for the future. Word is that thus far no machines have been removed from the AEG plant.

THURSDAY, 24 MAY

It's said that Herr Brendel and Dr. Reyss are still being held at Spandau citadel. I would so much like to fetch the gilded wooden temple and some more vases, along with the bambino, from the cellar on Xantener Strasse, but I'm not up to it. Our insufficient diet, especially the lack of any fat, is probably the reason for my weakness, which has rapidly worsened over the past few days. My diabetes is probably worse, too, and I keep wracking my brains about how I can get through this lamentable state with some dignity and grace.

There's a large billboard across the arches of the bridge at Charlottenburg train station (Wilmersdorfer Strasse): "The Red Army will provide the people of Berlin with food." On the radio, i.e. the crystal set,[67] we hear that 5,000 grocery stores are already back in business in Berlin. That's probably true, for I saw several shops open in the city with long lines of women waiting outside.

We're still living behind closed doors. Yesterday evening two Russian soldiers broke into our cellar rooms in search of radio vacuum tubes, even though the Russians have been forbidden to enter our houses without special permission from the commandant. Quite apart from the fact that all our watches have been stolen, we are constantly uncertain about what time it is. There are three different time zones: Moscow time, Central European daylight time, and standard time. Each an hour apart—a crazy hodgepodge!

There are nasty rumors about the punishment to be meted out to former party members. Some people say they won't be rehired at Siemens, that they'll be kicked out of their apartments and given the lowest level of rations; there are others, however, who believe they'll be deported or even shot. One poster in the Communist Party headquarters reads: "Those who like the werewolf rave, will join a hundred Nazis in the grave!" etc.

Thus far I've heard not one word from Siemens about the possibility of its being put back into operation. As long as Dr. Reyss and Herr Brendel are prisoners, you can hardly expect any news in that regard.

Unfortunately I don't enjoy the basic health and energy required for physical labor that Willi Schläger still enjoys, despite his illness. Sad to say, for now I have to spend my time at all sorts of puttering about the house: mending the garden fence, dipping candles, etc. What a bore! It's a mystery to me how, now that Irmi has been put to work, Mutti manages all the housework and still puts a meal on the table, when in reality she's physically weaker than I am.

SATURDAY, 26 MAY

Radio announces: Himmler was arrested on 21 May 1945 and committed suicide by taking cyanide on 23 May 1945. Göring, Darré, Backe, Speer, Hans Fritzsche, and others are reportedly under arrest. Irmi is feeling a little better, she'll have to return to work on Monday, since Frau Dr. Orlich can issue certificates only to those who are so seriously ill that they cannot work at all.

I was at the administration building at Siemens today. There's only a very slim chance I will be rehired there, at least according to Herr Fischer.

It looks for now as if most of the employees will be let go or given retirement. Rumor has it that the Russians will provide a pension of 90 marks
a month. Regular salaries are to be paid in four tiers: 1,150 marks, 2,250
marks, 3,350 marks, 4,450 marks a month.

Most recent reports have it that Robert von Siemens is still alive. Someone claims to have seen him near a water tank. No news about Dr. Reyss
and Herr Brendel. Fischer doubts that they're both still under arrest.

Irmi was at the police station to see if there's any chance of her being
able to travel to Bünde. The answer: "Passenger service has not been
restored. Perhaps in two weeks."

Sunday is to be reinstated as a day off. Dr. Schacht is to retain his old
post as the president of the Reichsbank. Today is Gudrun's ninth birthday!

TUESDAY, 29 MAY

Herr Steinberg and his wife visited us the day before yesterday. Steinberg is
very pessimistic. In his opinion, the Siemens concern will be restored, if at
all, to at most 15 percent of its former capacity. Hardly anything is left of
the firm's huge machinery plants.

Dr. Möhlmann visited me and brought me a letter from Frau Brendel,
whose husband has been held prisoner by the Russians since 5 May. While
on his way to the office, he was arrested outside director Bingel's house
along with Herr Backe and has not returned home since, whereas Herr
Backe was released after four days.

Frau Brendel is close to despair, especially since her husband has kidney
problems and was scheduled to undergo a kidney operation shortly before
Berlin was taken. Dr. Möhlmann says that Herr Steinberg saw both Brendel
and Dr. Reyss at the Spandau citadel some time back, although only from a
distance.

I was told that the West Power Plant is to be dismantled as well and that
a good number of the elevated's cars have already been shipped to Russia.
Mutti and I were on Xantener Strasse again and discovered the entire set of
metal and wooden idols that belong to the Chinese gold-enamel temple,
and we brought them back with us to Siemensstadt. We used the opportunity to stop by Dr. Hauser's apartment, where Herr R. lives now, whose
wife is expecting a baby in the next few days. While we were in the apartment, Mutti spotted a cup from our missing good china. The rest is probably there as well. Mutti bravely kept her concern to herself. The time is not

yet ripe to ask to search Herr R.'s and Frau Goll's apartments. We'll have to be patient.

Frau Fischer, Frau Brechelt, and Frau Wagner are all on the warpath with me since yesterday—their husbands as well, probably—because I insist that one must open the door when Russian officers urgently demand entry, as was the case yesterday, when three officers wanted to search Herr Brechelt's cellar for radio vacuum tubes, of which he has a large supply. The opposing party is of the opinion that one need not open the door. I have had no success thus far in pointing out that in such cases German soldiers would have broken down the door without hesitation, and that if we do not give in, our windows will be broken or something even worse will happen.

Dr. Möhlmann was quickly removed from his job at the Siemens carpentry shop. They are looking for a real carpenter, and not one's who self-taught. Dr. M. is now with the Berlin Transportation Company and is gathering up sections of broken trolley wire. Not pleasant or easy work. He looks very tired and drawn, for the work requires a great deal of walking. The Berlin rapid-transit system, some of whose cars, as I already noted, have been shipped off, is to be put back in operation with steam locomotives for now. Not very pretty, but better than nothing!

Together with Dr. Möhlmann, I went to see Herr Steinberg to let him know about Frau Brendel's letter and he promised that a letter from Frau Brendel would get through to Dr. Reyss. Both Herr Steinberg and I consider it totally pointless to try to approach the commandant on Herr Brendel's behalf. That sort of thing can only harm Brendel's cause.

You can't visit prisoners, either, to give them any advice, which could only consist of telling them to answer all the Russian questions truthfully and without equivocation. There is no other way to gain one's freedom! There is no point in trying to tell these people fairy tales or to hide the truth from them. We would not have behaved any differently in their place.

WEDNESDAY, 30 MAY

Mutti and I trekked out to the distribution office in Spandau today to get the ration cards for the sick and ailing (for fat and milk) that Frau Dr. Orlich had prescribed for us. It was a pointless trip unfortunately. There are no special ration cards for the sick. But since we were in Spandau, we visited Herr Gutmann, who, sad to say, does not know any way to help Herr Brendel, either.

Gutmann's living room is badly scarred by shelling. When the city was taken, a good many shots came right through the windows. G.'s sister-in-law, who was in the room at the time, lost an eye and her other eye was badly injured. It was 10 days before she was able to get medical help. She was there during our visit and looked so helpless it was downright pitiful.

Gutmann described a few especially horrible incidents that had taken place during the battle in Spandau. Among them, how 120 Hitler Youths lost their lives, while their leader, a man who'd been awarded the Knight's Order of the Iron Cross, got out alive. Gutmann accompanied us back home.

As we walked by, just looking at the ruins of the Siemens, Osram, airplane, Auto-Union works, etc. made us very sad. Fields of rubble everywhere you look! How can it all ever be rebuilt? You have the feeling that it will take decades just to remove the debris.

THURSDAY, 31 MAY

Money plays a very peculiar role in our current life. Our bank notes have no value for the Russians, who won't touch them. When I was arrested I had over 12,000 reichsmarks in my pocket, which were returned to me in full upon my release, whereas my watch fob, pocketknife, and fountain pen were confiscated, or simply got lost. The Russian soldiers have brought their own German bank notes along, with different colors from ours; but this occupation money is not in circulation. Since other than grocery stores, only the pharmacies are open as yet, you can't buy much with your money anyway. The price of food has stayed the same as before the occupation, so that we've noticed no difference in that regard, and since the Russians aren't selling any food but rather supplying it to us through German shops, there's almost no money of any kind in circulation. Willi and Irmi have left for work, Willi to dismantle the cable works, Irmi to dismantle the waterworks.

I'm still having these fainting spells, especially in the morning. My heart just doesn't want to function right. A man doesn't like to write about his own ailments, but I feel I must record them to explain why I'm no longer fit for any physical work or at least not fit at the moment. I run the danger of not being given a food ration card, or one with very low value, but, as much as I'd like to, I can't change that.

A directive has just come from the Antifascist Central Office that Jews, people of mixed race, and former political prisoners are to register. I'm actually one of the latter, even though I was a party member, but I hesitate to register; it goes against my grain to take advantage of the fact that I was temporarily held by the Gestapo. I'll make some inquiries shortly to learn what the real purpose of this directive is. Only a few people know about my experiences in China, which were connected with my arrest back then, and my fellow countrymen and neighbors would find them difficult to understand. Besides, the Gestapo let me go and didn't even throw me out of the party, although they had cause enough to do so because I had told the Japanese my opinion in no uncertain terms, but there was probably some fear of an international scandal if they punished me, since my activity as the head of the International Nanking Safety Zone was known worldwide.

If, as has happened on occasion, I were to be asked today why I remained in the party, I can only reply that those of us overseas never came into contact with the kind of people who were eyewitnesses to the atrocities that are said to have been committed by members of the SS, etc. We were "idealists of the first water" and it was our impression that any ugly stories were just rumors, nothing more than enemy propaganda, especially, since as I've mentioned, no one could say that he had seen the atrocities he was describing with his own eyes.

I must admit I shed tears of joy when I read that Germany had taken Bismarck's advice at last and formed an alliance with Russia. Which only made the shock all the greater when it turned out shortly thereafter that the Führer had no intention of joining forces with Molotov, and it was out of that that the war and all its hardships really began.

FRIDAY, 1 JUNE

Mutti has had to stay in bed today; her varicose veins are giving her trouble, she didn't wrap her leg for our walk to Spandau. I'm very worried about her. Without her we would all be helpless. Who is going to do the housework and round up food and prepare it, now that Irmi has been put to work?

I was at the administration building again yesterday and spoke with Herr Steinberg and Dr. Drescher. Steinberg tells me that the management of Siemens is optimistic about the future. That sounds very nice, but it's puzzling. I don't know what the basis for their optimism can be, and no one can explain it to me, either.

TUESDAY, 5 JUNE

According to an announcement of the "Antifas" [Antifascists], "party members and their kin," including the kin of dead, imprisoned, or missing party members must report in daily.

I've been to the administration building on several occasions, but always to no avail, for the present there isn't any chance that I'll be hired. My old division has apparently been left out of all calculations, they haven't even set up a "contact person," although they say Dr. Krohn has been trying hard to do something about it. Herr Brendel is still under arrest.

I visited Herr Scheichler today to ask whether I am among those people who are supposed to register as "former political prisoners." He took a very disparaging attitude, and accused me of having become a party member for personal advantage. I disputed this very energetically and pointed out that one reason among others for my joining the party was to receive a subsidy from the German Reich for our German School in Nanking. The fact that, with only a few exceptions, all the overseas Germans joined the party for the sake of solidarity, appears to be unknown here. As far as I know, no one gained any personal advantage from it. Scheichler then told me to go see a Herr Zienicke at the House of Comradeship.

In my attempt today to register somewhere for some kind of work to do at home, I ended up at the "Siemens Waterworks Registration Center" on Siemens Strasse, which could not use me. My chances of being rehired by Siemens are very dim. I don't know what will become of me. Will they put me on pension, perhaps? And would the money be enough to live on? All unanswered questions that weigh heavily on the soul.

It's obvious that our entire railroad system is to be reduced to single tracks. Even the Russian officers don't know why, but—they say—Stalin knows why, and *he* has never been wrong! The machinery plants at AEG have been dismantled and shipped off, too, by the way.

Our building got more Russians to quarter again today. Fifteen Russian soldiers have been placed in the building next door. Our worries seem to have no end. Let's hope we can stay in our apartment! We don't have enough food. So far this month the only supplies distributed in sufficient quantity have been bread and potatoes. In the west, however, with the Anglo-Americans and the French, things are even worse in this regard, or so we constantly hear.

THURSDAY, 14 JUNE

We don't have much to eat, but the bread and potatoes are adequate. The days just drag on. I'm a free man, but I feel like a prisoner. I don't have any real work to do. I've signed up at the Registration Office and the Labor Office, but have been given a medical certificate releasing me from work for the next two weeks.

We've had all sorts of sickness at home. Mutti sprained her left hand, Irmi is not feeling up to par, Willi has had a temperature of 104 for days now. He evidently can't go on doing such heavy physical labor—dismantling machinery at the cable works—much longer. He's very weak and helpless at the moment. His voice, which was never strong, has been reduced to a whisper that you can barely understand.

All this and the uncertain prospects of some paying job (nothing doing at Siemens!) is discouraging of course, particularly since we still have no news from the children. We're afraid that in the Anglo-American occupation zone they have even less to eat than we do.

Some progress is being made clearing debris in the city. The sidewalks have been shoveled clear in places, and a lot of the street barricades have been taken down. People are hammering away inside shops and putting up primitive displays out front. In a good many places you see announcements that a company will be opening again soon. We've got electricity again now, too. We still lack gas, and the same goes for mail and any public transportation. The subway is running in a few places, and there are a couple of buses, but no regular consistent schedule has been set up yet.

Frau Freier was given 60 marks of occupation money for sewing some pillows for the Russians, but she doesn't know if she can even use the notes.

SUNDAY, 17 JUNE

Yesterday we celebrated Mutti's 61st birthday. Our thoughts were with the children and grandchildren, who surely were thinking of us as well.

This evening, a visit from a Herr Vollbach, whom the Antifas delegated to inform me that for now, and probably later as well, there can be no administrative position for me as a former party member. For all that, he was very polite and very happy to be able to borrow a few books from me, because, as he said, his own library of 5,000 volumes had been lost in the horror of the bombing.

In response to my question as to what I could do, he suggested: Wait, stand back, and let time do its work. I can only hope that's possible for me. It takes money to live after all, and you have to work to get money. But what do you do when you can't find any work?

Herr V. provided me with a vivid description of the events that occurred in the center of town in the last days before the city was taken. After his apartment on Wilhelm Strasse had been bombed out, he and his wife fled to a huge bunker filled with thousands of refugees somewhere nearby (the Reich Chancery?). Once there, with only a little baggage and scarcely anything to eat, he was cut off from the outside world for days. On 1 May[68]— Siemensstadt had already been occupied on 24 April—a high-ranking officer, decorated with the Iron Cross, appeared and delivered the following speech: "Comrades! I have just come from the Führer, who sends his greetings and thanks you for having held out so bravely thus far. The Russians have already been pushed back across the Oder. Berlin will be freed very shortly. And to keep you from having to suffer here any longer, you are to be taken to a safer place. Follow me!"

And then they moved in procession through the subway tunnel, at times wading through water up to their chests, past corpses and debris of every sort, as far as Stettin Station—or was it some other train station? The exact name has slipped my mind—a procession that Vollbach said he would never forget till the day he died. Herr Vollbach is not the only person to describe this incident to me. Who would have thought it possible!

On 1 May, when the entire situation was already hopeless and the center of the city was about to be taken, they were still lying to the people. Was that necessary? Couldn't it have been done some other way, openly and honestly?

News on the radio today that Foreign Minister von Ribbentrop has been captured in Hamburg. Göring has been captured, too, it's said. Only Himmler and Goebbels took their own lives. The latter that of his wife and all his children as well. Nothing is said about Hitler. It's assumed that he fell in battle and is buried in some mass grave.[69]

MONDAY, 18 JUNE

All Nazis and their kin have to appear for work this morning at 7:45. Mutti and I as well! We don't know what will become of Willi, who is bedridden with dysentery. Frau Freier can look in on him perhaps. Irmi has to work, too. Yesterday, Thursday, she was gone from 8 in the morning till 8 at night. There is no one left at home to take care of things, find food, cook, etc.

FRIDAY, 22 JUNE

Instead of putting us to work cleaning up the administration building, as they had promised, the Russians took us to the transformer works, where cleaning up involves heavy physical labor. We had to move iron and brass rods, the debris left behind from both the bombing and the dismantling had to be cleared from the floor of the main hall. We spent two days of drudgery, scrubbing away the oily filth, ruining our clothes. From children of twelve to seventy-year-old adults—all of them party members or their kin—we were kept busy from 8 in the morning to 7 at night, with one hour's rest. The food, which was doled out at the dynamo works, was relatively good.

We've been laid off again now and can take care of our own personal business, to the extent we have any, at least we older folks can. Irmi still has to work 13 hours a day.

Herr Vollbach was here again yesterday to borrow some more books. I was able to help him out with some food as well. He told me that he and his wife have not had anything warm to eat for four days now. Why not? Don't the Antifas, with whom he's associated, take care of him? He doesn't go into it, but despite his incredibly threadbare clothes, he gives the impression of a well-mannered man of better than average education; and since Mutti and I help anyone who's in trouble, without asking the why's and wherefore's, we helped him out, too, to the extent we could.

Irmi has gone out today to find the authorities who can provide her with a travel permit so that she can return to Bünde. Let's hope she has some success. We can well understand that she's homesick. Dr. Rüsch has received news that both his parents, who were staying in the Uckermark, are dead. Poisoned? Suicide? There were no details.

A large number of Russians have departed, but have apparently been replaced by new troops. The Anglo-Americans have not yet shown their faces at any rate.

SATURDAY, 30 JUNE

The Russians are still here. This evening at 11 o'clock, Mutti goes to fetch whatever soup the Russian soldiers have left. She is not the only one who goes begging for soup, but we have no other choice: We don't have enough food.

I've heard from Dr. Rüsch that not only his parents but also his sister and her two children died in the Uckermark. Director Möhle from the assembly division and Director Lüschen (awarded the Iron Cross) both took their lives. Möhle shot his wife as well. Herr Brendel has vanished into some prison camp or other, perhaps has even been sent to Russia. Word is that he did not stick to the truth in his statements and said that Dr. Reyss would substantiate them. Instead Dr. Reyss contradicted them, and Brendel then admitted he hadn't told the truth: leading to solitary confinement and continued arrest. That's what Herr Steinberg told me. We ask ourselves if that's how it really was. Might not Brendel have been trying to protect Dr. Reyss? The latter has been released from detention.

MONDAY, 2 JULY

The Russians pulled out yesterday and took along much of the furniture from the apartments where many of them had been living. The English or Americans who drove their cars down Harries Strasse looking for quarters didn't want to move into any apartment where Russians had been living, and when they heard that Russian troops had been quartered everywhere in this neighborhood, they drove on.

We have very little to eat. Yesterday Mutti had to beg five potatoes from Frau Freier so that we could have something for our midday meal.

At midnight we heard screams for help coming from Riepelt Strasse and the Rohr Damm. We don't know what happened. We kept our clothes on all night again, but thank God we weren't molested.

There are only a few crusts of bread left in the house today. We haven't been able to buy potatoes for two weeks, but we're hoping that some will arrive today.

I spent yesterday making what repairs I could on my two model ships, which had been badly damaged by some Russians visiting our cellar. They look quite neat and trim again.

Things must have been dreadful in Landsberg. My three books (*The Life of Confucius, Pudge and Bones,* and the picture album with the silver corners) as well as all the clothing the children had to leave behind before their trip (at Christmas), have probably been lost, because Landsberg is currently occupied by the Poles, who are expelling all the Germans and not letting anyone in. In another week or so Irmi intends to try to travel to Bünde, although we're being warned on all sides, since no one is allowed across the Elbe.

24 AUGUST

I've not made any entries for a long time now—I'm tired, but will at least try to catch up with what I've left out. Only the most important things: We're hungry, but thank God we haven't starved yet. Often there aren't any potatoes, then again there's no bread; but each time, just when we were close to despair, something edible showed up and kept us alive.

On 12 July 1945, I was hired as the chief translator at the headquarters of the English military government. I was so happy, despite the fact that I had to walk to and from Spandau every day. I had to leave the English, who were very sorry to see me go, because former party members cannot hold such positions. Just as I left their service, the English were starting to be well-supplied with rations. What a shame I wasn't allowed to share in them, I could have brought home a nice snack now and then.

The English sent me on my way with a letter for the SSW (Siemens Schuckert Werk), saying they had nothing against my being rehired by Siemens. The official advisors at Siemens have nothing against it, either; but so far that has not been any help. There's no position open for me at SSW.

I'm at the end of my tether. Willi is back at work, which is to say, the Labor Office has put him to work clearing rubble. Hard labor—how long will he hold out? According to a decree of the military government, I have to register the rest of my Standard Life policies with the City-Kontor Bank in Spandau today. The policies, worth a total of £1,027—all that's left of £5,000—and for which I saved for so many years, are with Gretel in Bünde. I leave the receipts with the bank. The money's lost now![70] Last Sunday Mutti and I were on Xantener Strasse. Someone had forced open our cellar door and stolen my typewriter, our radio, and a long list of other items—*meyou faze!*[71]

Mutti weighs only 88 pounds in her clothes; we've both become very thin. Summer is drawing to a close. What will winter bring? Where are we to get fuel, food, and work? I'm translating Timperley's book *What War Means*—that won't bring in any money for now, but perhaps it will get us a better ration card.

At present, for every 300 marriages there are 200 births and 3,000 deaths! No comment.

28 AUGUST

On Wednesday 29 August, Irmi can perhaps travel to Hannover in an English car that's transporting released German prisoners. Lisl Hohmann can't go with her unfortunately, since she was never part of the Wehrmacht, which Irmi was. My attempts to convince the English military government in Spandau to make an exception and give Lisl a travel permit came to nothing. Lisl still intends to leave on Wednesday. But by train, at first as far as Eisenach.

Until now we've been unable to put together any provisions for the girls to take along on the journey, they must each have at least a loaf of bread. Mutti found a ride out to Lichterfelde (a walk of 5–6 hours) to beg a loaf from Frau Brendel; we got another one from a neighbor, Frau Haltermann, for ten cigarettes that an English fellow gave Willi.

This morning's breakfast was only two slices of bread. I saved one for lunch. I'm trying to adjust to the least quantity possible. Thus far we've always had something to nibble at, but what happens from here on is uncertain.

First, two loaves of bread will have to be rounded up for the girls' trips. For Irmi the trip is expected to take about two days, but it can take as many as four or six. And there's no telling how long Lisl Hohmann will be under way—she's trying to get to Essen to look for her mother. Perhaps she'll just have to depend entirely on the kindness of others. What a dreadful thought! But we don't have anything left to eat ourselves!

MONDAY, 3 SEPTEMBER

After two fruitless attempts to find shelter at the camp at Ruheleben before traveling on to the west with an English transport, Irmi was ordered to report to Falkensee and from there was sent to the camp in Staaken, which was supposed to be the starting point for a transport on 1 September. She hoped to be home by Sunday, that is yesterday. We hope so, too.

Lisl is still stranded in Ilsenburg in the Harz Mountains. Erika Brechelt returned home having got nowhere. Lisl will have to wait until a transport leaves; allegedly only 40 people are allowed over the border at a time.

I brought home two potatoes (two!) that fell off a Russian truck. Every passerby dives for precious booty like that now. You have to be quick, otherwise you come up empty-handed. Yes, that's what we've come to. Hunger hurts, but complaining doesn't fill your belly. Question: How long can a man hold out?

At school, the teacher told the children: "Death by starvation isn't fast, it's slow. You finally grow so weak that you die almost without pain." Why you would tell children that, I don't know. I suppose it's meant to console them.

SUNDAY, 14 OCTOBER

Finally news has come through from Gretel that she and the children, Ursi and Gudrun, are all right. As we learned from Dr. Möhlmann, who returned here a short while ago, Gretel has found a job with the English, where she hopes to get better rations. Irmi must have arrived in Bünde by now, too.

A letter has arrived from Otto's father-in-law, telling us that all the Stubenrauchs and Rabes are all right. A little boy was born to Otto and Eva on 12 May 1945. A letter from Otto came today, too, confirming the news.

The baby's name is Michael Detlef Nicolai. Meanwhile the Munich Rabes surely must have arrived in Mannheim, where they planned to move after their Munich apartment had to be returned to Herr Amann. Grandfather Stubenrauch is alive and working as a librarian in Mannheim.

As of 1 October 1945, I became a retiree, pensioned off by the SSW, which then hired me temporarily as a translator the very same day. I hope to God that I can keep the job, since the pension is very small.

Willi is a timekeeper for the English troops and returns home faithfully each day with his ration of corned beef and butter—small, very small portions, but absolutely essential for the three of us here, since we have so very little to eat. We have all been inoculated for typhoid now, which is rampant at the SSW. The furniture we had left with Dr. Selle in Xantener Strasse, or what was left of it, has now all been stored in our cellar here because our cellar on Xantener Strasse was badly pilfered by our fellow Germans.

We're moving into winter. There's no heat at the SSW, and only the kitchen is warm at home. Electricity and gas are rationed. Let's hope we stay healthy. Things are just as miserable for all Germans!

18 APRIL 1946

Tomorrow is Good Friday, and our mood fits the day. We have suffered hunger and more hunger. I didn't have much of anything else to report, which is why I stopped making diary entries. To supplement our diet, we ate acorn-meal soup, from acorns that Mutti secretly harvested last fall. For days now, ever since our supply ran out, we've been eating nettles, which taste as good as spinach.

My petition to be denazified was denied yesterday. Although as head of the International Committee of the Nanking Safety Zone I saved the lives of 250,000 people, Chinese people, my petition was turned down because I was temporarily the local group leader of the NSDAP in Nanking and—or so the newspaper writes—a man of my intelligence ought never to have joined the party.

I'll file an appeal with the Sector Commission in Charlottenburg, the next step up. If they take away my chance of continuing to work at the SSW, I don't how we're supposed to live, or to keep on fighting—I'm so tired.

I'm being interrogated daily by the English police (23rd Field Security Police, Spandau Detachment).

A member of the examining board for the Denazification Commission accused me of having been friends with the advisors to Chiang Kai-shek, who is driving his Chinese to their deaths—to wit: the news that he is fighting the Communists in Manchuria! What can you say to that?

If I had heard of any Nazi atrocities while I was in China, I would never have joined the party, and if my views as a German had clashed with those of the other foreigners in Nanking, the English, Americans, Danes, etc. in Nanking would never have chosen me to be *chairman* of the International Committee of the Nanking Safety Zone. The "living Buddha for hundreds of thousands" in Nanking, and a pariah, an outcast here! That would soon cure you of any homesickness.

I haven't reported this yet, either: Confidential Secretary Brendel and Director Dr. Bingel both died in the Russian detainment camp at Ketschendorf.

16 MAY 1946

As of 3 May, I'm no longer allowed to work officially in the Siemens office. A letter from a Mr. Coulden, deputy of Wing Commander McEvan, who is head of the Industry Department of the British military government and on vacation at present, forbade me from keeping my "former position." I think Mr. Coulden means my position with the English military government, but Siemens management wants to avoid complications of any sort.

As of 31 May 1946, then, I will be working at home, picking up my work from one of the directors (Herr Jäckel), who lives near Siemensstadt and has been very kind to me, and so for the moment I've been saved from direst straits—unemployment, etc.

So now I have plenty of time to attempt to prepare for my appearance before the Sector Commission, which is the 1st level of appeal. I don't know just yet when the hearing will take place. I'll be submitting my petition in the next few days, am already almost done with all the written material required.

In the meantime, on 12 May, little Michael was baptized on his first birthday, and on 13 May (Otto's birthday) Gretel arrived here from Bünde along with Ursi and Gudrun. We thank God that all three are here again, all with colds, but generally up and about.

7 JUNE

On 3 June, I was finally denazified by the Denazification Commission for the British Sector in Charlottenburg (District Office, Witzleben Strasse 3–4). The decision reads: "Despite your having been the deputy local leader in Nanking and although you did not resign from the NSDAP on your return to Germany, the commission has nevertheless decided to grant your appeal on the basis of your successful humanitarian work in China, etc." And with that, the nerve-wracking torture is over! Thank God! I've received congratulations from many friends and the directors at Siemens and been given a few days vacation by the firm to recover from the ordeal.

Mutti is off today with our Chinese carved wooden gods to see Dr. Krebs, who has provided us with food now and again and who is in love with our idols. We've sold my Chinese carpet, the runner given to us by Kong, to Frau Töpfer for three hundredweight of potatoes: You simply cannot do without food. And in such a plight a man has to part with his curios and keepsakes from China. I'm very happy that at my age I'm still allowed to work at Siemens.

The sweetest photographs have just arrived of Otto, Eva, and little Michael, who can already walk. If only the borders between zones were open, we could make the trip to Mannheim and see our little grandson. Travel is still not possible at present, that is private travel; and unfortunately I have no reason to travel on business, and I'd want to take Mutti along, since she's never even seen Eva. But we shall not be ingrates: We're simply thankful that fate has kept us all alive and healthy!

With that, John Rabe completed the last page of his diary. He never began another.

AFTERWORD

John Rabe's Last Years

HE HAD KEPT A diary for decades. It was his passion. He took pleasure in recording what he had experienced and observed so that he could understand it better. He could, as is surely obvious by now, write clearly and tell a story well. But after the Gestapo confiscated his Nanking diaries, the pleasure he once took in writing was apparently lost. Or perhaps he also thought it was too risky to put to paper what he was now thinking.

Since throughout the war, the only task assigned to him by his company was the job of looking after Siemens employees in foreign internment camps, he had plenty of leisure time to make a clean copy of what he had written in Nanking: seven not especially large volumes, covering the period from September 1937 to April 1938, intended as reading for his wife—and thus full of many remarks about the family and household problems—and interspersed with newspaper clips, letters, invitations, and documents that he had pasted into it. He gave these volumes the title: *Enemy Pilots over Nanking.*

And then he condensed it all into two volumes, a total of 800 pages titled *Bombs over Nanking—From the Diary of a Living Buddha*. The text is much the same as that found in the seven family diaries written for his wife. *Bombs over Nanking* also contains newspaper clips, letters, telegrams, minutes of Safety Zone Committee meetings, and a list of more than 400 cases of atrocities by the Japanese military. These two diaries contain an uninterrupted documentation of the bombardment of Nanking, the founding and work of the Safety Zone Committee, and those war crimes of which the committee was aware. This book is a selection of all the important entries in this work by John Rabe.

He did not begin his last diary until 24 April 1945. It is written in his fine hand and begins as if it were a direct continuation of *Bombs over Nanking*: descriptions of looting, rapes, arrests, people driven from their homes, executions. Not as bad as in China, but bad enough.

While on a visit to the Siemens Works he was arrested by the Soviets and kept locked up in a nearby house with other detainees. He was not subjected to a third-degree interrogation. The food and treatment were good, as he himself notes, but of course he did not like being under arrest. He was interrogated by a major whom he calls "Föderoff." There are claims that he was also received by Marshal Zhukov, but they are incorrect.

The Soviets asked him about his life in considerable detail, and he had to sign his statement as taken down by the Russians and give his word of honor to help the Soviets "restore order in Berlin."

He was then released, but they also ordered him to provide them with the names of all Siemens employees who had ever worked in the Soviet Union. "A difficult task," John Rabe writes. "I don't know how I'm going to carry it out." A colleague took over the job for him.

In Rabe's last diary, Hitler and the other leading National Socialists are mentioned only occasionally. He had come to his conclusions about them. He had written them off, they no longer interested him.

The Russians were followed by the British, who took over the sector in the northwest of Berlin. The military government hired John Rabe as its chief translator, but in August 1945, after only a few weeks, they tossed him out again because former party members were not allowed to work for them. He was now earning nothing and was burdened by the worry that as a former party member he would not be hired by Siemens, either.

He was often ill—heart problems, high blood pressure, and his old diabetes. The doctors blamed the eruption of a skin condition on a deficient diet. And yet he often had to work helping dismantle the heavy machinery at the Siemens Works.

The German Denazification Panel would not denazify him. As an intelligent man, he (1) should not have joined the party and (2) upon returning home in 1938, should have seen National Socialism for what is was and resigned at once.

He was finally denazified, however, on appeal, and his firm rehired him, but once again did not give him a position or real responsibility.

In 1934, he had written a lovely book, a bound manuscript of 215 pages titled *A Quarter Century with Siemens Company in China,* which contained old photographs of Peking and was dedicated to Carl-Friedrich von Siemens. It can still be found in the Siemens Archive. Rabe never wrote a single angry or critical word about his firm; but it is difficult to understand why they treated him as they did.

Upon his return to Berlin—after years of successfully managing one of the most important branches of Siemens China Company in Nanking; after serving as the mayor of Nanking who, in the unanimous opinion of both Germans and other nationals, saved its 250,000 inhabitants in a catastrophic situation, acting as manager, diplomat, negotiator, and chairman of the International Safety Zone Committee and, last but not least, providing splendid proof of his courage in many dangerous situations—he was given only a subordinate position in the personnel department.

He was never assigned tasks commensurate with his abilities. Why not? We can only guess. Because his education had stopped with the equivalent of a high-school diploma, because he was not an academic? Because he had not been part of the home team in the Berlin central office? Because people never forgot that he had stayed behind in Nanking, instead of representing the interests of Siemens China Company in Hankow? Surely the firm could have given him an appropriate position in China or Hong Kong after he was called back from Nanking. At one point there were hints from the Shanghai office that pointed in that direction, but then nothing more was heard of it. Why?

The Siemens Archive provides ample information about the excellent reviews given Rabe's work from 1911 to 1913. But it is silent about this question. After his diaries became public knowledge, the firm commissioned a Chinese artist to create a bronze bust of John Rabe, which was placed outside its new branch in Nanking in October 1997.

When they were bombed out of their apartment in Berlin-Wilmersdorf in 1943, John Rabe and his wife moved into one room of their son-in-law's apartment in Siemensstadt. John Rabe lived in this room until his death. They went hungry, and were perhaps not as clever as others who knew how to make better use of the black market for their needs.

When potatoes fell from a Soviet truck one day and John Rabe managed to pick two of them up off the street, it was an event that he considered worth recording in his diary. They made soup out of ground acorns his wife had gathered in the fall, and when the acorns ran out, they ate nettles, which according to Rabe tasted as good as other salad greens.

He did not complain, but remembered that others had things as bad or perhaps even worse. After beginning his diary with such élan, he then had to explain why later on he did not touch it for weeks, even months. "We have suffered hunger and more hunger," he wrote in the spring of 1946. "I didn't have much of anything else to report, which is why I stopped making diary entries."

He traded a Chinese carpet and his antique Chinese wooden figurines, including a Kuanyin, the goddess of mercy, for some potatoes. The cellar in his bombed-out building in Wilmersdorf was broken into and everything of value stolen—by his fellow Germans.

Early in 1947, he was pensioned off at age 65, but to augment his small pension he continued to work part-time for Siemens.

In Nanking he had once noted in a moment of depression: "Here I went and did the right thing, and now the company doesn't like it. What a mess! I truly am a 'Lame Jack'!"—or, as he might also have put it, a raven [German: *Rabe*] of bad luck.

"I am so tired," he writes in 1947. And again: "The 'living Buddha for hundreds of thousands' in Nanking, and a pariah, an outcast here! That would soon cure you of any homesickness."

He had resigned himself to his fate.

And then the Chinese military mission in Berlin found his address and saw to it that he got some extra food. Madame Chiang Kai-shek had her secretary inform him that she would be happy to help him out because of the great things he had done in Nanking. The Chinese offered him an apartment and a pension if he were willing to resettle in China. All he had to do was to be a witness for the prosecution at the Tokyo war crimes tribunal. John Rabe declined. In a message he left for his grandchildren, he explained: "I didn't want to see any Japanese hang, although they deserved it. . . . There must be some atonement, some just punishment; but in my view the judgment should be spoken only by their own nation."[1]

The wife of the American missionary W. P. Mills, who was still in Nanking, learned of Rabe's address as well. She sent him CARE packages. John Rabe went on working part-time for Siemens, he lived in poverty, but he no longer had to go hungry.

On 5 January 1949, John Rabe suffered a stroke while working at Siemens. He died that same evening. In attendance at his grave were his wife, his children, and a few friends.

DOCUMENTS

DOCUMENT I

From the German Ambassador in Nanking to the Foreign Ministry

Telegram
Cito!   Nanking, 3 December 1937, 0:55 a.m.
Top secret   Received: 3 December 1937, 1:50 a.m.
No. 2. from 2. 12.
For the Reich Minister

Chiang Kai-shek first expressed to me his profound thanks for Germany's peace efforts. China is ready, he said, to accept Germany's mediation because it regards us as a friend of China. I faithfully recapitulated the latest Japanese statement, to which Chiang Kai-shek then asked whether Japan's . . . [group missing[1]] were still the same. I replied that that was the case, saying that their telegram had spoken only of main points, but their previous conditions had also contained only main points. Whereupon Chiang Kai-shek said that he could not accept the standpoint that the Japanese had emerged as the victors in the battle. I replied that the whole world had admired the achievements of the Chinese army. At that,

Chiang Kai-shek . . . [group missing] that he could also not accept an ultimatum from the Japanese. I responded that this was not an ultimatum. Chiang Kai-shek then formulated the Chinese standpoint as follows:

1. China accepts these conditions as the basis for peace talks.

2. The sovereignty and integrity as well as the . . . [group missing[1]] autonomy of northern China are not to be violated.

3. Germany should be active as the mediator at all peace negotiations from the start.

4. China's treaties with third parties are not to be affected by peace negotiations.

As to Point 1: I told him that I considered it necessary for China to declare itself willing to discuss these conditions in a conciliatory spirit and with a desire to . . . [group missing]. Chiang Kai-shek declared that he would do this, but that he expected the same from Japan.

Point 2: I called Chiang Kai-shek's attention to the Japanese condition that the chief official in northern China be friendly toward Japan. Chiang Kai-shek responded that, of course, anyone chosen for such a post would not be anti-Japanese.

Point 3: I explained to Chiang Kai-shek that Germany would probably prefer not to be directly involved in peace negotiations, and certainly not to be in charge of them. We would rather try to do what we could to help China from behind the scenes. Chiang Kai-shek said he hoped that we would choose to be of such good service to the last.

Point 4: I called Chiang Kai-shek's attention to the Japanese demand of fighting Communism. I said I was of the opinion that this demand was not contrary to the Sino-Russian nonaggression pact. Chiang Kai-shek did not contradict me.

As to the cessation of hostilities, I told him that I imagined the procedure would be: that once Chiang Kai-shek's declaration had been delivered to the Japanese and Japan's agreement was in hand, the Führer and Reich Chancellor would appeal to both governments to cease hostilities. Chiang Kai-shek agreed. Finally, Chiang Kai-shek urgently requested that the Japanese government keep these preliminary discussions and, most especially, their conditions secret. That would be a precondition for peace. I believe we should support this request to the best of our abilities. Otherwise Chiang Kai-shek's position would be so badly undermined that he would have to resign and leave the government in the hands of those who hold pro-Russian views. Japan should attempt to do everything it can to make it possible for him to conduct negotiations. Since Chiang Kai-shek told me in my earlier conversation that it was impossible for China to accept the demand of an autonomous Mongolia, as that would mean the loss of two provinces, I asked him if he wished to say anything to me in that regard. He explained that the question of Mongolia could be negotiated with the Japanese. During the entire conversation Chiang Kai-shek was extremely friendly, in a good mood, and showed no signs of nervousness. He was optimistic about his capital's defense. I am traveling back to Hankow, where I shall await further instructions. All embassy staff and local Germans are all right.

Same message to Tokyo

TRAUTMANN[2]

DOCUMENT 2

From the German Ambassador in Tokyo
to the Foreign Ministry

Telegram
Top Secret!   Tokyo, 3 December 1937, 3:00 p.m.
No. 385 from 3. 12.   Received: 3 December 1937, 2:25 p.m.
Sent simultaneously to the Reich War Ministry and Reich Air Ministry

Ongoing discussions of our military attaché with the General Staff have resulted in the following situation as of early December: Northern China has been conquered, the major assault there has ceased, Japanese troops are being reorganized for occupation. No further battle for Shantung Province is expected.

In the main Shanghai theater of war, a rapid advance on Nanking, its fall assumed sometime yet in December.

In official Japanese circles resistance by Chinese troops is regarded as severely weakened, while new battle-ready troops cannot be brought up before summer 1938. Their battle supplies continue to dwindle, and any Chinese hopes that the Japanese economy will falter will prove to be in error.

Thirty airplanes have thus far been secured via Russian military aid, which number is allegedly now increasing to 200.

Within circles of the Japanese General Staff there is renewed consideration being given to accelerated peace negotiations with the Chinese, which serve China's purposes, given their heavy losses and disappointment at the failure of the Brussels Conference, and also serve Japan's, given the constant expansion of the theater of war and its costs.

According to personal and confidential information, the General Staff is holding back from Japan's taking steps toward peace because of radical opposition and an effort by several army groups to remove Chiang Kai-shek entirely. Given this situation, influential persons on the General Staff await an initiative from the Führer and Reich Chancellor that would open the door for negotiations; they believe that should the Führer and Reich Chancellor receive Chiang Kai-shek's fundamental consent to begin direct negotiations with Japan, the same request would receive Japan's consent as well.

In such a case, the General Staff emphasizes the necessity of full secrecy to avoid any interference by England and America, to which it would strongly object.

Official suggestions in this direction are not to be expected from the Japanese government at present.

DIRKSEN[3]

DOCUMENT 3

From Reich Foreign Minister von Neurath
to the German Embassy in Tokyo

Telegram
At once   Berlin, 4 December 1937
Secret   (Sent: 4.12., 9:15 p.m.)
No. 306 from 4.12.
For the Ambassador only

A. Your wires No. 385[4] and 386 have crossed with that of Ambassador Trautmann from Nanking on 2 inst. concerning his conversation with Chiang Kai-shek. According to Ambassador Trautmann's wire, almost all the essential points contained in the Japanese suggestions have been satisfied. I therefore believe we have come to a point where the Japanese government must take some step that would lead to an armistice in East Asia and in due course to direct negotiations between the parties.

In order to avoid all misunderstanding, it will be necessary to provide the Japanese government with a written statement of all German actions thus far. Let me again emphasize that these actions are not those of a mediator, but merely those of an informant passing on views brought to its attention by the two parties involved in the dispute. . . .

B. The necessity of delivering this foregoing detailed historical account [omitted here] to the Japanese, and soon thereafter to the Chinese government as well, arises from the great responsibility that the German government is assuming in its attempt to contribute to the cessation of hostilities and the restoration of peace, even if only in the role of a conveyor of information. That responsibility is further increased should the person of the Führer and Reich Chancellor be placed in the foreground at the appropriate moment.

During the presentation of the foregoing written historical account to the Japanese government, it will be your task to insure that it is on this basis that the Japanese government is prepared to take the steps leading to direct armistice negotiations and subsequent peace negotiations, first at the level of the Japanese and Chinese military authorities and later at the political level. I call to your attention that only this written account can be the valid and determinant basis for negotiations, so that no later reference to earlier objections or reservations (e.g., point No. 8 in your wire No. 386, 3 inst.) can be taken into consideration. As soon as Japanese consent is given, Ambassador Trautmann will be authorized to gain the same consent from the Chinese government, after first presenting it in the same written account. Once the secured agreement of both parties is obtained, this can be followed by a solemn appeal by Germany for both sides to cease hostilities for the purpose of restoring peaceful relations.

This appeal, which may very well be made by the Führer himself, would refrain from any political position whatever. It would be founded on the need for a restoration of peaceful conditions in East Asia, which is recognized worldwide and is most strongly felt by the two nations engaged in the conflict; but otherwise it would restrict itself to enjoining both governments involved to establish direct contacts for the purpose of ceasing hostilities, leading to negotiations to conclude a peace agreement. In your démarche, I would ask you to make it clear to the Japanese government the strong Chinese desire, which indeed corresponds to Japan's own express wish, that silence concerning preliminary negotiations must be maintained until the expected German appeal for peace is made. This wish of both parties is fully in accord with that of the German government. It can thus be assumed that all parties involved will comply.

VON NEURATH[5]

DOCUMENT 4

From Reich Foreign Minister von Neurath
to the German Embassy in Tokyo

Telegram
No. 313   Berlin, 10 December 1937
Private and Confidential
For the Ambassador

We, of course, understand that with the continuation of military operations, war goals of the parties involved can change. Despite this fact,

however, we are now no longer certain of our original readiness to forward whatever information that is made available to us and that might
contribute to those parties finding their way to the negotiation table.
There is, after all, a limit to the function of messenger that we have per-
formed thus far, when demeaning, unacceptable demands are made of
China. Nor can we allow ourselves to be put in the position of forwarding conditions to the Chinese, which, then, only a short time later the
Japanese deem to be in need of enlargement.

[. . .]   VON NEURATH[6]

DOCUMENT 5

*Memorandum of Secretary of
the Foreign Ministry von Mackensen*

Berlin, 3 November 1937

On the basis of impressions received thus far, the Reich foreign minister
does not believe that in Field Marshal von Blomberg's discussion scheduled for tomorrow with the Führer about the issue of withdrawing German military advisors from China, he will restrict himself to a simple
acceptance of such an order. Moreover, he—the Reich foreign minister—
will point out to the field marshal that counterarguments are necessary.
As a crucial argument I suggested the question of whether the Führer
would prefer General von Falkenhausen or a Soviet general on the side of
the Chinese.

MACKENSEN[7]

DOCUMENT 6

*From a Memorandum of Secretary of the Foreign Ministry
von Mackensen, Dated 8 November 1937*

*[When asked if in his meeting with the Reich War Minister, Hitler had clarified
the question of withdrawing German military advisors, General Keitel said the
issue had not been touched upon but]* . . . "the Führer had told Field Marshal
von Blomberg that the Reich War Ministry should see to it that it rids itself of the odor of pro-Chinese sentiments."[8]

DOCUMENT 7

Release to Chinese Press and Police of the International Committee for the Nanking Safety Zone, Dated 4 December 1937 [9]

Housing Plans.

1. The area is not yet ready for large-scale moving in of the population and the military situation does not yet make any such movement necessary.

2. In order to reduce the numbers of people that have to move when it becomes more urgent, the Committee suggests that individual families who can make private arrangements for houses with friends or others in the Safety Zone do so at once. The Committee reserves the right to put more people in houses later, if necessary.

3. Meanwhile the Housing commission is making a survey of housing facilities in the Safety Zone and will try to make arrangements for those who cannot make their own private arrangements. But these facilities will not be opened until absolutely necessary in view of the military situation. At that time definite announcement of the opening of the area will be made public.

4. In these private arrangements, only private houses are to be used. No public building or institutional building is to be used for this purpose.

5. No furniture or other movable property is to be brought into the Zone because all available housing space is needed for people. People moving in should only bring with them bedding, clothing, and food.

Food Plans.

1. The Zone is not ready for any large numbers of people to move into because there is not enough food in the Zone yet to feed them. All people moving in now should bring with them at least enough food for a week.

2. Private dealers are encouraged to move their stocks of rice, flour and other food supplies and fuel in and carry on their regular business.

3. Supplies of rice and flour assigned to the committee for use in the Safety Zone are to be held in reserve in case the stocks of private dealers run out. Then these reserve supplies will be

sold out through the private dealers having a license from the Committee.

Trucks and Autos.

The Committee needs trucks and cars badly and would welcome any given or loaned to the Committee for use in moving in supplies and other necessary services.

Time Zone will be opened.

The Zone cannot be opened as a Refugee Zone until all Chinese military establishments have been moved out of the area.

INTERNATIONAL COMMITTEE FOR SAFETY ZONE IN NANKING

DOCUMENT 8

Organization of Safety Zone Administration

I. Officers:

1. Chairman of International Committee: John H. D. Rabe.

2. Secretary of International Committee: Lewis S. C. Smythe.

3. Director: George Fitch.

4. 2nd Director: Dr. Han Liwu.

5. Treasurer: Christian Kröger.

6. Chief of Chinese Secretariat: Dean Tang.

II. Commissions:

1. Inspector General: Eduard Sperling.

2. Food Commission:
   Han Hsiang-Lin, Chairman.
   Hubert L. Sone, Associate.

3. Housing Commission:
   Wang-Ting, Chairman.
   Charles Riggs, Associate.
   Charles Gee.

4. Sanitation commission:
   Shen Yü-shu, Chairman.
   Dr. C. S. Trimmer, Associate.

5. Transport Control:
   E. L. Hirschberg, Chairman.
   R. R. Hatz, Associate.

DOCUMENT 9

Press Release, 5 December 1937

1. This morning the Committee received a direct reply from the Japanese authorities in Shanghai through the courtesy of the American Naval Radio.

2. This morning at 11:00 the Chairman of the Committee, Mr. John H. D. Rabe, the Inspector-General, Mr. Eduard Sperling and Dr. M. S. Bates called upon General Tang Sheng-chih concerning the question of moving military establishments out of the area proposed for the Safety Zone. In reply General Tang made the following three comments as explanatory of the letter he sent to the Committee on December 3rd.

    (1) If the proposed Safety Zone is clearly marked, the military will see to it that no new military establishments come in.

    (2) Furthermore, no military works including anti-aircraft guns will be continued in the area and all guns and armed men will be excluded.

    (3) Supplementary and service establishments, which comprise neither armed men nor active military units, will, of course, move out when it becomes necessary.

At a meeting this afternoon, the Committee decided to go ahead on the basis of these comments. The Zone will be marked with flags at a time to be agreed upon with General Tang in order to familiarize the people and military men with the boundaries of Zone. But the Committee will not declare the Zone in final effect until formal notification has been given by the Committee to both sides. That notification will not be given until all the conditions agreed upon have been fulfilled.

DOCUMENT 10

14 December 1937: Important Notice to the Refugees in the Safety Zone

1. From now on people should stay off the streets as much as possible.

2. At the most dangerous moment, everyone should get in houses or out of sight.

3. The Safety Zone is for Refugees. Sorry, the Safety Zone has no power to give protection to soldiers.

4. If there is any searching or inspection, give full freedom for such search. No opposition at all.

DOCUMENT 11

International Committee of the Nanking Safety Zone[10]

Letter to the Japanese Embassy, Nanking
For the kind attention of Mr. Kiyoshi Fukui, Second Secretary

17 December 1937

Dear Sirs:

In view of the statement of Consul-General Katsuo Okazaki yesterday afternoon that the International Committee had no legal status, some explanations of our position seem to be in order.

Vis-à-vis your Japanese authorities we are not claiming any political status whatever. But on December 1, Mayor Ma of the Nanking Municipality turned over to our Committee nearly all the functions of the City government for the emergency of transitions: police, supervision of essential utilities, fire department, housing regulation, food supply, and sanitation. Consequently, when your Army victoriously arrived in the city on Monday noon, December 13, we were the only administrative authority carrying on in the city. Of course, that authority did not extend outside of the Safety Zone itself, and involved no right of sovereignty within the Zone. . . .

The following morning, December 15, we were favored by calls by Mr. Tokuyasu Fukuda of the Imperial Japanese Embassy, and by Mr. Sekiguchi with cards from the Captain and Officers of the H.I.J.M.S. *Seta* at our headquarters. We presented our letter of December 14, referred to above, to Mr. Fukuda and assured Mr. Sekiguchi that we would be glad to cooperate in starting the electricity works. At noon, we had the pleasure of meeting the Head of the T'eh Pei Kwan Chang (specially delegated official) at the Bank of Communications and from him received a formal, oral statement in answer to our letter of December 14. In his reply, among other points, he said that they would station guards at the entrances to the Zone; that the civilian police could patrol within the Zone provided they were armed only with batons; that the Committee could use the 10,000 *tan* of rice it had stored and move in the other stores of rice assigned to it by the former City Government; and that it was essential to repair the telephone, electricity and water works as soon as possible.

But no answer was given to point 4 in our letter of the 14th excepting to say that people should return to their homes as soon as possible.

On the basis of this reply, we encouraged our police to go ahead with their duties, assured the people they would be well-treated now that we had explained to the Japanese officers, and started to move rice.

But since then any truck that appeared on the streets without a Westerner on it has been commandeered; the Red Swastika Society (working under our direction), which started trucks Tuesday morning to pick up dead bodies in the Zone, had its trucks either taken or attempts made to take them and now yesterday 14 of their workers were taken away. Our police were interfered with and yesterday 50 of them stationed at the Ministry of Justice were marched off, "to be killed" according to the Japanese officer in charge, and yesterday afternoon 46 of our "volunteer police" were similarly marched off. These volunteers had been organized by our Committee on December 13 when it looked as though the work to be done in the Zone was greater than the uniformed police—who were on day and night duty—could take care of. These "volunteer police" were neither uniformed nor armed in any way. They simply wore our armbands. They were more like Boy Scouts in the West who do odd jobs in helping to keep crowds in order, clean up, and render first aid, etc.

On the 14th our four fire trucks were commandeered by Japanese soldiers and used for transport.

The point we have been trying so hard to get across to your Embassy and to the Japanese Army is that we were left to carry on the City Government services for the civilian population of Nanking until the Japanese authorities could establish a new City Government or other organization to take over these functions in the city. But unfortunately your soldiers have not been willing to let us continue with our maintenance of order and services for the civilian population in the Zone. This resulted in a breaking down of our system for maintaining order and for providing necessary services which we had carried on up till the morning of December 14. In other words, on the 13th when your troops entered the city, we had nearly all the civilian population gathered in a Zone in which there had been very little destruction by stray shells and no looting by Chinese soldiers even when in full retreat. The stage was all set for you to take over that area peacefully and let the normal life therein continue undisturbed until the rest of the city could be put in order. Then the full normal life of the city could go forward. All 27 Westerners in the city at that time and our Chinese population were totally surprised by the reign of robbery, rapine and killing initiated by your soldiers on the 14th.

All that we are asking in our protest is that you restore order among your troops and get the normal life of the city going as soon as possible. In the latter process we are glad to cooperate in any way we can.

But even last night between 8 and 9 p.m. when five Western members of our staff and Committee toured the Zone to observe conditions, we did not find a single Japanese patrol either in the Zone or at the entrances! Yesterday's threats and marching off of our police had driven all our police from the streets. All we saw were groups of two and three Japanese soldiers wandering about the streets of the Zone and now, as I write, reports are pouring in from all parts of the Zone about the depredations of robbery and rape committed by these wandering, uncontrolled soldiers. This means that nothing has been done about our requests in our letter of yesterday, December 16, namely, point 2, that stray soldiers be kept out of the Zone by guards at the entrances.

Consequently, as a first step in turning over to your authorities the maintenance of order in the Zone, we suggest:

1. That the Imperial Japanese Army set up a system of regular military police to patrol the Zone both day and night with full authority to arrest soldiers found looting, entering houses, and committing rape or carrying off women.

2. That the Japanese authorities take over the 450 Chinese police assigned to us by the former Chinese Nanking City Government and organize them to maintain peace and order among the civilian population. (This order has never once broken down in the Zone.)

3. In view of the number of fires in the city yesterday and last night, fortunately not in the Zone, we suggest that the Fire Department be reorganized under your authorities and the four trucks be returned by your soldiers to such service.

4. We further respectfully beg to suggest that as soon as possible you kindly bring an expert in Municipal Administration to Nanking to manage the life of the civilian population until a new city government can be formed. (There is nothing left of the former city government excepting the police and firemen in our Zone and three clerks. All others left the city. Your army has taken the physical structure of the city of Nanking and the poorer sections of its population, but most of the trained, intelligent and active people have all moved further west.)

May we again reassure you that we have no interest in continuing any semi-administrative function left to us by the former Nanking City Government. We earnestly hope that you will kindly take up these functions as quickly as possible. Then we will become simply a relief organization.

If the depredations of the last three days continue, this relief problem is going to be multiplied rapidly. We organized the Zone on the basis that every family should make private arrangements for housing and food in order to reduce the administrative load suddenly placed on our *ad hoc* organization. But if the present situation continues, in a few days we are going to have large numbers of people facing starvation; their private supplies of food and fuel are running out; money, clothing and personal articles have been taken from many of them by wandering Japanese soldiers; and little normal business or other activity can be carried on because people are afraid either to open shops or appear on the streets.

On the other hand, since the morning of December 14, our supply trucks have been practically at a standstill. Before your troops entered the city we concentrated on getting supplies into the Zone and expected to carry out distribution later because the people had been urged to bring a week's supply of food with them. But in order to keep some of our camps from going without food over a day, Western members of our staff and committee have had to haul bags of rice to those places in their private cars after dark!

Besides the starvation facing the people if these services cannot be extended quickly, there is the stirring up of the people. Some families have had their houses entered, robbed and their women raped as much as five times in one night. Is it any wonder that the next morning they move out and try to find a safer place?

And yesterday afternoon while three officers of your Army Supply Department were asking us to help get the telephone service started, a small number of telephone workers wearing our insignia were turned out of their houses in the Zone and are now scattered to unknown places in the Zone. If this process of terrorism continues, it will be next to impossible to locate workers to get the essential services started.

It is hard to see how starvation may be prevented among many of the 200,000 Chinese civilians if order is not restored at once among the Japanese soldiers in the city.

Assuring you that we will be glad to cooperate in any way we can in caring for the civilian population of this city, I am

Most respectfully yours,
JOHN H. D. RABE
Chairman

DOCUMENT 12

List of Foreign Nationals in Nanking on 21 December 1937.[11]

NAME	NATIONALITY	ORGANIZATION
1. John H. D. Rabe	German	Siemens China Co.
2. Eduard Sperling	German	Shanghai Insurance Co.
3. Christian Kröger	German	Carlowitz & Co.
4. R. Hempel	German	North Hotel
5. Zaudig	German	Kiessling & Bader
6. R. R. Hatz	Austrian	Mechanic for the Safety Zone
7. Cola Podshivaloff	White Russian	Sandgren's Electric Shop
8. O. Zial	White Russian	Mechanic for the Safety Zone
9. Dr. C. S. Trimmer	American	University Hospital
10. Dr. R. O. Wilson	American	University Hospital
11. Rev. James McCallum	American	University Hospital
12. Miss Grace Bauer	American	University Hospital
13. Miss Ina Hynds	American	University Hospital
14. Dr. M. S. Bates	American	University of Nanking
15. Charles Riggs	American	University of Nanking
16. Dr. Lewis S. C. Smythe	American	University of Nanking
17. Miss Minnie Vautrin	American	Ginling College
18. Rev. W. P. Mills	American	Northern Presbyterian Mission
19. Rev. H. L. Sone	American	Nanking Theological Seminary
20. George Fitch	American	Y.M.C.A.
21. Rev. John Magee	American	American Church Mission
22. Rev. E. H. Forster	American	American Church Mission

DOCUMENT 13

Letter from Dr. Bates to Mr. Tanaka at the Japanese Embassy

University of Nanking   Nanking, 25 December 1937

Dear Mr. Tanaka:

I have tried for a couple of days to refrain from troubling you further. However, many difficulties occur every day, and today they are worse than usual. New parties of stray soldiers without discipline or officers are going everywhere, stealing, raping, and taking away women.
Some cases follow:

    1. Just now soldiers forcibly entered the university and towed away a truck used to supply rice to refugees.

2. In our Sericulture Building alone there are on the average more than ten cases per day of rape or of abducting women.

3. Our residences continue to be entered day and night by soldiers who injure women and steal everything they wish. This applies to residences in which Americans are now living, just the same as to others.

4. Soldiers frequently tear down the proclamations put up by your military police.

5. This morning an American member of our staff was struck by an officer who suddenly approached him and angrily tried to tear off the arm band supplied by your Embassy.

6. Other buildings not mentioned above are daily entered several times each, by soldiers who utterly disregard your proclamations, looking for women and for loot.

7. Despite this disorder caused entirely by soldiers, we have no guard whatever and no military police have been seen near us.

With thanks for your continued interest,
M. S. BATES

DOCUMENT 14

International Committee of the Nanking Safety Zone to Mr. Fukui of the Japanese Embassy (Excerpts)

Nanking, Ninhai Lu, 18 December 1937

Dear Sirs:

We are sorry to trouble you again but the sufferings and needs of the 200,000 civilians for whom we are trying to care make it urgent that we try to secure action from your military authorities to stop the present disorder among Japanese soldiers wandering through the Safety Zone.

There is no time or space here to go into the cases that are pouring in faster than we can type them out.

But last night Dr. Bates of our Committee went to the University of Nanking dormitories to sleep in order to protect the 1,000 women that fled there yesterday because of attacks in their homes. He found no gendarmerie on guard there nor at the new University library building. When at 8 p.m. Mr. Fitch and Dr. Smythe took Rev. W. P. Mills to Ginling College to sleep in a house near the gate (as one or more of us have been doing every night since the 14th in order to protect the 3,000 women and children, yesterday augmented to 4,000 by the panic), we were seized roughly by a searching squad and detained for over an hour. The officer had the two women in charge of Ginling College, Miss Minnie Vautrin and Mrs. Chen, with a friend, Mrs. Twinem, lined up at the gate and kept them there in the cold and the men pushed them around roughly. The officer insisted there were soldiers in the compound and he wanted to find them and shoot them. Finally, he let us go home but would not let Rev. Mills stay so we do not know what happened after we left.

This combined with the marching off of the men at the Ministry of Justice on December 16 (see separate "Memorandum"), among which were several hundred civilian men to our positive knowledge and 50 of our uniformed police, had made us realize that, unless something is done to clear up this situation, the lives of all the civilian men in our Zone are at the mercy of the temperament of searching captains.

With the panic that has been created among the women who are now flocking by the thousands to our American institutions for protection, the men are being left more and more alone. (For instance, there were 600 people in the old Language School at Siao T'ao Yuen up till December 16. But because so many women were raped there on the night of December 15, 400 women and children moved to Ginling college, leaving 200.) These public institutional buildings were originally listed to accommodate 35,000 people; now, because of panic among the women, this has increased to 50,000, although two buildings have been emptied of men: the Ministry of Justice and the Supreme Court.

If this panic continues, not only will our housing problem become more serious but the food problem and the question of finding workers will seriously increase. . . .

The second man on our Housing Commission had to see two women in his family at 23 Hankow Road raped last night at supper time by Japanese soldiers. Our associate food commissioner, Mr. Sone (a Theological Professor), has had to convey trucks with rice and leave the 2,500 people in families at his Nanking Theological Seminary to look out for themselves. Yesterday, in broad daylight, several women at the Seminary were raped right in the middle of a large room filled with men, women, and children! We 22 Westerners cannot feed 200,000 Chinese civilians and protect them night and day. That is the duty of the Japanese authorities.

Yesterday we called your attention to the fact that 50 uniformed police had been taken from the Ministry of Justice, and that 46 "volunteer police" had also been marched off. We now must add that 40 of our uniformed police stationed at the Supreme Court were also taken. The only stated charge against them was made at the Ministry of Justice where the Japanese officer said they had taken in soldiers after the place had been searched once, and, therefore, they were to be shot.

As pointed out in the accompanying "Memorandum on the Incident at the Ministry of Justice," Western members of our committee take full responsibility for having put some civilian men and women in there because they had been driven out of other places by Japanese soldiers.

Yesterday, we requested that the 450 uniformed police assigned to the Zone be now organized into a new police force for the city under Japanese direction. At the same time, we trust the above mentioned 90 uniformed police will be restored to their positions as policemen and that 46 volunteer police will either be returned to our office as workers, or we be informed of their whereabouts. We have on file a complete list of the 450 uniformed police assigned to the Zone, so can help you in this process.

Trusting that you will pardon our venturing to make these suggestions, and assuring you of our willingness to cooperate in every way for the welfare of the civilians in the city,

> I am
> Most respectfully yours,
> JOHN H. D. RABE
> Chairman

DOCUMENT 15

List of the Cases of Disorder by Japanese Soldiers in the Safety Zone

According to Rabe's diary, by 5 February the Safety Zone Committee had forwarded to the Japanese embassy a total of 450 cases of disorder by Japanese soldiers that had been reported either directly or indirectly after the American, British, and German diplomats had returned to their embassies. These are a few the cases from this list.

1. Six street sweepers of the second division of the Sanitary Commission of the Safety Zone were killed in the house they occupied at Kulou and one seriously injured with a bayonet by Japanese soldiers on December 15th. There was no apparent reason whatever. These men were our employees. The soldiers entered the house.

2. A carriage loaded with rice was taken on December 15th at 4:00 p.m. near the gate of Ginling College by Japanese soldiers.

3. Several residents in our second sub-division were driven from their homes on the night of December 14th and robbed of everything. The chief of the sub-division was himself robbed twice by Japanese soldiers.

4. On the night of December 15th, last night, seven Japanese soldiers entered the University of Nanking library building and took seven Chinese women refugees, three of whom were raped on the spot. (Full details of this case will be filed by Dr. M. S. Bates, Chairman of the University of Nanking Emergency Committee.)

5. On the night of December 14th, there were many cases of Japanese soldiers entering Chinese houses and raping women or taking them away. This created a panic in the area and hundreds of women moved into the Ginling College campus yesterday. Consequently, three American men spent the night at Ginling College last night to protect the 3,000 women and children in the compound.

6. At noon, December 14th, on Chien Ying Hsiang, Japanese soldiers, entered a house and took four girls, raped them, and let them return in two hours.

7. At 10:00 p.m. on the night of December 14th a Chinese home on Chien Ying Hsiang was entered by 11 Japanese soldiers who raped 4 Chinese women.

8. Last night, December 15th, Japanese soldiers entered a Chinese house on Hankow Road and raped a young wife and took away three women. When two husbands ran, the soldiers shot both of them.

9. On December 15th, a man came to the University Hospital with a bayonet wound and reported that six Chinese men were taken from the Safety Zone to carry ammunition to Hsiakwan and when they got there the Japanese soldiers bayoneted them all. He however survived and got back to Kulou. (*Wilson*)

10. On the night of December 15th, a number of Japanese soldiers entered the University of Nanking buildings at Tao Yuen and raped 30 women on the spot, some by six men. (*Sone*)

11. A man came to the University Hospital on Dec. 15th. He had been carrying his 60-year uncle into the Safety Zone and soldiers shot his uncle and wounded himself. (*Wilson*)

12. On the night of December 16, 7 Japanese soldiers broke windows; robbed refugees; wounded University staff member with bayonet because he had no watch or girl to give them; and raped women on the premises. (*Bates*)

13. December 18, 4 p.m., at No. 18 I Ho Lu Japanese soldiers wanted a man's cigarette case and when he hesitated the soldier crashed in the side of his head with a bayonet. The man is now at the University Hospital and is not expected to live. (*Fitch*)

14. On Dec. 16th, seven girls (ages ranged from 16 to 21) were taken away from the Military College. Five returned. Each girl was raped six or seven

times daily—reported Dec. 18th. Dec. 17th at 11 p.m. the soldiers climbed over the wall and took away two girls but they returned in 30 minutes. (*Tsan Yuen-kwan*)

15. There are about 540 refugees crowded in Nos. 83 and 85 on Canton Road. Since 13th inst. up to the 17th those houses have been searched and robbed many many times a day by Japanese soldiers in groups of 3 to 5. Today the soldiers are looting the places mentioned above continually and all the jewelries, money, watches, clothes of any sort are taken away. At present women of younger ages are forced to go with the soldiers every night who send motor trucks to take them and release the next morning. More than 30 women and girls have been raped. The women and children are crying all nights. Conditions inside the compound are worse than we can describe. Please give us help. Yours truly, All the Refugees. (Translation signed by *Han Siang-lin*.)

16. A Chinese girl named Loh, who, with her mother and brother, was living in one of the Refugee Centers in the Refugee Zone, was shot through the head and killed by a Japanese soldier. The girl was fourteen years old. The incident occurred in a field near the Kuling Ssu, a noted temple on the border of the Refugee Zone. The girl, accompanied by her brother, was gathering vegetables in the field when a Japanese soldier appeared. He made overtures to seize the girl who took fright and ran away. Thereupon the soldier fired at her and shot her through the head, the bullet entering the back of the skull and leaving through the forehead. (Signed *Ernest H. Forster*.)

17. On the afternoon of January 27th, yesterday, just after lunch, Mr. McCallum, business manager of the University Hospital, was called to escort two Japanese soldiers out of a back dormitory. When they got outside on the back road he pointed out the American flag whereupon they became angry and told him to come with them. So he thought he would go along to their headquarters to see. About 100 yards down the road south, one of the soldiers told him to go back. He said, no, he would go with them. Then the soldier drew his bayonet and made a thrust at Mr. McCallum's stomach, but since he stood his ground, the soldier put the point of the bayonet under his chin and gave a short thrust. Mr. McCallum jerked back his head so only received a slight skin cut on his throat. Then the other soldier took this man away. Some people gathered at the gate called to him and he looked around and saw a Consular Policeman coming in a horse carriage. So he got in the carriage with him and overtook the two soldiers at the corner. The Consular Policeman talked to them and got their names. Dr. Trimmer came along. The Consular Policeman said he would go to the Japanese Embassy to report and Dr. Trimmer went to the American Embassy to report. (A written statement was later made by Mr. McCallum to the American Embassy.) Later in the afternoon the

Consular Policeman came to the Hospital to apologize to Mr. McCallum and last evening he and two gendarmes came to 3 P'ing Ta'ang Hsiang to investigate and interview Mr. McCallum. (From a verbal report by *Mr. McCallum* to *L. Smythe*.)

18. Feb. 1st. This morning at 6:30 a group of women gathered a second time to greet Dr. Bates when he left the University. They told him they could not go home. Among other cases one woman who feared that she would lose her bedding when the camp was sealed, took her two daughters home yesterday, to Hsi Hwa Men. Last evening Japanese soldiers came and demanded to have a chance to rape the girls. The two girls objected and the soldiers bayoneted them to death. The woman says there is no use going home. If they are going to be killed at home they might just as well be killed at the camp by soldiers attempting to drive them out February 4th. (*Bates*)

19. Jan. 30th, about 5 p.m. Mr. Sone was greeted by several hundred women pleading with him that they would not have to go home on February 4th. They said it was no use going home they might just as well be killed for staying at the camp as to be raped, robbed or killed at home. They said, "You have saved us half way, if you let us go now what use is there unless you save the other half?" One old woman 62 years old went home near Hansimen and soldiers came at night and wanted to rape her. She said she was too old. So the soldiers rammed a stick up her. But she survived to come back. (*Sone*)

20. Feb. 1st. This afternoon about 2:30 a child came running to our house to tell Mr. Forster and myself that soldiers were after women in a house near us next to Overseas Building. We ran there and were admitted by a Chinese family. They pointed to a bedroom door which was locked but when no response was made to our knocking we smashed the door and found two Japanese soldiers in the room. One was reclining on the bed and the other sitting by the bed. The girl was on the bed between them and the wall. One soldier immediately jumped for his belt and pistol and went out through a hole in the wall. But the other one had his trousers down and was so drunk he could not get away quickly and moreover left his belt so his pants would not stay up. We had to help him out through the hole in the wall. Out on the road he wanted to shake hands. Mr. Forster ran ahead to find a military police while I walked behind the soldier. We delivered him to the two sentries at the opening of Shanghai Road where it joins Chung Shan Lu. We were told that the girl was raped before we got there. (*Magee*)

21. Feb. 1st, 11:00 p.m., three Japanese soldiers came to the Nanking Theological Seminary, climbed over the wall, grabbed a girl in a hut, but she ran away and yelled. This woke the camp and they all turned out and yelled. The soldiers climbed back over the wall and drove away. (*Sone*)

22. Jan. 29, evening, Nos. 43, 44, 45, 46 Yin Yang Ying were all visited and searched by soldiers for money and raping. In No. 44 four Japanese soldiers raped one woman and beat her husband.

23. Jan. 30, morning, Tai-ping Hotel, at Sze Hsiang Chiao a woman was dragged by Japanese soldiers to the door and killed at the spot.

24. Jan. 31, Sze Hsiang Chiao an old woman over 60 was first raped and then was stabbed by a bayonet in her vagina and killed.

25. Feb. 3rd, a.m. Mrs. Liu returned home and while she was walking in front of the door of Sung Yuan, Er Tien Hong, Hsi Hwa Men, she was pulled by three Japanese soldiers to a foreign style house and was raped there and also her garment was bayoneted. (Chopped by her right hand 2nd finger.)

Note: These are only sample cases we have had time to check up on more carefully. Many more have been reported to our workers.

LEWIS S. C. SMYTHE
Secretary

DOCUMENT 16

Description of Some Shots from a Film by John Magee, a Missionary

See Rosen's report to the Foreign Ministry of 10 February 1938, p. 187

1. December 16th, 1937. Chinese women on Shanghai Road, Nanking, kneeling and begging Japanese soldiers for the lives of their sons and husbands when these were being collected at random on the suspicion of being ex-soldiers. Thousands of civilians were taken in this way, bound with ropes, carried to the river bank in Hsiakwan, to the edges of ponds, and to vacant spaces where they were done to death by machine-guns, bayonets, rifles, and even hand grenades.

2. This man, Liu Kwang-wei, an Inquirer in the Chinese Episcopal Church at Ssu Shou Ts'un, the model village at Hsiakwan, came into the Refugee Zone with fellow-Christians before the occupation of the city by the Japanese. On December 16, he was carried off by Japanese soldiers with thirteen others of this Christian group. They were joined to another group of 1000 men (according to his estimate), taken to the river bank at Hsiakwan, arranged in orderly lines near the Japanese wharf and mowed down with machine guns. It was dusk but there was no chance to escape as the river was behind them and they were surrounded on three sides by machine guns. This man was in the back immediately next to the water. When the lines of men began to

fall, he fell with them although uninjured. He dropped into shallow water and covered himself with the corpses of those about him. There he stayed for three hours, and was so cold when he came out that he could hardly walk, but he was able to make his way to a deserted hut where he found some bedding. Here he took off his wet clothing and wrapped himself in the bedding, staying there for three days without food. He finally became so hungry that he left the hut to find something to eat, putting on his clothing which was still damp. He went to the China Import and Export Lumber company, a British concern in which he had been employed, but found nobody there. Just then he met three Japanese soldiers who struck him with their fists, led him off to Paohsing Street, Hsiakwan, where they made him cook for them. After several days he was released, being given a note signed with the seal of two of the Japanese soldiers. This enabled him to get through the city gate and back to his family in the Refugee Zone.

3. Yü Hsi-Tang, an employee of the Telephone Office in Hsiakwan, was among four thousand men refugees living at the University of Nanking. On Dec. 26, Japanese officers came there to effect registration, a requirement for all grown Chinese in the city. The officer told them that if any of them acknowledged that they had been soldiers their lives would be spared but they would be given work; that if they did not acknowledge it and were found out they would be killed. They were given twenty minutes to think it over. About 200 men then stepped forward. They were marched off, and on the street many more men were picked up, whom the Japanese claimed were soldiers. Yü was one of these taken on the street. He said they led him with a few hundred others to the hills near Ginling College and there the Japanese soldiers started bayonet practice on them. After being bayoneted in six places, 2 in the chest, 2 in the abdomen, and 2 in the legs, he fainted. When he came to, the Japanese had left and somebody helped him to get to the Mission Hospital. The picture was taken while Dr. Wilson was operating, at which time there did not seem to be much hope of the man's recovery; but he did recover.

4. This woman was taken with five others from a refugee center to wash clothes for Japanese officers. She was taken upstairs in a building apparently used as a military hospital. During the day they washed clothes and at night entertained Japanese soldiers. According to her story, the older and plainer women were raped from 10–20 times per night, while the younger and prettier one was raped forty times per night. The woman in the picture was the one of the plainer ones. On Jan. 2, two soldiers motioned her to come with them. She followed them to an empty house where they tried unsuccessfully to cut

off her head. She was found in a pool of blood and taken to the Mission Hospital where she is recovering. She had four deep lacerations along the back of her neck, severing the muscles to the vertebral column. She also has a slash on her wrists and four on her body. The woman has not the slightest idea why they wanted to kill her, nor does she know the fate of the other women.

5. On December 13th, about thirty soldiers came to a Chinese house at No. 5 Hsing Lu Koo in the southeastern part of Nanking, and demanded entrance. The door was opened by the landlord, a Mohammedan named Ha. They killed him immediately with a revolver and also Mr. Hsia, who knelt before them after Ha's death, begging them not to kill anyone else. Mrs. Ha asked them why they had killed her husband and they shot her dead. Mrs. Hsia was dragged out from under a table in the guest hall where she had tried to hide with her one-year-old baby. After being stripped and raped by one or more men, she was bayoneted in the chest, and then had a bottle thrust into her vagina. The baby being killed with a bayonet. Some soldiers then went to the next room, where were Mrs. Hsia's parents, aged 76 and 74, and her two daughters aged 16 and 14. They were about to rape the girls when the grandmother tried to protect them. The soldiers killed her with a revolver. The grandfather grasped the body of his wife and was killed. The two girls were then stripped, the elder being raped by 2–3 men, and the younger by 3. The older girl was stabbed afterwards and a cane was rammed into her vagina. The younger girl was bayoneted also but was spared the horrible treatment that had been meted out to her sister and her mother. The soldiers then bayoneted another sister of between 7–8, who was also in the room. The last murders in the house were of Ha's two children, aged 4 and 2 respectively. The older was bayoneted and the younger split down through the head with a sword.

After being wounded the 8-year-old girl crawled to the next room where lay the body of her mother. Here she stayed for 14 days with her 4-year-old sister who had escaped unharmed. The two children lived on puffed rice and the rice crusts that form in the pan when the rice is cooked. It was from the older of these children that the photographer was able to get part of the story, and verify and correct certain details told him by a neighbor and a relative. The child said the soldiers came every day taking things from the house; but the two children were not discovered as they hid under some old sheets. All the people in the neighborhood fled to the Refugee Zone when such terrible things began to happen. After 14 days the old woman shown in the picture returned to the neighborhood and found the two children. It was she who led the photographer to an open space where the bodies had been taken afterwards. Through questioning her and Mr. Hsia's brother and the little girl, a clear knowledge of the terrible tragedy was gained. The picture shows the bodies of the 16 and 14 year old girls, each lying with a group of people slain at the same time. Mrs. Hsia and her baby are shown last.

6. The case of a Buddhist nun and a little apprentice nun (between 8–9 years old). This child was bayoneted in the back, although she ran a fever for weeks after the incident. The adult nun has a compound fracture of the left hip, caused by a bullet wound, from which an extensive infection developed. If she recovers, which is questionable, a very specialized operation will be necessary to enable her to walk. She and some other nuns occupied a building behind a temple in the southern part of the city. When the Japanese entered the city they killed a great many people in this neighborhood. The tailor who brought her to the hospital estimated that there were about 25 dead there. Among the dead was the "Mother Superior" of this nunnery, 65 years of age, and a little apprentice nun between 6–7. They wounded the nun and the little apprentice shown in this picture. They took refuge in a pit where they stayed for 5–6 days without food or drink. There were many corpses in this pit, and an old nun of about 68 years of age was either crushed or smothered to death by the weight of the bodies. After 5 days the wounded nun heard a soldier say in Chinese, "What a pity." She thereupon opened her eyes and begged the man to save her life. He dragged her out of the pit and got some Chinese to carry her to an army dressing station, where an army doctor attended to her. Eventually she was brought to the Mission hospital by a neighbor.

7. On January 11, this boy, between 13–14 years of age, was forced to carry vegetables to the southern part of the city by three Japanese soldiers, who then robbed him of all his money and bayoneted him twice in the back and once in the abdomen. About one foot of the large intestine was protruding when he reached the Mission hospital two days after the assault. He died five days after admission to the hospital. The boy was so ill at the time this picture was taken that the doctor did not dare to remove the dressings to show the wounds.

8. Having heard that his mother had been killed, this man left the Refugee Zone, established by an International Committee, to investigate. He went to the Second District, an area which had been designated as safe by the Japanese and to which they were urging the people to return. He could not find his mother's body, but met two Japanese soldiers who stripped him and a friend of all their clothing except their trousers. (It was an icy cold day, about Jan. 12, 1938.) They also tore up their registration cards which they had received from Japanese officers after the general registration. The soldiers bayoneted

them both, throwing them into a dug-out. About an hour later, when this man recovered consciousness, he found that his friend had disappeared. He was able to make his way back to the Refugee Zone and eventually to the Mission hospital. He had six bayonet wounds, one of which penetrated his pleura giving rise to a general subcutaneous emphysema. He will recover.[12]

DOCUMENT 17

From the Japan Advertiser, 7 December 1937[13]

Sub-Lieutenants in Race
to Fell 100 Chinese
Running Close Contest

Sub-lieutenant Toshiaki Mukai and Sub-lieutenant Takeshi Noda, both of the Katagiri unit at Kuyung, in a friendly contest to see which of them will first fell 100 Chinese in individual sword combat before the Japanese forces completely occupy Nanking, are well in the final phase of their race, running almost neck to neck. On Sunday when their unit was fighting outside Kuyung, the "score," according to the *Asahi*, was: Sub-lieutenant Mukai, 89, and Sub-lieutenant Noda, 78.

Contest to Kill First 100 Chinese
with Sword Extended When Both
Fighters Exceed Mark

The winner of the competition between Sub-Lieutenant Toshiaki Mukai and Sub-Lieutenant Iwao Noda to see who would be the first to kill 100 Chinese with his Yamato sword has not been decided, the *Nichi Nichi* reports from the slopes of Purple Mountain, outside Nanking. Mukai has a score of 106 and his rival has dispatched 105 men, but the two contestants have found it impossible to determine which passed the 100 mark first. Instead of settling it with a discussion, they are going to extend the goal by 50.

Mukai's blade was slightly damaged in the competition. He explained that this was the result of cutting a Chinese in half, helmet and all. The contest was "fun," he declared, and he thought it a good thing that both men had gone over the 100 mark without knowing that the other had done so.

Early Saturday morning, when the *Nichi Nichi* man interviewed the sub-lieutenant at a point overlooking Dr. Sun Yat-sen's tomb, another Japanese unit set fire to the slopes of Purple Mountain in an attempt to drive out the Chinese troops. The action also smoked out Sub-Lieutenant Mukai and his unit, and the men stood idly by while bullets passed overhead.

"Not a shot hits me while I am holding this sword on my shoulder," he explained confidently.

DOCUMENT 18[14]

Letter from the Representatives of the District Superintendents and Camp Managers of the Nanking Safety Zone to John Rabe

Dear Mr. Rabe:

We have the honor to transmit to you the following resolutions which were passed on February 15th by the Sixth Joint Meeting of the Superintendents of the Nine Districts and the Managers of the Twenty-five Refugee Camps of the Nanking Safety Zone.

To extend to Mr. John H. D. Rabe, Chairman of the International Committee for the Nanking Safety Zone, a vote of thanks for his valuable services in connection with the organization and administration of the Zone and of the relief work which was followed upon its establishment. We would assure Mr. Rabe of our deep appreciation of his efforts on behalf of the people of this city. His name will ever be held in grateful remembrance among us.

It was further resolved that a copy of the above resolution should be sent to Messrs. Siemens China Company and to the German Embassy, that they also might be made aware of the Nanking Community's gratitude for Mr. Rabe's presence and work among us during this time of crisis.

The undersigned were also instructed by the above mentioned Meeting to convey to Messrs. Siemens China Company the earnest desire of the District Superintendents and Camp Managers to have you continue, if possible, your residence in Nanking and your services as Chairman of the International Committee. Though the need for the Zone as a place of special refuge has of course ceased to exist, nevertheless the need for relief among the people is as great as ever, or even greater, and it is with reference to this work that the Superintendents and Camp Managers would like to have your services continue. The proposed departure of so tried and true a friend as you have been is indeed to us a cause for deep regret.

We therefore earnestly trust that Messrs. Siemens China Company will give favorable consideration to our desire that you should be permitted to continue your good work here in Nanking, and we hope that with their concurrence you yourself will decide to remain among us for a least some time longer. But if this should not be possible, we will still look forward to your early return to Nanking and to a renewal of that constant association with you which has meant so much to us during these recent months.

Believe us, with gratitude and affection,
Sincerely yours,
Representatives of the District Superintendents
and Camp Managers of the Nanking Safety Zone
J. M. TONG, Y. S. SHEN, HSÜ CHUAN-YING, FRANCIS F. J. CHEN

DOCUMENT 19

Declaration of the Members of the
Committee of the International Safety Zone

The resident members of the International Committee for a Safety Zone in Nanking (now become Nanking International Relief Committee), desire to express our hearty appreciation of the services of Mr. John H. D. Rabe, who has served as our Chairman during three critical months. Mr. Rabe's leadership in difficult tasks of benevolence has been fearless and gentle. It will long be remembered among the entire population of Nanking, and among great numbers connected with them by ties of blood and of interest. Our Chairman has combined most splendidly the qualities of effective effort in a large enterprise, with those of close personal sympathy and care for individuals in need.

Among the Chinese community there is grateful recognition of this unselfish service. Among the foreign community there has been set a lasting example of devotion to human welfare transcending commercial duty and national interests. The Siemens China Company, which Mr. Rabe has so ably represented in Nanking, is held in heightened respect because of its contribution to a great public service through the recent work of our Chairman. Likewise the whole standing of German enterprise and of the German community in China has been brought new honor through the well-deserved reputation of Mr. Rabe.

Nanking, February 21, 1938.

Signed with personal affection and regard:

W. P. Mills	John Magee	Eduard Sperling	M. S. Bates
Lewis S. C. Smythe	Chas. H. Riggs	C. S. Trimmer.	

We, the remaining non-official foreign residents of Nanking, desire to associate ourselves with the expressions of the International Committee as to Mr. Rabe and his services:

Minnie Vautrin,   Cola Podshivaloff,   O. Zial,
Ernest H. Forster,   R. Hempel,   Hubert L. Sone,
Grace Bauer,   Jas. H. McCallum,   R. Rupert Hatz,
Ina Hynds,   Robert O. Wilson

DOCUMENT 20

Letter from Ernest H. Forster
(Written in German) to John Rabe

Nanking, 22 February 1938

Dear Herr Rabe:

I do not wish to let the opportunity pass to express to you my deepest thanks for everything that you have done here in Nanking over the last few months. It often happens that there is a gulf between commercial people and missionaries that cannot and is not easily bridged; but that bridge is the love of God, Who reveals Himself through our love for our neighbors. And through your selfless devotion to the plight of all classes, you, Herr Rabe, have revealed that love in rich measure during these difficult times. I would like to thank you as well for the precious friendship that you showed me as a newcomer in Nanking. I hope that you and Frau Rabe will have a safe trip back to Germany and a refreshing vacation in your homeland, and then a happy reunion with us here in Nanking.

God be with you!
Yours sincerely   ERNEST H. FORSTER

DOCUMENT 21

Report of the Nanking Office of the German Embassy
to the Foreign Ministry, 26 February 1938

The local representative of Siemens China Co., Herr John H. D. Rabe (Party Member), left a few days ago for Shanghai in order, after a short stay there, to return home on a well-deserved vacation.

As I have frequently reported before, Herr Rabe has done meritorious service as the chairman of the International Committee for the Nanking Safety Zone, risking his life and personal safety for thousands of poor refugees, and by his energetic actions has enhanced the regard in which the German cause is held overseas. Both foreigners and Chinese alike appreciate the fact that German businessmen have shown that they not only stand in the front ranks when it comes to doing good deeds during peacetime, but also at the risk of their own lives have proved their solidarity with China even in its terrible need as it battles for its honor and freedom.

In a touching farewell ceremony, both foreign and Chinese members of the International Committee expressed their gratitude to Herr Rabe and presented him with warmly felt resolutions, of which I enclose a copy. On the day following the Führer's recent important speech, a Chinese physician asked Herr Rabe to tell the Germans that the Chinese are not and do not wish to become Communists. That they are simply a peaceable nation that wishes to live in quiet cooperation with all other nations, and that China needs the continuing friendship of Germany.

Herr Rabe can presumably be reached in Berlin through the Siemens-Schuckert Works, and he would like to call on the Foreign Ministry and asks especially to meet with Bohle, head of the foreign section of the NSDAP.

Because of poor postal connections with Hankow, I am sending this report directly to the Foreign Ministry. The embassies in Hankow and Tokyo as well as the consulate general in Shanghai will receive carbon copies.

ROSEN[15]

NOTES

FROM JOHN RABE'S NANKING AND BERLIN DIARIES

1. Hapro—*Handelsgesellschaft für industrielle Produkte* [trading company for industrial products] was the cover name for a firm that secretly delivered weapons to the Chinese army. The firm was originally answerable to the War Ministry in Berlin, later to Göring.

2. "Tummy-not-good," i.e., diarrhea.

3. A suburb of Nanking that served as its port on the Yangtze.

4. This remark by someone on the embassy staff refers to a directive from Hitler. The German embassy in Nanking had telegraphed the Foreign Ministry, asking whether, for their own protection, Jews of German nationality who lived outside international concessions (as for instance in Tientsin or Shanghai) were permitted to display the Reich flag with swastika. This suggestion had originally come from the Japanese general consul in Tientsin. In an express letter to the Reich Interior Ministry dated 9 September 1937, Legation Councilor Hinrich, an official of the Foreign Ministry, noted that he was aware that "in general there should be only a limited extension of protective measures to Jews living abroad." But then he added that conditions in China were quite different. "In practice, then, we are left with no other means by which to make the property of German nationals of Jewish blood recognizable than by displaying the German flag." Moreover, this was not in any way a "display of the flag in a legal sense." And it was the view of the legal department for overseas organizations—in effect, of the NSDAP—that there was no problem with displaying the flag of the German Reich as a way to make Jewish property recognizable. Herr Hinrich requested a reply by return mail. The deputy state secretary of the Reich Interior Ministry responded that he, too, had no objection; but just to con-

289

form with regulations, he suggested that the matter be "submitted to the Führer and Reich Chancellor for decision." The director and state secretary of the Reich Chancery passed on Hitler's answer on 4 October:

> The Führer and Reich Chancellor has decided against granting German nationals of the Jewish race permission either to display our national flag because of the warlike confusions in China or to make themselves recognizable by the wearing of armbands of a similar nature. It is the Führer's view that German nationals of the Jewish race can protect themselves and are adequately marked by displaying white flags or armbands, on which, if necessary, their association with the Reich can be indicated in German or some foreign language.

This trail of letters shows that officials at the Foreign Ministry and even the Reich Interior Ministry were less rigorous in their treatment of "German nationals of Jewish blood" than was the Führer and Reich Chancellor. A telegram reflecting Hitler's directive was then sent to the embassy in Nanking (Federal Archives, Berlin, R 43 II/1286).

5. Rabe's son.

6. The reference is to the widespread sympathy among intellectuals for Mao's cause.

7. Rabe's daughter and son-in-law, who had returned to Germany.

8. Horse-drawn wagon.

9. Dr. Horst Baerensprung, the former police chief of Magdeburg and a Social Democrat. Emigrating to China in 1933, he first became an advisor to the Police Academy in Nanking and then in 1937, an advisor to the military police at the headquarters of Marshal Chiang Kai-shek.

10. Taken from Wolf Schenke, *Reise an der Gelben Front: Beobachtungen eines deutschen Kriegsbereichterstatters* [Journey to the Yellow Front: Observations of a German War Reporter] (Oldenburg and Berlin, 1943), pp. 60 ff. (excerpt).

11. The code dictionary of the Foreign Service, in which every German word was replaced with a five-digit number. It offered no top-secret protection and was therefore not used for confidential telegrams.

12. *Curio* was a term used by old China hands for Chinese works of art, which most of them did not especially value. It was not until about one hundred years ago that Westerners discovered Chinese art and began collecting it. John Rabe owned a small collection.

13. A high ministerial official in Chiang Kai-shek's government.

14. Ret. Lieutenant Colonel Hermann Kriebel, acting as General Ludendorff's representative, took part in Hitler's putsch attempt in 1923 and was sentenced to prison along with him. He first joined the NSDAP several years later. From 1929 to 1933, he was a German military advisor to Chiang Kai-shek, including one year during which he served as director of the advisory staff; then in 1934 he became consul general in Shanghai. Because of his pro-Chinese views, he was called back in 1937 and after an eighteen-month hiatus, became the head of personnel in the Foreign Ministry. He had long since lost any influence he once had with Hitler.

15. Read: his great-grandfather, Ignaz Moscheles.

16. He had established a Safety Zone in Nantao/Shanghai.

17. Code address: American Embassy Nanking.

18. Lautenschlager was actually legation councilor.

19. Rabe is punning on his own name here, since in German *Rabe* means "raven."

20. China had a silver coin, originally called the tael, but when it began to be minted in Mexico it became the so-called "Mexican dollar," whose value in the thirties fluctuated between 2.4 and 2.7 reichsmarks.

21. Foreign Ministry.

22. 1 tan = 133 lb.

23. From the political archives of the German Foreign Ministry, China-Japan, Pol. VIII, 28, vol. 19.

24. The Chinese Red Cross.

25. In those days, a term for lunch commonly used by foreign nationals in China and India.

26. "There are Japanese soldiers who are very bad."

27. Identification card.

28. Virgins.

29. Little children.

30. "The hundred old family names"—an affectionate term for the Chinese people as a whole.

31. Policemen.

32. Chiang Kai-shek's brother-in-law, Prime Minister H. H. Kung.

33. The Chinese pronunciation of Scharffenberg.

34. On 12 December, the American river gunboat *Panay* was attacked and sunk by Japanese bombers about twenty-five miles upriver from Nanking. The incident led to a serious diplomatic confrontation between Washington and Tokyo. See pp. 71–72.

35. Rabe is confused here. He apparently means Rosen's grandfather, Georg Rosen.

36. In the Federal Archives, R 9208 / 4439, pp. 74–79.

37. The text reads: "Wind up business yourself and Han return Shanghai soonest."

38. Rabe's handwritten notation: "Received in Nanking 14/1/38—Rabe."

39. Firm, a firm's property or compound.

40. The official in charge of the administration of a diplomatic embassy or consulate was given the official title of "chancellor." Scharffenberg's memoranda were forwarded as his personal reports to the Foreign Ministry.

41. Germans were told, and erroneously believed, that black French troops were incited by such promises during World War I.

42. Chang Hsueliang, son of the warlord Chang Tsolin from Manchuria, had inherited his father's army and continued to lead it in northern China. In December 1936, he took Chiang Kai-shek prisoner while the latter was visiting the city of Sian but after a few very tense days released him again under pressure from Mao and Zhou Enlai. Chiang Kai-shek pledged that from then on he would stop fighting Mao and fight the Japanese. News that Chang Hsueliang had been shot and killed in January 1938 was not true. He was arrested in Nanking, and in 1949 Chiang Kai-shek took him with him to Taiwan, where he lived under house arrest until his death.

43. Edwin Erich Dwinger's books tell about the war on the eastern front and in the Baltic.

44. Foreign Ministry.

45. "Better dead than a slave," from "Pidder Lüng," a poem by Detlev von Liliencron (1844–1900).

46. The national group leader for China of the Overseas Department of the NSDAP, with offices in Shanghai. For a discussion of the man, see Erwin Wickert, *Mut und Übermut* [Courage and Arrogance] (Stuttgart, 1991), pp. 313 ff.

47. Ambassador Trautmann had requested the Medal of Honor of the Red Cross for all three.

48. Chinese: woman of the house.

49. The official Japanese news agency.

50. The copy made in Shanghai at the request of Legation Secretary Rosen arrived in Berlin via courier on 12 April 1938, that is, three days before John Rabe's arrival. But the bureaucrats at the Foreign Ministry were apparently bewildered by the idea of purchasing a copy of the film. The report of the embassy in Hankow reads: "The general consulate in Shanghai advanced the sum of 60 Chinese dollars for the preparation of the aforementioned film document. This amount is recorded in Part III of the official ledger of the general consulate—not of the embassy—in Shanghai as a nonbudgeted expenditure for January / March 1938. Signed: *Trautmann.*"

Apparently the purchase of a film seemed highly unusual to the accounting department. The embassy's report was therefore forwarded to political desk VIII "with the request that a decision be made whether and on what basis the costs are to be defrayed by official funds of the Foreign Ministry and whether such funds are then to be collected from some other source." Whereupon political desk VIII replied in a marginal note: "Inasmuch as, once the Europeans had evacuated from Nanking, there were as good as no foreign eyewitnesses to the atrocities attributed to the Japanese in Nanking, the acquisition by the office of the German embassy in Nanking of a film made by an American missionary and recording several such occurrences is, in this particular and exceptional instance, deemed of official interest. A showing of this film at the Propaganda Ministry (and on other closed occasions) has been planned under arrangements made by the Foreign Ministry. Respectfully resubmitted herewith to the Division Pers. R." But that in no way resolved the matter of cost. The desk in the personnel department therefore prepared a new file document, which reads:

> In the case at hand it is to be recommended that the small sum of approximately 45 reichsmarks be taken from the political budget, given the political nature of this material, which, given our position vis-à-vis Japan, one would not gladly make available to a broader public; there would be some danger of that, however, were the sum to be recorded in an open account. Moreover, funds for such purposes are not available to the Pers. R desk. Herewith presented to Legation Councilor Dr. Dienstmann, respectfully requesting his approval. Berlin, 22 April 1938.

> Marginal note: approved (signature).

The document was resubmitted several times, and in the end, there is this final notation: "Accounting instructions have been given. The matter of finances is settled. Respectfully returned to the East Asia political desk VIII. Pers. R, 4 June 1938 (signature unreadable)."

51. Martin Fischer, later consul general and assistant to the ambassador in Shanghai.

52. Literally "fast horse"—midwife.

53. A reference to "Hans Huckenbein, der Unglücksrabe" [Lame Jack, the bird (literally, raven) of ill omen] by Wilhelm Busch.

54. See note 30.

55. See the diary entry for 12 December 1937, p. 62.

56. The Chinese business manager of a firm. The word comes from the Portuguese.

57. Piefke was a Prussian military band conductor, who in 1864 composed the Düppeler Sturmmarsch on the occasion of Prussia's victory over the Danes. Ever since, the term "Piefke" has been a pejorative nickname for a chauvinistic Prussian.

58. Willi Schläger was the husband of Rabe's daughter Gretel.

59. A distant relative.

60. A colleague's daughter.

61. Hitler had already committed suicide in the "Führer's bunker" near the Reich Chancery on 30 April, only a few miles from Rabe's apartment in Wilmersdorf.

62. The capitulation of the entire German Wehrmacht had been signed by General Jodl in Reims, France, on 7 May. This surrender was repeated on 9 May at Soviet head-quarters in Karlshorst, where among the signatories were General Keitel and Count Schwerin von Krosigk, who was still acting head of government.

63. Gretel, John Rabe's elder daughter and the wife of Willi Schläger, together with her daughters Ursula and Gudrun; Rabe's son Otto and his wife, Eva.

64. There was no armistice with Japan until 15 August 1945.

65. An early autobahn west of Berlin, also used as a race track.

66. The Chinese goddess of mercy.

67. That is, without using outside electrical current.

68. Hitler was already dead, see note 61.

69. Herr Vollbach's report is full of improbabilities.

70. Long after Rabe's death and with the help of Dr. Rosen, Rabe's daughter recovered some of these monies.

71. Chinese. "Doesn't matter."

AFTERWORD

1. From a small manuscript that Rabe left for his grandchildren and titled *Lest We Forget*.

DOCUMENTS

1. This means that a coded five-digit group of numbers signifying a particular word was never transmitted or was mangled in transmission and was therefore unreadable.

2. *Akten,* vol. 1, no. 528.

3. Ibid., no. 529.

4. See Document 2, above.

5. *Akten,* no. 532.

6. Ibid., no. 538.

7. Ibid., no. 513.

8. Ibid., no. 519.

9. From John Rabe's diary.

10. Ibid.

11. Ibid.

12. *Politisches Archiv des Auswärtigen Amts, Pol. VIII, Chinesisch-japanischer Konflikt, 1937–1938* [Political Archives of the Foreign Ministry, Pol. VIII, Sino-Japanese Conflict, 1937–1938] and John Rabe's diary.

13. Article of the English-language newspaper *Japan Advertiser*, Tokyo, 7 and 14 December 1937. The newspaper was owned by Americans. Quoted from H. J. Timperley, *What War Means: The Japanese Terror in China* (London, 1938).

14. Documents 18, 19, and 20 are taken from John Rabe's diary.

15. *Politisches Archiv des Auswärtigen Amts, Pol. VIII, Chinesisch-japanischer Konflikt, 1937–1938.*

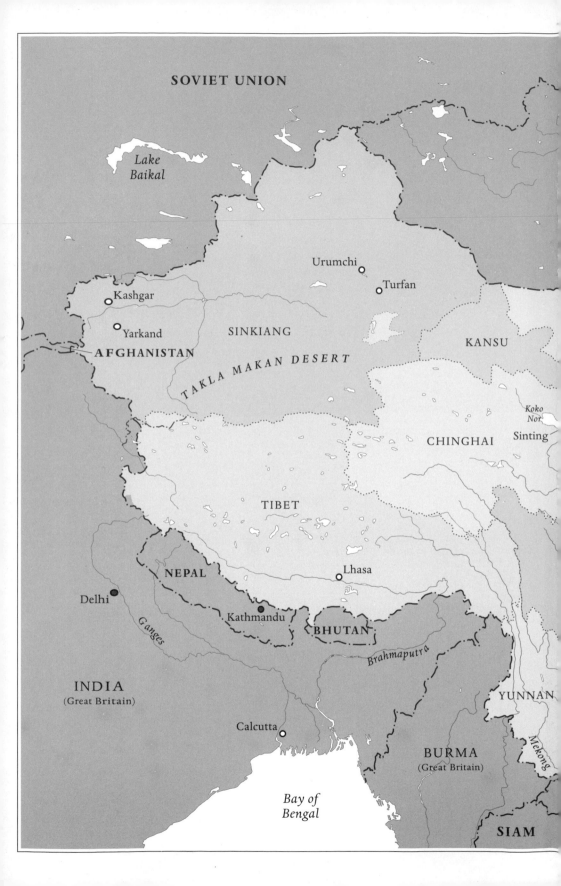